HOW TO MAKE IT IN
HOLLYWOOD

HOW TO MAKE IT IN

* * * * * * * * * * * * * * * *

Hollywood

* * * * * * * * * * * * * * *

ALL THE RIGHT MOVES

LINDA BUZZELL

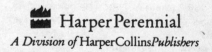

Harper Perennial

*A Division of HarperCollins*Publishers

HOW TO MAKE IT IN HOLLYWOOD. Copyright © 1992 by Linda Buzzell. All rights reserved.
Printed in the United States of America. No part of this book may be used or repro-
duced in any manner whatsoever without written permission except in the case of
brief quotations embodied in critical articles and reviews. For information address
HarperCollins Publishers, Inc., 10 East 53rd Street, New York, NY 10022.

HarperCollins books may be purchased for educational, business, or sales promotional
use. For information, please call or write: Special Markets Department, HarperCollins
Publishers, Inc., 10 East 53rd Street, New York, NY 10022. Telephone: (212) 207-
7528; Fax: (212) 207-7222.

FIRST EDITION

Designed by Helene Berinsky

Library of Congress Cataloging-in-Publication Data

Buzzell, Linda.
    How to make it in Hollywood : all the right moves / by Linda Buzzell. — 1st ed.
        p.   cm.
    Includes index
    ISBN 0-06-055305-7 (cloth) — ISBN 0-06-096596-7 (paper)
    1. Motion pictures—Vocational guidance—United States.   I. Title.
    PN1995.9.P75B89   1992
    791.43'023'73—dc20   91-58469

92 93 94 95 96 CC/RRD 10 9 8 7 6 5 4 3 2 1
92 93 94 95 96 CC/RRD 10 9 8 7 6 5 4 3 2 1 (pbk.)

To my dear husband, Larry Saltzman, who believed in me and this book before I did.

To Ruth, Sarah, Ellen, and Hannah.

And to the readers of this book, whose fresh talent, vision, and stories Hollywood desperately needs.

In Hollywood, anything can happen. Anything at all.

—RAYMOND CHANDLER
The Long Goodbye, 1953

Contents

★ ★ ★ ★ ★ ★ ★ ★ ★ ★ ★ ★ ★ ★ ★ ★ ★

PART IV ★ ALL THE RIGHT MOVES

Preface

★ ★ ★ ★ ★ ★ ★ ★ ★ ★ ★ ★ ★ ★ ★

WHY SHOULD THE HUSTLERS HAVE ALL THE FUN?

Right now there's a story going around Hollywood about a sitcom writer who everyone agrees is only minimally talented. Most of the scripts he's written in the past have been disappointments. He is, however, a master pitcher. He used to be a stand-up comic. Once again this year, he spun a story in such an entertaining way that unsuspecting network executives gave him yet another order for a pilot script, passing over other more talented writers.

Hollywood insiders roll their eyes in exasperation when they tell this tale. Why is it that skills other than talent are so often rewarded in Tinseltown? Why do the hip hustlers frequently succeed while many of the truly talented languish in career disappointment?

The results of this unfortunate reality can sometimes be seen on the screen. Too often the job or the green light goes to the expert deal maker, pitcher, or shmoozer, not the inspired filmmaker.

Do you ever find yourself looking at a film or TV show and saying "Hell, I could do better than that!"?

Perhaps you could.

But can you pitch a story on a sports club treadmill without missing a beat? Can you romance a recalcitrant producer's secretary by "giving good phone"? Can you grow "rhino skin" so thick that you could coolly take tea at Trumps with an agent who makes Attila the Hun look like a wimp? Can you overcome self-sabotage, lack of self-confidence, and procrastination? Can you shmooze with the best and out-chutzpah the most outrageous, determined, and entertaining people on the planet?

Before Hollywood will hand you a multimillion dollar canvas to paint on, you'll have to learn some skills they don't teach you in film school. Many people wish that these skills weren't necessary, but in today's Hollywood they are just as important as knowing how to write, perform, shoot, or direct.

Why should the hustlers have all the fun? In this book I hope to put into your hands some of the tools you *really* need to make it in showbiz.

No one gave me these "insider tips" when I came to Los Angeles. I picked them up by working in and around Hollywood for over twenty years. I kept my eyes open and watched carefully, observing who made it and who didn't. Both as an industry employee (in development and production) and as a psychotherapist and career counselor, I've worked with people at every level in the business: ambitious film students, hot directors, showbiz lawyers, frustrated assistant directors, flavor-of-the-month screenwriters, overworked production managers, insecure TV and movie stars.

One thing I've learned is that it's not enough to be talented. The people who really succeed in Hollywood not only have talent but also have learned to play the Hollywood game and to make the right moves.

I can't give you talent. God does that.

I can't teach you your craft. That's what film schools are for.

But I *can* help you learn to play the game to win.

My dream is to make it a little easier for truly talented people to create quality films and TV shows in Hollywood. I hope this book will be a road map for you so that you can bring your fresh ideas, stories, and vision to Hollywood and share them with billions of people around the world.

PART I

THE RIGHT GAME

1

☆

The Hollywood Game

★ ★ ★ ★ ★ ★ ★ ★ ★ ★ ★ ★ ★ ★ ★

IS IT FOR YOU?

MOM, CALL HOLLYWOOD!

For director Patrick Read Johnson, the road to success in Hollywood started in Wadsworth, Illinois (pop. 750), and ended on Mars.

At the age of ten, young Patrick set his Christmas train set on fire and filmed the spectacle with his dad's movie camera. By the time Patrick was thirteen, his mom was so sick of driving to Chicago to buy movie magazines for him and hearing him complain that he hadn't yet been discovered by Hollywood that she picked up one of the magazines herself—it turned out to be *American Cinematographer*—and called a name off the masthead: Herb Lightman, editor.

A determined Mom got through to Herb in Los Angeles. "Listen, Herb, I've got a kid here who's been making 8-millimeter films since he was ten. He's thirteen now. He wants to be Stanley Kubrick. I don't know anybody. I don't know what I should do with him. Should I send him to film school? If I put him on a plane and get him a place to stay with friends in L.A. for a week, will you introduce him to some of his heroes?"

Luckily for Mom and Patrick, Herb turned out to be one of the Hollywood good guys. He chuckled. Who knows, maybe Mom reminded him of his own mother's exasperation with a youngster obsessed with films and filmmaking. He agreed to Mom's proposition and a week later Patrick was on a plane to Hollywood, explaining to the astonished guy in the next seat that he was going to visit a special effects wizard named Douglas Trumbull.

Not only did Patrick meet Doug Trumbull, but Herb let him tag along as he visited the set of a new movie Doug was working on, *Close Encounters of the Third Kind*, where an ordinary-looking guy in a trucker's cap who asked him if he wanted a Coke turned out to be the director, Steven Spielberg. Patrick's last day in Hollywood was spent watching the rough cut of a film called *Star Wars* that everyone thought was going to be a nice, small, kids' movie.

After that introduction to the business, it's no wonder that young Patrick couldn't wait to get back to Hollywood. He finally went back in 1980 and worked in special effects for a few years. He also co-wrote and directed a low-budget film about a group of wayward alien invaders who land on earth Halloween night. Steven Spielberg looked at it and called his buddy Jeffrey Katzenberg at Disney to suggest that they release the picture—which became *Spaced Invaders*, a Touchstone release. Patrick is now one of the new, hot directors in town, romanced by studios, producers, and agents. He's hard at work on his next film, which will be coming soon to a theater near you.

Sometimes Hollywood dreams do come true. Just ask Patrick's mom.

THE HOLLYWOOD GAME

The Hollywood game isn't always this easy, of course. And those of us without a lucky mom for an agent need to learn the rules.

In spite of recent belt-tightening, entertainment is still one of America's most successful export industries. While many other U.S. products can no longer compete in the global economy, American entertainment talent and "software" (films, TV programming, music, etc.) are eagerly consumed around the globe. In fact, the Hollywood entertainment industry has become so desirable that major international corporations have invested billions of dollars in Tinseltown.

Unfortunately this doesn't mean that there are plenty of jobs waiting for you in Hollywood, especially during bumpy economic times. The entertainment industry is now more ruthlessly competitive than ever. The world's best and brightest in every job category—performers, directors, executives, technicians—are flooding into Hollywood in ever-increasing numbers.

To succeed in the entertainment industry—even as a hermitlike independent—one must not only have great talent and do outstanding, original work but also understand the Hollywood game and its players. There is an entertainment industry culture that characterizes the show business game as it's played all over our rapidly shrinking planet. With telecommunications and air travel linking the far corners of the globe, the industry is becoming increasingly unified in its rituals, habits, and mores. Industry people in Los Angeles, London, Cannes, and Hong Kong have more in common with each other than with hometown friends in accounting or insurance.

Newcomers—and even many industry veterans—have trouble understanding this arcane system and its unspoken rules. And many people are put off or intimidated by the blatant wheeling and dealing, the ruthless tactics, and the dramatic personalities.

As an introduction, I'll give you a "person from Mars" view of this fascinating industry culture, taking a closer look at the colorful natives, strange behavior patterns, rituals, and language idiosyncrasies that characterize show business and make it different from every other manufacturing industry.

This is the way it *is*—not necessarily the way it *should* be. If, once you're established in the industry, you decide to make some changes to the system—more power to you!

In the meantime, my advice to those of you who decide to make show business your life is to learn the game, appreciate the people, and relax and enjoy the craziness. A sense of humor about the whole scene will keep you sane.

But as veteran director Melvin Van Peebles has observed: "If you're not in the game, you can't win." You don't have to indulge in the more obnoxious customs and practices yourself, but you will need to know how to deal with people who do.

THE OBJECT OF THE GAME: TO MAKE MY PICTURE, MY WAY

For the huge corporations that have bought up many entertainment industry studios, networks, TV stations, and production companies, the goal is, of course, no different from the goal of every other corporation on the planet: to make profits. And many corporations have additional reasons for getting into this unique business. Some firms want to own important pieces of the global telecommunications puzzle. Some lust after studio real estate or film libraries. Others want new software to drive their hardware sales. Still others just want to have some fun and mingle with the stars.

But for most people below the top corporate level, the goal is a creative one: I WANT TO MAKE MY PICTURE, MY WAY!

Money, credits, and perks are nice, but the true mark of power in the entertainment industry is creative control. It's not enough to be rich or famous. Will your "yes" greenlight a picture? And can you get that picture made your way? Few people have this power; they may be actors, directors, producers, or studio or network heads. Whoever they are, they are the most popular and powerful people in show business.

Everyone wants to *be* them or get next to them.

These are the "players" who run show business. Membership in this exclusive club is fairly fluid—people are always joining or being ousted as they rise to prominence or fall from grace. For example, a few years ago writer Shane Black was a lowly UCLA student with a script. But when the script became *Lethal Weapon* the club members began to rush him. His next spec script, *The Last Boy Scout*, was the object of a bidding war and he was paid $1.75 million for it. He's now a member in good standing, rubbing shoulders with the "A"-players, treated with respect by other members.

How can you join the club? Simple. Have something that club members really want: incredible talent, a potent script, money to make films, sales wizardry. Success is the only requirement for membership. A hit picture and you're almost in. Two hits and you're a very popular person!

But even before you make your two hit pictures, you'll be dealing with the members of the club. You need to understand their culture.

THE RATING GAME

Because of the normal up-and-down cycles of show business, club members are by nature insecure. This year's hot producer may be next year's bombmeister. Everyone in town—producers, studio execs, talent—is constantly rated by everyone else. Are you an "A-list" player, a "B-list," a "C-list," or a "forget it"? It's just like high school or fraternity life.

The in-crowd mentality isn't unique to show business, of course, but it's perhaps more blatant and dramatic in this industry.

Many Hollywood people are constantly "taking their temperature" to see where they currently stand in the pecking order. Am I perceived as a B-player who slipped to a C after my last bomb? Am I seen as an up-and-coming C+ or B−? Actors are particularly vulnerable to this malady, and their psychic thermometers see plenty of action. Things can change so quickly and you have to keep up not only with your own rating but the ratings of others with whom you play the game. Richard Gere, for example, was a former A-list actor who had slipped to a B until *Internal Affairs* made him a B+ and *Pretty Woman* revived his A rating!

ARMANI JACKETS, MASERATIS, AND MALIBU MANSIONS

Because there's little established hierarchy (even studio heads often don't hold their coveted jobs for long), many show business people spend a lot of time and money trying to look like A-players even if they aren't. This is the reason for the ostentatious display of wealth and power in the Hollywood game. It's not that industry folks lack modesty and subtle taste (although that can certainly be true for many). It's a matter of how they appear in the town. It's business. You have to look and act like a player or your club membership could be revoked very quickly at the first sign of a slipping career.

THE DRESS CODE: PSEUDOCASUAL

The need to look like a serious, powerful player isn't unique to show business, of course. Lawyers, stockbrokers, and executives dress for success too. But, as always, things are a little more extreme in Hollywood.

What's the dress code? Check out the top players in your chosen niche. There are different looks for different jobs. Studio development execs and agents don't look like directors or cinematographers or grips. In most creative jobs, the look is "expensive play clothes." It's casual (or "pseudocasual," as a friend of mine describes it) but expensive and hip. This is an industry dependent on rapidly changing public taste, and you need to communicate that you are plugged into the current zeitgeist.

What about traditional business wear? Directors, performers, writers, and crews often call industry people who have to wear suits and ties "suits" (e.g., "Heads up, guys, there are suits on the set."). It's not a complimentary term. Typically, creative and business executives, agents, lawyers, and accountants are suits.

CAR FADS

The need to look like a successful player extends to cars also. Los Angeles is awash in Mercedes-Benzes, Rolls Royces, Jaguars, and Maseratis. As with clothes, the fads change every year and each job has its favorite cars. Porsches and BMWs used to be popular with creative talent. Now expensive "play" cars are in—beautifully restored 1957 red-and-white Buick convertibles or sporty Range Rovers. With car phones, of course. With or without second phones, call waiting, and car faxes.

How do people afford this ostentatious consumption? Often, they really *can't* afford it, but do it anyway, fearing that a failure to keep up with the Katzenbergs and Spielbergs will be a signal that they aren't serious players. (David Puttnam's Audi was considered a slightly disreputable choice for a studio chief.) This financial overextension was the cause of much of the anguish during the last strike, when many had to sell their expensive toys and homes.

THE HOLLYWOOD DIAMOND

Homes are the most expensive toys of all, especially in Los Angeles. Aaron Spelling's outrageous, sprawling mansion has been the subject of scandalized gossip in national magazines (is it coincidence that he built it just as his career was waning?), but thousands of other homes rival it in extravagance.

The rule of thumb in Hollywood is that serious players (and serious wannabes) live in the "Hollywood Diamond," within easy commuting distance of the important studios and production companies. To locate the Hollywood diamond, get a map of Los Angeles and put four dots on it: Santa Monica, Culver City, Burbank, and Malibu. Join the dots. Voilà: an odd-shaped diamond, within which most industry people live and work. Many of the most powerful agencies and law firms are located in the center of this diamond, in Beverly Hills or Century City.

The West Side of Los Angeles (including Santa Monica, Malibu, Brentwood, the Pacific Palisades, Bel Air, Holmby Hills, and the now less-than-chic Beverly Hills) and the Hollywood Hills are popular home bases. Newcomers can find less expensive but fairly convenient houses or apartments in Hollywood, Venice, Culver City, West Hollywood, and the San Fernando Valley. Try to live where you can quickly commute (a relative term given the current state of the L.A. freeways) to meetings, screenings, parties, or jobs in the diamond.

DECORATING GAMES

When players find an abode appropriate to their wished-for status, they then proceed to dress it for success. Hollywood has its A-, B- and C-list interior decorators. But even they may not be enough for some top Hollywood talents, who call upon their favored production designers to create an appropriate setting.

Styles come and go with blinding speed. Barbra Streisand used to be fond of Art Deco, but soon she was being advised on the finer points of the Craftsman movement by producer and Frank Lloyd Wright aficionado Joel Silver. The Santa Fe look appealed to many Hollywoodites for a second; then Memphis; then English country; then fifties turquoise and pink and boomerang tables; then the Western look. . . . By the time you read this, who knows what look will be catching the community's fancy?

OFFICE DECORATING GAMES

The decor of one's office is perceived as an important power statement. Agents and lawyers negotiate redecorating money as part of their clients' contracts.

The objects of this game: to obliterate all traces of the previous inhabitant, to demonstrate one's creative pizzazz and with-it-ness, and to impress all visitors with the amount of money the studio was willing to pay you in redecorating fees.

Tell-all producer Julia Phillips was an expert player: in the spring of 1984 she extracted $75,000 from Fox ("a pittance by Hollywood standards, but a whole lot more than they wanted to spend on me"), with which she "obviated every last gray tile of Dan Melnick's by having a spray-paint artist replicate Georgia O'Keeffe's *Sky above Clouds* ad infinitum." Take that, Danny!

Players also consider the impact of the art on their office walls. Insecure types put up posters from their successful movies, plus photos of themselves hobnobbing with important "friends."

True heavy hitters display serious art. This is a big-ticket hobby that separates the moneyed players from the hopefuls—which is, of course, its purpose. You have to be doing very well indeed to keep up with Creative Artists Agency mogul Michael Ovitz's Picassos and Lichtensteins, Steven Spielberg's Norman Rockwells, or Madonna's Frida Kahlos.

TROPHY SERVANTS: THE "GREAT AND FAMOUS" GAME

To demonstrate your status as an A-player, you need to be surrounded by A-servants and services: the best chef, the "great and famous" surgeon, the "in" caterer, the poshest nanny, the trendy hairstylist, the talk-show-hosted personal trainer, the well-known shrink, the most-sought-after decorator, the noted nutritionist, the celebrities' masseuse, the famous architect, the hippest xeriscaper (landscaper specializing in drought-tolerant plants). . . . In all the power spots, you'll overhear Hollywood people crowing about the merits of their "trophy" servants.

The trophy mentality also extends to industry hiring practices. Players like to employ trophy talent—"name brand" editors, cinematographers, composers—people who are not just the best but are "great and famous" in their own right.

TROPHY DATES AND SPOUSES

Trophy servants can be a relatively harmless game, but trophy families are something else again. Hollywood has its tragic examples of people who choose their loved ones not on the basis of their personal value but because they enhance the player's standing in the general pecking order. A lot of Hollywood "dating" is less an expression of genuine romantic interest and more a matter of enhancing one's perception in the industry.

TRENDY TINSELTOWN: LIVING IN SEARCH OF THE NEXT BIG THING

Hollywood is in the business of predicting the future. What will audiences want to see next year or the year after? The entertainment industry has more "what's in" and "what's out" lists than does *W* magazine.

Will the nineties be the Green Decade? Has Spago-style designer pizza been supplanted by nostalgic Mom's meat loaf? Are soothing earth tones this year's look? Is the male-oriented action film dead? Will political activism rise again? Is romance back in style? Are children's films the happening genre?

Because of the lag time between the writing of a script and the screening of the final product, the ability to see into the future is an important survival skill for Hollywood players. That's why many of them fear being seen in last year's clothes, last year's car, last year's decor, or last year's restaurant.

THE PACK MENTALITY

Insecure players, like insecure stock investors, like to travel in packs. Because, as veteran screenwriter William Goldman observed about Hollywood, "nobody knows anything" about what will succeed next year, most industry people are nervous when faced with the necessity of making decisions. Every yes or no is a gamble that could come back to haunt them. Who wants to be the person who said yes to a flop or no to a hit? The easiest thing is to say no unless there is extreme pressure to say yes. "Extreme pressure" means that other Hollywood people are enthusiastic about the person or property you're considering. "Extreme pressure" means that the current Hollywood conventional wisdom is on your side ("Big-star vehicles are out this year," "Action pictures don't draw crossover audiences," "Women don't like to watch pictures about women," etc.). "Extreme pressure" means that known, "proven" Hollywood elements are attached to or supportive of your decision.

There are perhaps 8,000 people seriously playing the Hollywood game at any given time. By anyone's definition, that's a cottage industry. The small size of the group often leads to a myopic, inbred, provincial mentality. There are still, thank goodness, a few brave, independent souls in the entertainment industry who are willing to gamble on their own tastes and instincts, but by and large, Hollywood is a small town with a herd mentality.

THE HOLLYWOOD PECKING ORDER

Things may change in the future, but right now the pecking order is: Oscars, Emmys, Aces, Grammys, Clios.

Major-studio feature film people are at the front of the pecking order. Independent, foreign, and "art" filmmakers are seen as classy and interesting. Documentary filmmakers are unfortunately perceived as high-minded but irrelevant (unless they make a hit film like *Roger & Me*).

Feature film people are still quite snobbish about the difference between film and television, although that prejudice is gradually fading as more TV stars like Michael J. Fox and Bruce Willis make it on the big screen. But this doesn't stop film people from feeling just a cut above the folks toiling away in TV.

In the television world, prime-time people lord it over daytime denizens. Series score higher than TV movies and miniseries, which in turn outrate specials, reality series, game shows, news, sports, children's shows, documentaries, and cartoons ("The Simpsons" notwithstanding). Broadcast network folk still feel superior to the plebeians in cable and home video. National TV outranks local. Industrials and corporate video are thought to be at the periphery of the business.

The music industry is inaccurately perceived as peripheral to the "real" entertainment industry, and music stars, producers, and executives are often eager to move over and up into TV and features.

Commercials are seen as a source of new ideas and talent, as are music videos.

Studios also have a pecking order, which constantly changes with the fortunes of each season's product and shifts in management. They compete ruthlessly with each other to be known as the most desirable place to make one's films or shows, thus attracting Hollywood's brightest and most creative talent.

PECKING ORDER INSECURITIES LEAD TO HOLLYWOOD PHONE GAMES

How can Hollywood people tell if they are perceived to be A-, B-, C-, or D-players? Simple: by how fast their phone calls are returned. This is the reason for the industry's obsession with the phone.

People read volumes into how rapidly their phone calls are responded to. If Jeffrey Katzenberg takes your call immediately, even though he's in an important story meeting with a prominent director, you know your rating is A +. If the call is returned the same day, you still have clout. If days go by, increasingly desperate callers may have to resort to phoning during off-hours (7:00 P.M. calls will often find the power player at his desk picking up his own calls after the secretary has left) or to odd locations (the car, the vacation home, the hotel room, a lover's home, etc.). Some rely on fax to get the message through.

CALL DUMPING AND "WHO'S ON FIRST?"

Busy players receive hundreds of calls a day and can't possibly return all of them. Some resort to an annoying survival tactic called "call dumping," where they have their secretaries "dump" messages during lunch or at night when the callee is sure to be unavailable. They *did* return your call, so how can you complain? Now the ball's back in your court. Telephone tag continues.

When players finally connect, who gets on the phone line first is thought by many to determine one's place in the show business pecking order. Secretaries duel with each other to make sure that

Player B must wait on the line before Player A picks up. One rather sadistic producer I know used to deliberately wait up to a minute after his secretary told him that the caller was on the line—just to see how long he'd wait, which would tell him how desperate he was to do business with him.

Another nasty phone game involves the speaker phone. A player may put a caller on the speaker and conduct a very public conversation, not telling the caller who else is in the room listening. This move may be calculated to embarrass the caller by revealing indiscreet statements to an audience or to humiliate the people in the room by making them invisible. Proper Hollywood etiquette dictates that the player should announce the names of the people listening in on the call. Folks with clout often refuse to talk unless they are taken off the speaker phone or told who else is in the room.

But even if the call is on a seemingly private line, callers shouldn't assume that no one but the player is listening. Powerful producers and agents routinely allow their trusted lieutenants or clients to tune in unannounced on another phone.

THE CREDIT GAME: WHOSE PICTURE WAS THIS ANYWAY?

People in Hollywood fight over power (who gets to make their picture, their way), money, and credits. Credits are important because they affect how one is perceived in the town (one's rating). And how one is perceived in the town determines whether or not one will work again any time soon and how much one will be paid.

One rule of thumb to keep in mind, to protect you from future pain is: "If it's a hit, it's mine. If it's a bomb, it's yours." The most powerful person involved gets to make that call. I remember a number of years ago when a filmmaker friend sat fuming at the Oscars while his boss—an executive producer who had barely been involved in making the picture—gave himself "producer" credit and picked up the Oscar. It's not supposed to happen that way, but sometimes it does.

RABBITS' FEET, GOLD DUST, AND LUCKY CREDITS

Since no one knows where Lady Luck will strike next, Hollywood is a superstitious town.

If you worked on a picture that made $200 million or won an Oscar—even if you were a lowly grip or production assistant—this will definitely sprinkle gold dust on your resume (the "halo effect"). People will enjoy being associated with you (and, by extension, the hit you worked on). Some may even hire you as a sort of lucky charm, hoping your good fortune rubs off on their project too. You become a trophy employee ("Well, you know my editor just worked with Martin Scorsese on *GoodFellas*").

But the opposite holds true as well. (Hollywood people are not going to boast that you did the production design on *Hudson Hawk* or *Howard the Duck*, are they?) Even if you did a terrific job of shooting or art directing or crewing on a bomb, some Hollywood people may superstitiously avoid hiring you. In a notoriously insecure business, "losers" are avoided as though failure were a communicable disease.

You can frequently see these phenomena at work at Academy Awards time. Each year a number of creative and technical awards seem to go to people who worked on Oscar's favorite pictures, rather than to those who actually did the best work in the category.

WARRING EGOS

Film and TV have two major problems as artistic media: (1) they're outrageously expensive; and (2) they're necessarily collaborative—even superrich, superpower players can't do everything themselves. These two facts are the cause of the incessant fighting that is a normal part of the culture of show business. The L.A. canyons echo with the sounds of giant egos clashing morning, noon, and night. Lawyers and agents thrive because their services are needed as mediators, litigators, negotiators, and power brokers. Actor A has walked off the set over "creative differences" with Actor B . . . Director C is threatening legal and guild action because the producer is overstepping his bounds . . . Network Executive D has nixed Writer E, favored by the studio.

It's a paradox of life in show business that everyone—even people with absolutely no creative background or training—thinks they know what's best for a picture. Because we all watch film and TV, we're all convinced we know better than the writer, actor, or director. Everyone believes that their vision is the right vision. Everyone is sure their taste is terrific. Everyone feels they're an artist, much to the frustration of the genuine artists in the industry.

So we have the phenomenon of "too many cooks" with their fingers in the soup, all squabbling at once. If you enjoy the fun of a good squabble, jump right in. If you are a person who values peace and tranquility—think twice before making film and TV your life!

As former Vietnam War reporter and novelist Martyn Burke, who sold the screen rights to his book *Ivory Joe* for $950,000, told the *Los Angeles Times:* "I quickly realized the big similarity between Hollywood and Vietnam. I looked at all the infighting, at all the bodies strewn around, at all the people trying to survive for just one more day. . . . Anyone who wants to write, direct or produce in Hollywood should be shipped to a war zone first. That's a perfect crash course."

WHEELING AND DEALING

The incessant wheeling and dealing raise the decibel level still further. It's hard to find peace and quiet in a lively bazaar. But a bazaar can be an exciting and stimulating environment, especially when it's filled with colorful characters bartering over high-concept tales and gorgeous talent.

To make a picture, producers and studios have to put together the "elements" (which may not be easy if the potential elements have "history" and bear the scars of previous squabbles). They're buying raw materials, just the way a cook buys fresh vegetables or a nail factory buys spools of uncut steel wire. What's different is that the raw materials in this case are ideas, stories, and people. But the process of haggling is no different from the ages-old bargaining in a bazaar over the price of camels or pomegranates.

Novelist Jim Harrison, whose book was turned into Columbia Pictures' film *Revenge,* starring Kevin Costner, discovered that it's not a difficult game to learn. "As a farmer, I come from a long generation of horse traders. It's not all that much different."

What bothers many people, of course, is the idea that this is a "human meat market." People's lives and dreams are the raw materials the wheelers and dealers are arguing over. And you may be that fine piece of talent the power players are bidding for against each other. The difference between you and the hapless horse or camel is that you get to say yes or no to your potential buyer. But to know whom to say yes to (and whom to avoid like the plague) you need some information about the power players and how to deal with them.

2
☆

The Power Players

★ ★ ★ ★ ★ ★ ★ ★ ★ ★ ★ ★ ★ ★ ★

LARGER-THAN-LIFE PERSONALITIES

The men who work in this town, and, to a lesser degree, the women, display behaviors that would undo them in any other profession. Egomania and greed that would disgrace an executive in, say, the insurance or aerospace industries are here rewarded. And even for those who run afoul of the law and are convicted of crimes, there is an apparently bottomless well of forgiveness. "Nobody cares about that shit," one studio head said recently. "If you're a money-maker, or if they think you can be a money-maker, you could have killed and eaten your own children. It doesn't matter as long as there is the perception that you can make somebody some money."

—CHARLES FLEMING
"Failing Upward in Movieland,"
M, January, 1992

The folks doing the wheeling, dealing, and bidding can be an intimidating lot; anyone who has risen to the top in the most competitive creative business on the planet is, by definition, a tough cookie. Hollywood is a Darwinian environment. The meek don't last long.

That's not all bad. If you're going to team up with a producer, an agent, a manager, or a lawyer, you'll *want* them to be tough survivors and good street fighters. Otherwise they're no use to you. The ideal model is probably a friendly (and maybe even creative) Terminator 2. Newcomers often make the mistake of getting involved only with "nice people" with "good intentions" who may or may not be effective warriors, able to win the battles required in order to get projects off the ground.

THE HOLLYWOOD ZOO

Unless you've been asleep for the last forty years, you're probably aware of some of the Hollywood types you may encounter. The industry has always been full of strange characters and larger-than-life personalities—not all of them nice. To succeed in show business, you need to learn to recognize the more dangerous creatures and to be prepared to deal with them.

THE BULLIES AND ABUSERS

When twenty-one-year-old Matthew went to work as an apprentice film editor, he was seated in front of an editing bench at a small production company and was ordered to rewind reels. He was relaxing into this mindless task when a tense, fast-talking, fast-walking producer in his late thirties rushed up to him, grabbed a film can, and started pounding it violently against the wall, screaming names at him at the top of his lungs. Matthew was shocked.

At lunch the older hands in the cutting room reassured him. "That's just Joe. He does that all the time. Don't take it personally."

There's actually a happy ending to this story. Twenty years later, Matthew and Joe are still on friendly terms. Joe is a talented film-maker with a good eye—he just had a unique and rather eccentric communication style, which has fortunately mellowed with the years.

Some folks are outraged that people who behave like this aren't thrown out of the industry or locked up in jails or mental hospitals. But in Hollywood there are only two sins: to be dull and to be desperate. Bullies are neither. If they make successful shows, all is forgiven. Creativity and achievement are valued. Politeness is not.

This tolerance for outrageous conduct is nothing new. Show business has always been a haven for unusual people. Beyond-the-norm conduct is the norm. Since the industry was founded at the turn of the century, extravagant behavior has been part of the scene. Stifling odd or emotional people might mean stifling creative impulses, some believe.

What's the best way to deal with the bullies and ragers? If you can't avoid them, you need to grow "rhino skin" to cope with their antics. A sense of humor also helps. And above all, *never* take it personally.

This is an especially sensitive issue for people who were abused as children. Some therapists feel that the entertainment industry is an inherently abusive environment for adult survivors of child abuse, and recommend they seriously consider another career.

Who are these bullies? They are the famous and not-so-famous producers, studio executives, directors, casting directors, and other power players who can't resist the chance to abuse the weak and the desperate. They are insecure, dysfunctional people who cover their low self-esteem with grandiosity and bluster. Since many of them are very successful in Hollywood, they're hard to avoid, but do your best to steer clear of the worst offenders. And if you can't avoid them, ask your lawyer, agent, or career counselor to advise you before you deal with them. Also, keep in mind the good advice your mom or dad gave you when you were dealing with schoolyard bullies: stand up to them. Don't cower. Fear only irritates them. They'll respect you if they think you're as tough as they are.

It's easy to spot the bullies—they're notorious. Everyone in town talks about them and stories of their legendary tantrums travel fast. Jokes are written about them. Profiles of them appear in national magazines.

THE YELLERS AND SCREAMERS

Many Y&S types are also bullies, but some are really pussycats in disguise—they just get excited, talk loud, and swear a lot. They're dramatic, passionate, big personalities, not meanies. Try getting excited and yelling with them. They may enjoy the opportunity to conduct a conversation at their preferred decibel level. Or stay calm and respond to them as if they had communicated in dulcet tones. Just don't let them freak you out and put you off your game.

THE SMILING COBRAS

Everyone who's successful in Hollywood has some ability to be charming and seductive when they need to be. Even the most notorious bullies and Y&Sers can turn it on with people they want something from. Just remember that charmers, like whores, seduce for a living—they don't really love you. To survive, you may want to develop your own brand of charm—hopefully more sincere than the usual variety.

THE CASTING COUCH LOTHARIOS

Hollywood people joke about the fact that in today's high-pressure entertainment industry, no one seems to have the time, energy, or medical courage for sexual adventures anymore, but that's just talk. In a town of professionally attractive people, it would be too astonishing if everyone's libido were defunct.

Sometimes the libido in question belongs to a player who preys on unsuspecting wannabes. The *Los Angeles Times* calls this "the powerful exploiting the desperate." Unfortunately, sexual harassment still happens all too frequently. Actors are the traditional victims of this ploy, because they are often the most desperate of the desperate, but these days the casting couch extends to other creative types and even to executives. And male Lotharios have been joined by a few ruthless women who enjoy the sexual aura their success creates.

What should you do if a Power Player comes on to you? Be friendly, and beware. Put him off and go away and think about it seriously. Would you go out with this person if he lost his job? If the answer is no, pass. Some of you may think that a little recreational sex (safe sex only, of course—how many other people do you think they're sleeping with?) might do wonders for your career. But if this affair ends badly, whose career do you think will suffer, yours or his?

That said, it would also be less than honest to claim that sleeping with or marrying a player has never enhanced anyone's career in Hollywood. Just last week in my office, a tearful young hairstylist told me a sad tale about how a competitor of hers had slept with the director and talked him into replacing her with his paramour.

What if a player won't take no for an answer? Or what if he implies that not going to bed with him will get you fired or hurt your chances of success on the job? Anyone who watched the Hill-Thomas hearings will tell you that this is sexual harassment, pure and simple. Get advice from people in the business whom you trust. You may want to contact Women in Film or Cinewomen, a support group for women in the industry (Dinah Perez, one of Cinewomen's founders, told *Entertainment Weekly* that "the men in this business expect you to put up with harassment—and to put out"), or your lawyer.

THE RUTHLESS CLIMBERS

Ruthless climbers are single-mindedly obsessed with getting ahead in the industry. The acid test: talk to them about something unconnected to show business. If their eyes glaze over, bingo, you've got a genuine climber on your hands. A cartoon that circulated around town a few years ago beautifully captures the essence of the true climber: A young woman presses her hand to her head in a dramatic gesture of despair. In the background a nuclear mushroom cloud erupts. The woman's wail: "But I had a development deal at Fox!"

These people are everywhere, so it's hard to avoid them. The best thing to do is understand their single-minded nature, and use them. They're usually very well connected and knowledgeable about what's happening in the business and they will be happy to trade information and "baseball cards" with you if you have useful tips and gossip to share. But don't expect them to return your calls once they feel you are no longer helpful to their careers.

Climbing is a disease many people in Hollywood catch, at least for short periods. If it happens to you, pray that your loved ones will kick your behind and get you into a treatment program (a vacation in a nonindustry spot may do the trick). Left untreated, this disease will rot your soul and warp your creative spirit.

THE TRICKY THIEVES AND THE "SUE ME" SHARKS

In the industry, as in the horse trading business, it's not unusual for a seller or a buyer to be dishonest. The most innocent form of this is the ubiquitous hype about projects, talents, and accomplishments. The horse who's described as a yearling sired by a Kentucky Derby winner may be an old nag with a dye job. Take it all with a grain of salt. Keep your sense of humor. And *always* check the horse's teeth. If a producer tells you that the project has been greenlighted at Fox or that Sigourney Weaver is set to play the lead, call around to see if Fox and Weaver's agent agree.

More serious crimes occur. Art Buchwald recently sued Paramount for stealing his work—and won. But getting his share of the "net" profits will prove no easy task—Hollywood's "creative accounting" is legendary. Even a blockbuster hit will mysteriously yield no profits to be shared by participants.

David Begelman drew national attention when, as head of Columbia Pictures in the late 1970s, he forged actor Cliff Robertson's name on a check. Begelman's wrongdoing was passed over lightly. The victim, Robertson, who blew the whistle on industry insider Begelman, didn't work in Hollywood for six years.

This explains why few have the courage to sue the thieves, and why the thieves continue their shady practices. "I know a number of producers whose attitude is 'Sue me and I'll settle for less money later,' " says a studio executive quoted in an article in the *Los Angeles Times* on Hollywood ethics (a contradiction in terms!). "If the contract says you're owed $100,000 and it costs $50,000 for you to sue, you might choose to take a $60,000 settlement and be $10,000 ahead. The producer saves $40,000."

The trick to dealing with the thieves is simple: buyer beware. Let your entertainment attorney advise you about how to protect yourself as you walk through the mine fields. The lawyer's hourly fee may seem high, but you're paying for his or her years of dealing with every dirty trick that has ever been pulled. Consider it an insurance policy.

But even with the best of advice, you may get ripped off a few times. Everybody does. Don't get hung up on it. Persevere toward your goal. Keep your eye on the ball: getting work that allows you to be creative and getting projects made. If you let fear of the bad guys stop you from getting on the playing field, you'll never score.

THE GOOD GUYS

Yes, Virginia, there really *are* a few good guys still hanging out in Hollywood. Patrick Read Johnson's mom found one of them. You'll need to find some too. They're what makes it all worthwhile.

The best of these are the creative people. They're folks like you who came into the industry burning with the desire to creatively express themselves in film and television and who haven't lost that passion.

They're bright, talented, and wonderful to spend time with. Sure, some can be prima donnas or a little neurotic at times, but they're never dull. These fantastic people will keep you going when the bad guys get you down. They'll help you remember why you got into this crazy business in the first place. Treat them like gold.

There are also some good people in the industry who truly love creative folks and want to help them get what they want and deserve. These good guys may be accountants, business affairs executives, managers, agents, consultants, teachers, technical people, producers. But whoever they are, say thank you!

3
☆

The Right Reasons and the Wrong Reasons for Going into Show Business

★　★　★　★　★　★　★　★　★　★　★　★　★　★　★

After meeting some of the animals, you may wonder why anyone in their right mind would go into the entertainment industry zoo. Well, there are right reasons and wrong reasons. Let's start with the wrong ones.

THE WRONG REASONS

"I'LL SHOW THEM I'M SOMEBODY"

You feel bad about yourself. It probably started with painful childhood experiences, but it may also involve your ex-spouse or ex-boss. You think that if you make it big in Hollywood it will prove you're OK and show them all that you really *are* a special and worthwhile person. (It will also show them up for the idiots they were in not seeing your true value.)

The problem: It doesn't work. Making it in Hollywood isn't going to make you love yourself any more. And without good self-esteem you may find yourself being used and abused by the industry in exactly the same way you were as a child and in your personal life.

It's also win–lose thinking. If you win, you'll expose their mistake in underestimating you—in other words, they lose. You may think that sounds just fine, but when it comes right down to it, it doesn't feel very satisfying to hurt your family and loved ones, even if they've wronged you. In my practice I see people who continue losing, year after year, as a way of protecting their families from the pain of being proved wrong.

All in all, not a good reason for going into show business.

"YOU LOVE ME, YOU REALLY REALLY LOVE ME"

Sally Field's Oscar speech to the contrary, show business (or any business, for that matter) isn't really a great place to get your unmet love needs satisfied. In fact, it's a good idea to keep your work and your love life reasonably separate. Love needs should be met in your private, personal life. If they're not, you're incredibly vulnerable in the work sphere to abuse or rejection by employers and audiences. If you're starved for emotional approval, you commit the second of the two cardinal Hollywood sins: you're desperate.

"I DON'T WANT TO GROW UP"

A few years ago I asked a director friend of mine why he became a director. "Because I didn't want to grow up," he quipped. Show business seems to offer a refuge to those of us who are perennial Peter Pans.

While it's true that there's more tolerance for creative temperament and unconventional behavior in show business than in many other fields, corporate-owned Hollywood is now a very no-nonsense, bottom-line-oriented, grown-up place. The struggles required to make your picture your way are definitely adult struggles, and wide-eyed perennial children are often among the first casualties of war.

"I'M ADDICTED TO FAME, GLAMOUR, ACTION, POWER, GAMBLING, AND A CHAOTIC ROLLER COASTER LIFE-STYLE"

Some people believe the entertainment industry is like a dysfunctional family (complete with ragers and abusers) and that addictive personalities, narcissists, and adult children from alcoholic or abusive families are drawn to it in disproportionate numbers. To "adult survivors," the chaos and insecurity feel "just like home."

Even if this sounds a little far-out to you, it's worth asking yourself if you're just in it for the excitement and so-called glamour (which rubs off very quickly), or if you have better, deeper reasons for making show business your life.

HOLLYWOOD: THE NEW NATIONAL LOTTERY

For many writers and would-be writers, Hollywood has become the new Las Vegas, to be approached like playing lotto or scratching the numbers. Thousands of people around the country are taking screenwriting classes and writing "speculative screenplays" in an effort to get in on the action.

The gambling fever has been fueled by media stories on unknown or novice writers who have hit the jackpot. The headlines scream: *"Radio Flyer*, a spec script by a first-timer, sells for $1 million!" "Wunderkind Shane Black's spec script *The Last Boy Scout* gets $1.75 million!" "Spec script *Basic Instinct* brings $3 million!" (Few stories appear in the press about the hundreds of thousands who fail to win.)

Even novelists are getting involved. Walt Disney's Hollywood Pictures purchased rights to first-time novelist Chris Moore's *Practical Demon Keeping* for over $700,000 after a bidding war. Until he sold the script, Moore was a waiter in Cambria, California.

By 1990 things had gotten a little absurd. Los Angeles's Century City Shopping Center hosted a forty-eight-hour "Scriptathon" inviting shoppers to collaborate on churning out a screenplay called *Hot Property*. The nonprofit Independent Writers of Southern California charged writer wannabes $40 for ten minutes for the privilege of entering this newest version of the Hollywood lottery. (No word yet on whether anyone has bought the script.)

Lately the cost-conscious studios have become much more cautious about buying big-ticket spec screenplays or literary properties, trying to develop more projects in-house. But the lottery still continues and is fueled by every new sale that's made.

"Screenwriters are flooding in by the busload," New Line creative affairs VP Marjorie Lewis told *Esquire* magazine. "The teeming masses from film school are driven here not by love of writing but by the chance to go from poverty to success in one week. It's like winning a game show."

What's wrong with writing a novel or screenplay and going for the big bucks? Nothing, if you're doing it for the right reasons.

THE RIGHT REASONS

Truly special raw talent plus a strong need for creative self-expression (or to work with creative people) are the best reasons for going into show business. A natural affinity for the life-style is also a plus, as long as it's based on who you really are and not on running away from personal problems.

If you're an unusual and artistic person, a maverick, or a dramatic "big personality," you may find this free-wheeling industry a natural habitat and a refuge from the strictures of more traditional life-styles. If you have special gifts—as a storyteller, interpreter, performer, organizer, executive, salesperson, visual artist—that can find their best expression only in the media, this is probably the right field for you.

ARE THERE ALTERNATIVES TO THE HOLLYWOOD GAME?

If Hollywood-style mainstream film or TV sound like a turn-off, why not consider the alternative markets? Each is highly competitive in its own way, but perhaps they will be a better match for your personality, interests, and values.

News, home video, local programming, documentaries, public television, educational programming, children's fare, industrials, animation, corporate media, music video, and commercials all offer opportunities for creative work. Check them out.

But don't be surprised if you find aspects of the Hollywood game increasingly invading these outposts as well. Many producers feel that PBS, for example, is an even more competitive and cutthroat market than mainstream, Hollywood-style TV. And many books have been written about the ruthless search for ratings in the news world.

Cable still offers a number of interesting possibilities for nonmainstream people, although more and more Hollywood folks are invading that arena every year as the power of the big three broadcast networks shrinks. And some people are trying the home video route, creating tapes that can be sold directly to viewers.

THE INDEPENDENT FILM MOVEMENT

The independent film movement attracts many filmmakers who are discouraged by the daunting competitiveness and superficiality of the Hollywood scene. Championing their cause is the mission of the Independent Feature Project in New York, which has branches in Los Angeles, Chicago, Minneapolis, and San Francisco. IFP presents an important annual market, the Independent Feature Film Market, in the fall in New York City. The IFP and its branches present seminars that provide information on how to make your own independent films and get them distributed. The Association of Independent Video and Filmmakers in New York City is also a helpful resource for independent filmmakers.

The Sundance Institute and Sundance Film Festival in Park City, Utah, also support the efforts of independent filmmakers, by linking independents with Hollywood professionals who act as "resource" people. Sundance has offices in Burbank as well as Utah. It offers labs for screenwriters, directors, playwrights, producers, composers, and choreographers. Getting into the labs is very competitive, but if you're interested in independent film you may want to start by attending the annual Sundance Film Festival, which showcases independent features and documentaries.

The independent route isn't easy, and there are ongoing problems with raising money and distributing films. But many creative people believe that the artistic freedom and creative control are worth the hassle. After all, Hollywood certainly has its hassles too, and the odds against your becoming powerful enough to get total creative control in Hollywood are long indeed!

The independent movement has been a breath of fresh air for moviegoers, and I believe its influence will grow even stronger as more and more filmmakers decide to just make their projects first—sometimes for very little money—and then bring them into the marketplace. Breakthroughs in technology and the decreasing price of equipment should make this an increasingly viable option.

But becoming an independent—especially if you're successful—doesn't guarantee you freedom from Hollywood. Industry people keep tabs on new talent, including independents. Many belong to the IFP and attend its events. Once your talent becomes apparent, you will be approached by Hollywood studio execs, agents, and producers who will try to entice you into the system with promises of big money, big budgets, big distribution, and big marketing that may be hard to resist.

NOW FOR THE TOUGHEST QUESTION

Could you be happy in any other line of work? If so, do it! Please!

Take time for some serious soul-searching. If your life could be happy without pursuing a show business career, let it go. As your loved ones will be quick to tell you, this is the toughest business around. There are definitely far easier ways to make a living. If there is any other career that would give you equal happiness, do yourself and your family a favor and pursue it. But if your soul-searching leads you to the conclusion that you must give this your best shot or you will be unhappy and disappointed for the rest of your life, then *go for it!* You will have no peace until you find a way to express the creative passion in your soul.

PART II

THE RIGHT STUFF

4

☆

Focus

★　★　★　★　★　★　★　★　★　★　★　★　★　★　★

TO KNOW WHERE YOU'RE GOING YOU HAVE TO KNOW WHO YOU ARE!

> The way to find out about your happiness is to keep your mind on those moments when you feel most happy . . . not excited, not just thrilled, but deeply happy. . . . What is it that makes you happy? Stay with it, no matter what people tell you. This is what I call "following your bliss."
>
> —JOSEPH CAMPBELL
> *The Power of Myth*

Focus is perhaps the single most important factor in a successful career in the entertainment industry. Show business insiders are allergic to people who have only a vague notion of who they are and what they really want. "Well, I thought I might like to direct . . ." is a line that guarantees a cold shoulder.

How well people know themselves is also directly related to how well they can sell themselves, their skills, their talent, and their projects. So take the time to do your homework on yourself—even if you think you're certain of who you are and where you're going, a little soul-searching couldn't hurt.

In this chapter I'll invite you to explore your dreams, interests, values, tastes, temperament, and passions to help you focus on the specific entertainment industry career goals that are most appropriate for you.

YOUR DREAMS

Hold onto your dreams. Don't let anyone take them away. Never give up.

—*Dances with Wolves* screenwriter
MICHAEL BLAKE at the 1991 Academy Awards

It's important to be honest with yourself about what you *really* lust after. I've found that many people (especially performers who are often warned by "caring" families to give up their passion for performance) try to "protect" themselves from possible disappointment by focusing on secondary dreams while ignoring primary ones ("I want to open a dancing school" instead of "Well, to be honest, I really want to dance myself, not teach others to dance").

Don't panic if your answers to the following questions seem unrealistic. You may still run that dance school, but at least you'll know that dancing is your first love and that in order to be really happy you may need to include plenty of opportunities for performance in your life in addition to teaching.

Answering these questions will take time. When you're ready, find a quiet place and answer each question as fully as you can, to help you get as clear an idea as possible of your own unique dreams, values, interests, tastes, and passions.

WINNING THE LOTTERY

Imagine that you've won the lottery—twenty-five million big ones are yours. Now that you no longer have to focus on making a living, what will you do with your time and your life? What do you want to experience? What do you want to accomplish?

GLINDA, THE GOOD WITCH OF THE NORTH

Shades of *The Wizard of Oz* . . . your fairy godmother appears in a rosy bubble. With a wave of her wand, she *guarantees* you success in any career you choose. But just one! What will you pick?

GLINDA II: INSTANT SEX CHANGE

Glinda waves her wand again and this time you're the opposite sex. What career would you pursue?

GLINDA III: THE FOUNTAIN OF YOUTH

Glinda keeps busy by waving the wand yet one more time. You get to start over. What schooling and careers would you tackle if you had it to do all over again?

THE LITTLE GREEN MONSTER

Whose job do you secretly covet? Barbara Walters's? Keenan Ivory Wayans's? Ridley Scott's? Meryl Streep's? Dawn Steel's? Superagent Mike Ovitz's? Or is there a job you'd like that no one currently holds? If so, what would it be?

WRITE YOUR OWN EPITAPH

You're ninety-nine years old. You've had a great, full life—accomplished what you wanted to accomplish, experienced what you wanted to experience. Write your own epitaph. It can be as long as you like. "Here lies Jane Doe. She did _____ and enjoyed _____ . What meant most to her was _____ ." This will help you pinpoint what you truly care about.

Life has finite limits—even if you're given ninety-nine years. Are you currently spending only a low percentage of your life's hours doing things you really enjoy? Are you wasting the precious days you've been given on things that aren't meaningful to you?

GOD FORBID

What if, God forbid, the clock were to stop on your life right now. What would you regret not having accomplished or experienced?

THE GLOBAL BROADCAST

If you could satellite-broadcast twenty-four hours of programming to millions of people around the globe (better than the Academy Awards!), what would you air? You can choose already-existing programming or programming you would specially create for the occasion. This exercise will help you pinpoint the kind of films or TV shows you care about and the themes or issues you believe are important.

DO YOU HAVE A LIFE MISSION?

Do you feel you have a "mission," something special to say or to contribute to the world during your stay on this planet?

If you haven't already discovered your mission in life, let me suggest one way of approaching this important question. I believe that each of us, as a result of our genetic inheritance and our life experiences, is endowed with a pattern of traits and talents that is as unique as a snowflake, a fingerprint, or an individual seed or bud. It's our job to discover, appreciate, and then share our best gifts with those who need them. This mission is a good recipe for happiness and fulfillment in life. People who follow the "golden thread" of their natural gifts—wherever it leads them—find deeper pleasure and satisfaction than those who try to fit themselves into a mold set out for them by their families or society at large.

YOUR LIFE-STYLE/WORK-STYLE VALUES

What matters to you in life-style—friends, working environment? The following questions will help you determine which life-style and work-style factors are most important to your happiness on any job.

What kinds of people do you like to work with? What age groups? What temperament? Do you prefer down-to-earth, practical colleagues and friends? Ambitious fast-trackers? Creative types?

Would you prefer to work in a big city or are you more comfortable in a smaller town? Do you like to devote most of your time to your work or is it important to you to have plenty of free time for relationships and play? Do you like intense competition with others? Do you enjoy fast-paced work or prefer a more leisurely atmosphere? Do you like to work under pressure?

Do you like to work on your own or with other people? Are independence and freedom to make your own decisions important to you? Do you like to work in an office or do you like to move around or work outdoors? Do you prefer a secure, predictable work situation with reliable salary and benefits or a more exciting, high-risk career? Do you like a steady job or do you prefer the free-lance life-style? Do you prefer variety or predictability? Is it important to you to do work that helps others and benefits humanity?

Is it important to you to do work with artistic and aesthetic merit? How important to you is creative expression? How important to you are high earnings?

Look over your answers to the above questions. List the five factors that are most important to you on any job:

1. _____

2. _____

3. _____

4. _____

5. _____

Will a Hollywood career satisfy these requirements?

ENTREPRENEURIAL SPIRIT

Do you enjoy excitement, adventure, and risk more than security and a predictable routine? Are you a self-starter? It's important to be honest about this one. Folks with high security needs are seldom happy in the entertainment industry. This is a field for independent-minded self-starters who love the free-lance life-style and the excitement of roller coaster ups and downs. Even heads of studios can only look forward to an average of three years' employment in any one place. Adventurous souls who don't mind taking risks thrive in this environment. Timid or passive souls shrivel.

YOUR ENERGY LEVEL AND STAMINA

Do you have high levels of physical, emotional, mental, or intellectual energy? Can you work long hours without getting tired? Energy is important for a successful Hollywood career.

THE "P" WORD

Most successful entertainment industry people are very driven. They care so deeply about film, television, or music that they can be obsessive and ferociously competitive in their pursuit of success. Don't be fooled by all the low-key interviews players give on "Entertainment Tonight" or in *Premiere* about how they "just fell into it" or were "lucky." Industry insiders will tell you that almost no one who makes it in the entertainment business lacks a burning passion to succeed. They have "fire in the belly." Be honest with yourself about the level of raw drive you bring to this career. How bad do you want it?

When I teach seminars at the American Film Institute, the TV Academy, or the Directors Guild, I invite guest panelists who are successful in the industry to speak to the audience about what they look for in someone they hire. Almost without exception, they say passion.

The reason for this is simple. To become successful in this industry, you must be passionate about what you're doing. Entertainment is a tough, survival-of-the-fittest business and only the truly passionate have the guts and drive to keep going against the odds.

By definition, almost all employers are themselves truly passionate or obsessed about the medium they work in and the product they sweat so hard to make. That's how they've survived and become successful enough to be in a position to hire you. And when they pick talent or choose an employee, they naturally tend to look for someone like themselves who is passionate about doing whatever job needs to be done.

But it's not enough just to be passionate. You must also be able to clearly and entertainingly describe *exactly* what you're passionate about.

YOUR TASTE

Whatever area of the entertainment industry you enter, even the so-called noncreative fields, should have some relationship to the kinds of film, video, or music product you personally enjoy. Otherwise you might as well work in widget manufacturing or banking, which are a lot less hassle than the dream-making business.

YOUR TOP TEN MOVIES OF ALL TIME

You probably wouldn't even be considering a career in show business if you didn't love films. Take the time to list your favorites. Think about what they have in common. Are you a *film noir* buff? Do you love melodrama, comedy, action, detective stories? What is it about these particular films that lights your fire?

YOUR TOP TEN FILMS OF THE LAST YEAR

What have you seen this year that turned you on? Again, what does this list tell you about yourself and your taste?

MORE TOP TENS

While you're at it, list your top ten TV shows, kids' shows, commercials, documentaries, soaps, videos, songs—whatever appeals to you most. Keep exploring until you can clearly articulate what kind of show business "product" you'd like to make or be associated with in your career. This information will come in handy when you're out there selling yourself. People you meet in the industry (including potential employers) will respond positively to your clearly articulated enthusiasm and passion.

YOUR NONFILM INTERESTS

Some industry people joke that "show business is my life," but hopefully you have a few other interests as well. (Filmmakers with few outside interests find themselves making movies that constantly refer back to other movies rather than saying something original about real life.)

Take a few minutes to make a list of five to ten things (besides showbiz) that fascinate you. It could include chess, ancient music, making pottery, global politics, Native American folklore, speaking Chinese, Cray computers, the environment, forties jazz, whatever. This list may tell you something about the areas of show business where your passions would be strongest. Later in this book we'll talk about how this list of interests on your resume can spark an employer's involvement with you or come in handy when you're shmoozing at a party. Be ready to tell a few entertaining anecdotes about your interests.

If you're having trouble identifying your interests, try the following exercises:

THE BOOKSTORE

You have an hour to kill in a bookstore while a friend is shopping elsewhere. What sections (besides Film/Performing Arts) are you drawn to? Psychology? Gardening? Travel? Computers? Mysteries? Biography? Mythology? Business? Anthropology? Sports? What specific subjects would you look for within your favorite sections? Jot down a rough list of subject areas and topics that interest you:

	Section	*Specific Subject Area*
1.	_____	_____
2.	_____	_____
3.	_____	_____

THE MAGAZINE RACK

The bookstore also has a terrific magazine section. You're given a coupon that entitles you to five free magazines. List them below and then list the general subject area covered by the magazine:

	Magazine	*Subject Area*
1.	_____	_____
2.	_____	_____

3. _____   _____
4. _____   _____
5. _____   _____

THE NEWSPAPER

When you read the newspaper, what are your favorite sections (besides Film/TV)?

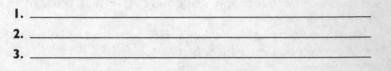

1. _____
2. _____
3. _____

From all of this information, put together a list of your favorite nonfilm interests. Enter the top five below:

Five of My Favorite Nonfilm Interests

1. _____
2. _____
3. _____
4. _____
5. _____

YOUR ACHIEVEMENTS AND ACCOMPLISHMENTS

What accomplishments in your life are you most proud of? Don't just think in terms of work, but also include other areas of your life—leisure activities, relationships. Think of times when you tackled a challenge, enjoyed working on it, and felt great about achieving it. Perhaps it was selling lemonade when you were a kid to make money for a present for Dad . . . getting an A on a tough test . . . marrying someone you really loved . . . editing a sequence the director was crazy about . . . reorganizing an office . . . getting a great agent . . . overcoming a personal problem and healing your life . . . directing a difficult actor and getting a terrific performance . . . taking good care of an elderly parent . . . writing a dynamite script for a screenwriting class . . . bearing a child . . . winning a film festival award.

Don't forget things you've learned "the hard way." Sometimes the most painful things in your life turn into your greatest victories.

Make a list of all the accomplishments, big and small, that come to mind. For those of you who are very hard on yourselves, try to put your internal critic to one side as you do this exercise. I know you've accomplished *something* in your life, even if you're not valuing it very highly right now. As you start to write things down you may be surprised at how much you really have done that you can feel pleased about.

When your list gets long enough, pick your top five favorite accomplishments and enter them here:

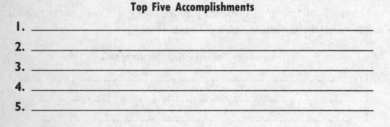

Top Five Accomplishments

1. _____
2. _____
3. _____
4. _____
5. _____

As you look at this list, you may become aware of certain skills that you enjoy using to accomplish your goals.

THE SKILLS YOU LOVE TO USE

You will have the greatest chance of success if you pick a career where they need someone to do just what you're naturally good at and enjoy doing—where you're a round peg in a round hole. The most miserable people in the world are the square pegs trying to jam themselves into that round hole—which might be perfect for someone else but is a bad fit for them. The trick is to find out exactly what you're good at and avoid jobs in which you don't get to exercise your best skills.

THE SKILLS-I-LOVE-TO-USE CHECKLIST

Here's how to take this minitest: get two different-colored pens or pencils. Start with one color and go through each skill, giving it one check if you can do it, two checks if you can do it well. Then, with the second color, go through the list again and put one check beside those skills you enjoy, and two checks beside the skills you truly *love* to use.

Then draw circles around the skills that have four checks. These are your favorite skills and any job that doesn't let you use most of them will be a disappointment to you. Also, keep this list handy so you can use it when writing your resume or creating your "basic pitch." People will want to know what you're good at.

__ Analyze
__ Coordinate
__ Speak in front of large groups
__ Speak to small groups
__ One-on-one communication
__ Start things
__ Move things forward
__ Finish things
__ Work as part of a team
__ Head up a team
__ Work directly for a powerful person
__ Work directly for a creative person
__ Use your charm/charisma
__ Good looks/sex appeal
__ Work with hands
__ Work with body movement
__ Work with equipment
__ Work with information
__ Express emotions
__ Create organized systems
__ Teach
__ Interview people
__ Create images
__ Arouse emotions in others

___ Create fantasies
___ Perform
___ Take physical risks
___ Take emotional risks
___ Take financial risks
___ Advise/coach
___ Edit (images, words, objects)
___ Write
___ Compose music or create sounds
___ Get people together
___ Create ideas/brainstorm
___ Tell stories
___ Intuit others' feelings
___ Predict public taste, future trends
___ Judge talent
___ Put together shows or movies
___ Take care of people
___ Read
___ Make people laugh
___ Cook
___ Enhance or change appearance (clothes, hair, makeup, costume)
___ Create models, effects
___ Carpentry/construction
___ Organize
___ Persistence/follow through
___ Research/track things down
___ Track information and detail/keep records
___ Solve problems on the spot/troubleshoot
___ Create a plan of action, strategy, tactics
___ Memory for names and faces
___ Observe people
___ Observe detail
___ Visual design/good eye
___ Negotiate
___ Persuade others/motivate
___ Sell
___ Budget/track financial information

__ Set policy
__ Make it happen/put a plan into action, carry it out
__ Make decisions
__ Test/evaluate
__ Use mechanical abilities
__ Make friends/hang out with people
__ Move objects
__ Work with animals or plants
__ Welcome people and make them comfortable
__ Head up a project or organization
__ Set and supervise others' work
__ Other: _____
__ Other: _____

From the above list, pick your five favorite skills:

Top Five Favorite Skills

1. _____
2. _____
3. _____
4. _____
5. _____

YOUR SPECIAL TALENTS AND GIFTS

In a supercompetitive industry, it's not enough to be good. You've got to be special!

The "Skills-I-Love-To-Use" exercise helped you to identify areas where you have both passion and talent. Now it's time to define what's really special about you in even more detail. You may have an uncanny ability to project presence on film . . . a photographic memory for names and faces . . . an intuitive, almost visceral sense about which actors will make it and which won't . . . a martial arts black belt plus a winning on-screen persona . . . a never-say-die persistence . . . a silver tongue . . . go-for-the-throat negotiating savvy . . . a great set of rock and roll pipes . . . a deep instinct for story . . . a delightful visual imagination . . . a wacky sense of humor . . . an analytic and strategic mind . . . a wicked smile (which hasn't hurt Jack Nicholson, Bruce Willis, or Tom Cruise!) . . . technical genius . . . marketing savvy . . . sex appeal . . . the ability to bring order to chaos . . . a natural empathy . . . sales talent . . . a knack for numbers . . . a great eye . . . an amazing ability to pick the hits . . .

Take a few minutes to jot down a paragraph describing two or three of your extra-special talents. Go into as much detail as you can.

WHEN IN DOUBT, ASK A FRIEND!

If you're having difficulty with this exercise, try asking a few close friends what they think your special talents and gifts are. Sometimes other people can see us much more clearly than we can see ourselves, especially if we're self-critical. Also, sometimes we devalue the things that are easiest for us to do. A friend may tell you that you're a genius at putting other people at ease. "Oh, that," you may think. "That's nothing. It takes no effort at all." Exactly. This may be one of your best and most special talents, the thing you do "like falling off a log." Value it. It may bring you your biggest success.

THE ADJECTIVES LIST

Another way to pinpoint your special gifts is to make a list of five adjectives that best describe your strongest, most distinctive strengths and qualities—gutsy, funny, conscientious, intense, reliable, sexy, organized, fiery, logical, creative. Ask your friends to contribute to it, in case you've forgotten anything.

DUNCAN BURNS'S SPECIAL STRENGTHS

Duncan Burns is a film editor whose credits include *Tropical Snow*, a feature starring Madeline Stowe and David Caradine that was shot in Colombia and New York for Paramount Pictures, and *Routes of Rhythm*, a three-part PBS documentary narrated by Harry Belafonte that was produced by Gene Rosow and Howard Dratch.

To pinpoint his best strengths so he could pitch himself more effectively, Duncan wrote this list describing his special strengths. Perhaps it will help you in preparing yours:

★ **QUICK**—Physically quick with film and in the work space. Mentally quick in problem solving.

★ **ORGANIZED**—Adept at staying organized. Able to develop systems that are efficient for each particular phase of a project, systems that don't get in the way of creativity.

★ **GOOD IDEA MAN**—Can supply an array of solutions with ease concerning choices that can be made, paths that can be taken.

★ **PRECISE**—Accurate in knowledge of material. I care about details.

★ **WORK WELL WITH OTHERS**—Bring out the best in everybody.

★ **SOLID CREDITS**—Experience in documentary and feature films has given me a broad ability. I can bring the film to a high artistic and technical level without excess expense.

★ **INTERNATIONAL WORK EXPERIENCE**—Documentary experience has taken me to India, Japan, Guatemala, Peru, and Honduras.

Sounds like a good guy to have around the cutting room, right?

Whatever your special talents are, be able to describe them vividly and entertainingly. They are your tickets to success in show business.

My Special Talents and Qualities

1. _____

2. _____

3. _____

THE TALENT CROSS

Yet another way to get at what's distinctive and special about you is to describe yourself in a popular form of Hollywood shorthand called the talent cross. In the cross, a new person is described in terms of already-familiar talents: "She's a cross between Teri Garr and Geena Davis." "He has a Spielberg sensibility with a Joel and Ethan Coen twist." "She's this year's Kathy McWorter" (a twentysomething writer whose spec screenplay *The Cheese Stands Alone* was auctioned for $1 million). "He's as intense and ambitious as a young Mike Ovitz." A very talented client of mine could be described as a cross between Lucille Ball and Anna Magnani. Sounds interesting, right?

A great TC gives you an instant picture of the distinctive qualities of the person. Try putting together your own TC.

YOUR TEMPERAMENT

Personality "typing" is all the rage now in business and psychology circles. And with good reason. It's helpful to know how your pattern of preferences compares with the patterns of people who are successful in various fields. A number of excellent books exist to help you determine your personality type and code (see Resources). These books are based on an important psychological test called the Myers-Briggs Type Indicator, which scores people on four personality dimensions. I'll briefly summarize each of the four temperament preferences it deals with and talk about how they relate to choosing an entertainment industry career.

A word of caution as you read: if your code doesn't seem to "match" a particular job you'd like, don't let that discourage you. Just because many writers are introverted, for example, doesn't mean that an extrovert can't succeed in writing. You just have to adjust your working style to match your personality.

ARE YOU AN EXTROVERT?

The first dimension is extroversion-introversion. This has to do with where you get your energy. Extroverts (Es) get energy and ideas when they're with others. They like to think out loud and bounce things off people. They're good at doing more than one thing at once. They're lively and popular.

Introverts (Is) need to be by themselves to refuel and they tend to be more single-minded, focusing deeply on one thing at a time. They think before they speak. They're calm, private.

No one, of course, is 100 percent extroverted or introverted. We all fall somewhere on a continuum between the two extremes and can be different things at different times in different situations. But generally people will have a *preference* for one or the other.

It's important to your career success for you to know who you naturally are and to find the place where that is most appreciated. Show business, for example, is generally an extroverted career. It's run by the Extroverts, and extroverting is a highly valued skill, as you'll see from the chapters on pitching and shmoozing. If you're an Introvert, you may do well as a writer, an editor, or a model maker or in any job where you meet briefly with the extroverted creative or business types and then they leave you alone to do your thing. But in this highly relationship-oriented business, even the Introverts have to learn to do a certain amount of extroverting because that's how people get hired to do jobs.

There are a few industry jobs, however, in which too much extroverting can be a problem. Some extroverted writers, for example, have bright, creative ideas and are terrific pitchers but can't hack the long, lonely hours in front of the computer screen and therefore can't finish a screenplay by themselves. They need introverted writing partners. This can be a great team: the Extrovert hops around, sparking good ideas off his partner and pitching up a storm in meetings. The Introvert goes off and grinds out a draft, and in regular meetings and rewrite sessions the Extrovert contributes comments, dialogue, and editing. The Introvert is spared the excruciating agony of having to carry the ball in stormy studio story sessions and the Extrovert gets to work in intense spurts.

SENSING OR INTUITIVE?

This dimension is a little tougher to define. Sensors (Ss) gather information about the world through their hypersensitive senses. They are interested in what they can touch, see, smell, hear, and taste. They're often down-to-earth, physical, sensual, practical, and realistic. They favor specifics over generalities, facts over theory.

Intuitives (called Ns, to distinguish them from the Introverts) sometimes live with their heads in the clouds. They filter reality through their minds and often love to create their own worlds. Many Ns get off on fantasy and the abstract. They love to think about possibilities, not just realities. They are visionaries. They pay less attention to what is and more attention to what could be. They favor generalities and see the forest well, while Ss see the trees and the bright green leaves on the branches.

The entertainment industry has lots of room for both types. Many performers, hands-on production folks, administrators, and salespeople appear to be Sensors. Many writers, directors, lawyers, execs, and creative producers are probably Intuitives.

THINKING AND FEELING

How do you make decisions—with your logical, analytical head (a Thinker) or with your heart and guts (a Feeler)?

Thinkers are rational people, and in the entertainment industry they can often be found trying to bring some logic into a basically illogical business. (This is definitely a Feeler-type industry!) Thinkers try to be objective. They work strategically or tactically. Both Thinkers and Feelers can be creative, but in different ways and about different things. Thinkers often have a scientific or administrative bent. Many industry lawyers, accountants, producers, production managers, technical types, and executives (and even some directors!) seem to be Ts.

Feelers go from (and for) the heart or gut. They're subjective about things. They can be very persuasive. Many are empathic. "Creative" types are often Feelers. After all, the entertainment industry manufactures a product designed to make an audience *feel* even more than think. The manufacturers need to hire workers with feeling sensibilities to craft the film, TV, music, or theater experience that arouses laughter, tears, fear, anger, or pleasure. People love having these feelings stimulated and they are willing to pay high ticket prices for the privilege.

If you're a Thinker, be prepared to experience frustration with the illogical Feelers. But learn to appreciate them, because there wouldn't be a show in show business without them.

If you're a Feeler, welcome home! But learn to develop your Thinker side enough to deal effectively with the industry powers that be who often are Ts.

JUDGMENT AND PERCEPTION

"Judgment" and "perception" are the terms the Myers-Briggs test uses for this dimension but I prefer to use "organized" and "spontaneous." Judgers are orderly people. They have a plan. They carry a well-organized Daytimer. They have neat desks. They don't procrastinate. They like closure and are good at finishing things. Perceivers tend to wing it. If they make lists, they don't live by them. They improvise. Sometimes they avoid closure and wait to the last minute to get things done but are incredibly productive under deadline pressure. They are terrific at on-the-spot problem solving and troubleshooting, which can throw the more rigid Judgers. Both Judges and Perceivers can be creative, but in different ways. Js need time to plan things, but Ps can be creative on demand.

A word of advice for the Judgers in the industry: learn to loosen up a bit or you'll be unhappy. Enjoy the spontaneous creativity of the Perceivers around you.

Advice for the Perceivers: stop beating yourself up for not being a step-by-step person. As long as you actually make the deadline and do good work, who's to say that it would have been better to do it by working one hour a day for fifteen days rather than fifteen hours the day and night before the deadline? To be really successful, learn to incorporate a little more discipline in your life (find a loose system that works for your temperament), work on completing things, and don't lose your spontaneous creativity in the process.

THE ENTERTAINMENT INDUSTRY CODE

You've probably guessed by now that this is basically an EN/SFP (Extroverted-iNtuitive/Sensing-Feeling-Perceiving) industry—full of creative and action-oriented types who like to extrovert. Even the Introverts have to learn to extrovert their creativity around other people when they need to. The Thinkers need to learn to enjoy emotional people. The Judgers must find a way to cope with creative chaos.

WHAT'S YOUR CODE?

You may have already figured out your basic code, or you may want to read one of the suggested books to further define it.

Whatever your code is, however, you need to respect it and discover how it best fits into an EN/SFP industry. If you're an ISTJ (Introverted, Sensing, Thinking Judger), for example, you'll probably enjoy working as an accountant or administrator or production person but might find yourself swimming upstream as an actor or writer. (However, I know a very talented ISTJ actor whose finely tuned powers of detailed observation enable him to specialize in accents and dialects, where his talent for exact sensing shines!) For maximum career success, it's usually wise to choose a job that takes advantage of your strongest preferences, not one that requires your "inferior functions." Otherwise you'll be like a right-handed person trying to write with your left hand (or vice versa). You won't do your best work, and both you and your employers will be unhappy with the results.

SOME TYPICAL ENTERTAINMENT INDUSTRY "TYPES"

Using the Myers-Briggs coding system, one can create certain "archetypal" codes for various industry jobs.

For example, the successful hands-on producer (who may hold the title of producer, line producer, unit production manager, etc.) is often, in my experience, an ESTJ (Extroverted, Sensing, Thinking Judger) or ESTP (Extroverted, Sensing, Thinking Perceiver): an extroverted, practical, rational planner or implementer. Many other production people share these codes. Stunt people, for example, will probably be either ESTPs or ISTPs (Extroverted or Introverted, Sensing, Thinking Perceivers). The SP (Sensing, Perceiving) combination usually describes a person who loves action.

The actors and performers in my practice usually turn out to be ESFPs (Extroverted, Sensing, Feeling Perceivers) or ENFPs (Extroverted, iNtuitive, Feeling Perceivers), although some are Introverts who can "turn it on" in front of an audience or camera. The ESFP code is considered "the Entertainer" code, and many actors, salespeople, and agents appear to be ESFPs.

Writers I've tested tend to be INFPs or ENFPs (Introverted or Extroverted, iNtuitive, Feeling Perceivers), which is logical when you think about what they do: create fantasy worlds (an intuitive function) that evoke feeling. Many writers wish they were more organized (the judging function), but it appears that the NP (iNtuitive Perceiving) combination is usually more creative than the NJ (iNtuitive Judging) combination. There are thinking writers as well as feeling writers, and these Ts tend to take a strategic approach to writing and to be terrific at story structure.

The directors I have tested often score as ENFPs (Extroverted, iNtuitive, Feeling Perceivers) or ENTPs (Extroverted, iNtuitive, Thinking Perceivers). Executives are often ENTPs or ENTJs (Extroverted, iNtuitive, Thinking Judgers). ENTJ is the classic chief executive officer code. I have encountered INTJs (Introverted, iNtuitive, Thinking Judgers) who are superb media arts administrators, teachers, nonfiction writers, and researchers.

ISTJ (Introverted, Sensing, Thinking Judger), as mentioned above, is the classic accountant code. SJs (Sensing Judgers) prefer order, stability, and traditional ways of doing things, and are often frustrated by the insanity of a creative business, even though they are secretly attracted to it. Their factual, thorough, systematic and dependable nature makes them highly valued in any company or project, however.

Support people (managers, assistants, hairstylists, etc.) often have extroverted feeling preferences. ESFJs (Extroverted, Sensing, Feeling Judgers) might be helpful to others in hands-on, practical ways, while ENFJs (Extroverted, iNtuitive, Feeling Judgers) could excel at coaching and training, public relations, media arts administration, and career management.

If your code doesn't seem to match the typical code for a particular career you've targeted, however, don't let this dissuade you from pursuing your dream. Perhaps your pattern of strengths may be unusual for this job, but if you approach the tasks at hand using your strong suits, you may turn out to be very successful.

Until more research is done (and I hope to do some of it myself), we won't really know what percentage of people in various entertainment industry jobs have what codes. But until then, let common sense guide you. Unless there are strong reasons for doing otherwise, focus on a career target in which your natural temperament and preferences will give you an edge over the competition.

TAILOR YOUR JOB SEARCH STRATEGIES TO YOUR TEMPERAMENT

Adjust and translate the job search advice in this book (and any others you may read) to suit your temperament. "Go out there and network" may be music to the ears of an Extrovert but sounds like a dentist's drill to the Introvert. Networking is a must in show business, as you'll learn in the chapter on shmoozing, but Extroverts and Introverts will have to take different approaches to it. For Introverts, research, one-on-one or small-group contacts, and a systematic plan can substitute for the natural socializing and party-going that work for the Extrovert. It's the final result that counts, not how you go about it.

If you're a Sensor, a practical, step-by-step approach will probably appeal to you and get you into action. If you're an iNtuitive, focusing on future possibilities may motivate you. Try creating a "career collage" out of magazine photos illustrating your future life-style and hang it over your desk to inspire you.

Thinkers tend to like a strategic (NT—iNtuitive Thinking) or tactical (ST—Sensing Thinking) approach to job search. Feelers can use their emotions to connect with other people and to create enthusiasm in those people about hiring them or working on projects with them.

Judgers like an orderly approach. They make lists and work their way through them. Perceivers, on the other hand, need to put themselves in situations where they can improvise and shine.

WHAT IF I *STILL* CAN'T SEEM TO FOCUS?

If you've done all the exercises and answered all the questions above and your goal still seems unclear, you may want to seek out a professional career counselor who can work with you to help you clarify your direction.

But sometimes, in spite of extensive career counseling and testing, things *still* don't come into focus. Then it's time to look at the possibility that underlying personal issues are preventing you from focusing. The chapter on self-sabotage (Chapter 19) explores the problem of lack of focus in greater depth.

ADD UP THE GIFTS YOU BRING TO HOLLYWOOD

Add it all up. This is what you bring with you to Hollywood. This is what you have to sell. In the following chapters you will discover how and where your best gifts fit into the Hollywood game. On a separate piece of paper, summarize your results.

My Most Important Dreams
My Most Important Life Values
My Mission in Life
My Work Values
My Passion
My Taste (the kinds of entertainment projects I'd like to make or be associated with in my career)
My Interests
My Accomplishments
My Favorite Skills
My Special Talents and Qualities
My Temperament

PART III

THE RIGHT NICHE

5
☆

Producers, Script Doctors, Best Boys, Dolly Grips, and Wranglers

★ ★ ★ ★ ★ ★ ★ ★ ★ ★ ★ ★ ★ ★ ★

INDUSTRY JOBS AND WHAT THEY REQUIRE

The easiest way to categorize entertainment industry jobs is to list them in the order they would appear on a typical film or television production budget. Remember that film/TV is a manufacturing industry: the core of the business consists of the "line" people who design and manufacture the product. Everyone else is "staff"—they are there to help the line people get the product made. The writers dream up the product; the creative producer decides which product to manufacture and pulls together all the elements, including the money; the director and hands-on producer supervise the creative and practical aspects of the actual manufacturing.

CHECK OFF THE JOBS THAT INTEREST YOU

Here's how to use this chapter: as you read, put one check next to those jobs that interest you and two checks next to those you're sure you'd *love*. If you're unsure of exactly what's involved in a particular job, consult the books mentioned in the Resources section for this chapter or do further research at an industry library or bookstore.

When you've finished reading the chapter, go back and pick your top five job titles. Then you'll be ready for the next chapter, on targeting the specific industry niche that is right for you and will give you the maximum chance of success.

__ **WRITER.** In the beginning is the word—or the high concept, as the case may be. It may be the writer's or the producer's or even the star's idea, but then it must be turned into a film or TV script by a writer. There is no "career track" to becoming a writer. If you're a writer, just start writing. If you learn your craft, learn to sell, and have really special talent, sooner or later someone will buy what you've written. Take classes and learn dramatic structure and concept development. Take a pitching seminar. Some writers believe that time spent as a story analyst will improve writing skills. Others think it's the kiss of death. There's no magic here. Just start writing and keep writing.

__ **PRODUCER.** "Producer" is perhaps the most misunderstood job title in the entertainment industry. What exactly does a producer do? And what's the difference between a plain-vanilla producer and an executive, associate, or supervising producer? In the entertainment industry there are roughly two broad categories of producer: the "creative" producer and the "line" or "hands-on" producer. Sometimes the same person does both jobs and sometimes they're quite separate.

Creative Producer: may be the true "auteur" of a project. The best creative producers are artists in their own right. They may create or discover an idea, hire a writer to write it or supervise the development of the script, and sell it to talent and financial backers. This person may be the first involved with a project and the last off the project, following it for the many years that can elapse between initial story development and the last ancillary markets. The creative producer is usually an entrepreneur, heading up his or her own company. The company may make a "housekeeping" deal with a studio, being given free rent and possibly a substantial sum of money to give the studio "first look" at projects it develops. Outsiders often imagine producers as wealthy hustlers in gold chains picking up starlets in bars, but Hollywood cynics know that the majority of creative producers are the worst-paid people in the industry, because whatever money they make on a project must be divided by all of the days they've worked on it. According to that math formula, few creative producers make more per hour than the lowliest gopher. (And of course there are no guarantees they'll ever sell their project in the first place, let alone collect their producer fee or see the mythical "back end" money they're owed by a studio or distributor!)

"Going Indie Prod": The Hollywood trade papers, *Variety* and the *Hollywood Reporter*, often tell of studio or production company executives who are leaving their posts to "go indie prod." Insiders nod knowingly, assuming the executives in question have been fired. For who would go willingly into independent creative production if they didn't have to? The term "independent producer" is sometimes synonymous with "unemployed" or "between jobs." But of course Hollywood *does* have some very successful and wealthy creative producers. Those who succeed tend to have the following characteristics: (1) taste and vision—they have a good sense of what audiences will respond to; (2) access to creative talent; (3) sales ability; (4) entrepreneurial spirit and a taste for risk; (5) business savvy; and (6) amazing persistence and drive.

Essentially, a creative producer is part creative talent (a person with ideas and vision, a hit-picker with good guts) and part salesperson. If you hate high-stakes, risky business situations and if you hate to sell, don't choose this job! The creative producer may also be a "business" producer, handling financial and legal issues for his or her own projects. Many creative producers, however, hire others to do these tasks. Their staff include legal advisors, "business affairs" executives who negotiate deals, and financial wizards who pay attention to stock prices and bean counting.

CAREER TRACK: How do you become a creative producer? Those Hollywood cynics I mentioned a few minutes ago would tell you that there are no qualifications required to be a producer—just money. That's partly true. If you're a millionaire and you'd like to finance your own film—you're the producer! Or if you're the person who has access to the money, you can probably demand and get producer credit. And a lot of people who write or option a script dub themselves producer and make the rounds, selling the project. But if you're serious about creative producing as a long-term occupation, there are more rational ways of approaching your career track. The University of Southern California's Peter Stark program in the Graduate School of Management specializes in training people for the business side of show business. A sales background is a huge plus, even if it's in another industry. Becoming an agent or a manager of high-powered acting, writing, or directing talent is excellent preparation for creative producing. Story analysis and development are steps in the right direction. Creative executive positions at a production company or studio provide excellent training. Even studio chief is often a stepping stone toward a successful creative producing career. People have moved into creative producing from acting, writing, legal affairs, marketing, and distribution.

Line Producer: a hands-on person, organizing the practical aspects of a production to make it actually happen. The creative producer hires a line producer when the money is actually in place, so this job is less speculative than creative producing, although it is, like most industry jobs, primarily free-lance work. Line producers and production managers are responsible for budgeting, scheduling, and implementation. Although creative suggestions from the line producer are sometimes welcome, it's important to keep in mind that this is *not* primarily a creative job. The line producer's task is, to use Captain Picard's line from *Star Trek: The Next Generation,* to "make it so." You would be an excellent line producer if you (1) are a good team player and can also be a team leader, putting together and heading up an effective crew; (2) are good with numbers and budgets and can find creative ways of cost-cutting to bring a project in on or below budget; (3) are good at organizing, scheduling, logistics, and tactics—seeing that things get done right, on time; (4) have a high energy level and can work long, intense days during production; (5) are a good on-the-spot troubleshooter; (6) keep your eyes and ears open and pay attention to what's going on around you; and (7) get along well with creative types.

CAREER TRACK: Line producing is a job you work your way up to. You can start in an entry-level production job—perhaps production assistant, gopher (as in "go for" coffee), production secretary, production coordinator, location scout—and work into location management, production management, associate producing, and then line producing.

Can't I Do Both? Absolutely. Producing isn't always either/or, and many successful producers combine elements of both creative and line producing. But if you're interested in producing as a career, it's important to be honest with yourself about which aspects you love most and are strongest in.

What's In a Title? Now, about the titles. On a film, "Producer" is usually the most desired and most powerful producer credit. You can tell by where it appears on movie credits—right before the director. The producer also picks up the Best Picture Oscar. The person who gets this credit may have been the creative producer or the line producer, so the credit doesn't tell you much except that the person has enough clout to demand and get that title. Sometimes it's the director, the writer, the star, or the star's manager! In these cases, the unit production manager or the line producer probably did the actual hands-on producing and the creative producer may have been bumped upstairs as executive producer.

Speaking of executive producer, that can also be the person who got the money for the project . . . or the star's manager . . . or the head of the production company. You see the problem. The executive in charge of production may be the line producer with bangles on, or the star's uncle, or a studio old-timer, or an important executive. You never know. In television, the executive producer of a series is often the writer-creator of the show. In this case the producers are often lesser writers or line producers. Steven Bochco, for example, would probably take executive producer credit on all episodes of series he creates. Associate producer can be a working credit (on a TV series the associate producer often supervises postproduction) or a vanity credit (given to a studio executive, writer, development person, relative, or hanger-on with clout). If you discover the project and don't have the power to demand producer credit, you might be given associate producer credit as a consolation prize. The credit is also sometimes given to writers as a bonus. Co-producer (not to be confused with joint producers who share producer credit) is another confusing category. You have to know who did what on the project to determine the credit's worth. Supervising producer credit can go to a TV writer or to a line producer with clout. Sometimes there's no way to interpret these credits accurately without asking someone who worked on the show exactly what the person given the title actually did!

Additional producer credits:

Segment Producer: creates segments for reality shows. Often includes writing and supervising the editing.

Promo Producer: creates promos and trailers (ads) for upcoming TV shows (includes writing and editing).

Video Press Kit Producer: creates video stories and clips that promote upcoming movies or events.

Trailer Producer: creates trailers for upcoming movies.

__ **DIRECTOR.** This is the most glamorous title in show business (after "star"). The director tells the cameraperson where to aim or tells the actors (if there are any) what to do. Sometimes a "furniture mover" and sometimes a creative artist with a vision.

CAREER TRACK: This is another catch-22 job: the only way to become a director is to direct—or to write a screenplay someone wants enough to let you direct it. If you want to direct, try both. Direct a showcase film that demonstrates your talent for working with actors and story. Direct commercials, music videos, second unit, whatever you can direct that demonstrates your talent. The following are some titles that include the magic word. Unfortunately most are not as creative and exciting as they sound.

First Assistant Director: in Hollywood, usually not a stepping stone to directing, although some assistant directors go on to become TV directors or unit production managers. This is more of a line production function than a creative one. You need a commanding presence, leadership ability, and a knack for tactical organization to be a successful first assistant director. The Directors Guild has a special program to help outsiders break into this end of the business. It's tough to get into, but if you get in, you'll have an exciting and fairly lucrative career to look forward to.

Second Assistant Director: liaison between production office, first assistant director, and talent, including extras; basically a coordinator.

Associate Director (videotape): assists the director in videotape.

Second Unit Director: directs sequences (action, scenics, inserts, etc.) that usually don't involve the actors.

Technical Director (videotape): works the switcher and heads lighting crew.

DGA (Directors Guild of America) Trainee: Take a test with many other applicants at the Directors Guild of America and you may land one of these coveted internships.

___ PERFORMER.

Actor
    film drama/comedy actor
    TV drama/comedy actor
    voice-over
    commercials actor
    on-camera host
    on-camera reporter (includes writing, producing), anchor
    announcer
    interviewer
    extra
    stand-in

Dancer

Choreographer

Singer/Musician

Acrobat

Stunts
    stunt coordinator
    stuntperson

CAREER TRACK: I don't have to tell you how tough it is to succeed as a performer. Acting is especially competitive. Becoming a working actor in today's Hollywood is an entrepreneurial endeavor. No one's going to discover you in the mythical Schwab's pharmacy. Directors and casting people seem to prefer known commodities, and it's your job to turn yourself into a desirable, brand-name performer. Many books have been written on how to make it as an actor, and you should check them out. An agent once said that unless you fall into one of the following categories your chances of success as a performer in Hollywood aren't great: (1) you're gorgeous and sexy; (2) you're very funny; (3) you're incredibly talented. If one or more of the above criteria apply to you, you need to find a way to showcase your talent so that casting directors can discover you. Many agents and managers feel that theater in L.A. or New York is an excellent way to demonstrate your talent (writers and directors use it to showcase their talents too), provided you play exactly the type of roles you want to be cast in, which are very natural for you and demonstrate your best gifts. This is not the time to stretch. Other tips: Work in student films. Do stand-up if you're funny. Know your "type" and the kinds of roles that have your name on them (sinister bad guys, fiery seducers, goofy but lovable pals). Do your Adjectives List (the five words that best describe your special qualities) and take it to your photographer. Ask him or her to make sure that your head shots illustrate those qualities. If you have more than one natural type, get pictures that demonstrate each type and be sure the appropriate shot is sent out for each role. Unfortunately, Hollywood directors and casting people are often rushed and don't have time to imagine how you *might* fit the role, so go to auditions in character (and sometimes in costume).

HOLLYWOOD'S LOVE/HATE RELATIONSHIP WITH PERFORMERS

The entertainment industry, like the culture at large, is ambivalent about performers. On the one hand, actors are called narcissistic "children" and are treated like dirt. Cattle calls and casting sessions are frequently abusive. Hollywood says things about actors that it no longer dares to say openly about minorities. Some directors wish they could make movies without performers; car crashes and special effects are easier to control. At the other extreme, once actors become successful, Hollywood treats them like royalty, handling them with kid gloves, coddling them like Little Lord Fauntleroy. If actors sometimes seem to be taking revenge for their previous impotence by using their newfound power in excessive or self-destructive ways, perhaps only other actors who have endured Hollywood's abusive treatment of performers can understand why.

The real underlying issue is our culture's attitude toward emotion. Western countries generally value reason over feeling. Is expressing emotion for a living considered "real work" or just self-indulgence? The fact is that Hollywood makes its money by selling emotional experiences to audiences. Movies that don't make people feel something—excitement, sadness, fear, anger—fail at the box office. The entertainment industry can't manufacture good product without the emotional artists it loves to hate. Hollywood wouldn't be Hollywood without its great actors. Portraying feeling is a subtle and instinctive art and craft.

Even if your career goals lie elsewhere, take an acting class to meet actors and appreciate what they do. You'll be amazed at the wealth of fine artistic talent in Hollywood's acting pool. Smart industry players treat performers with respect.

PRODUCTION JOBS

This next section describes the large category of skilled and entry-level production and postproduction jobs. These are the "hands-on" people who get projects made, putting in long hours under enormous time schedule pressures to bring other people's creative visions to the screen. They are mostly unsung and unknown except to each other and to the usually grateful directors, writers, producers, and actors who could not make movies without them. The rewards are generally good to outstanding pay (except for the entry-level jobs), extensive travel opportunities, the satisfaction of practicing a skilled craft, and the thrill of knowing that millions of people are watching and enjoying your handiwork. Be aware that video is redefining some of the jobs and that many nonunion shoots have people double up in more than one job category. And a word about Hollywood unions: once upon a time they were almost impossible to get into. Even today it is no easy matter. But it is not impossible so persist, persist, persist. Learn about all their rules and regulations and all the requirements for letting new people in. And although people are not usually penalized for starting out by working nonunion, do be careful that you don't do anything that will make it impossible to get into the union when you're ready to do so.

— PRODUCTION STAFF. In a film or video budget, the category of production staff includes key people whose duties involve coordination, implementation, and crew management. It also includes jobs that keep the production office (command center of any project) humming along, sometimes around the clock and certainly for many more hours than most normal jobs require. To succeed in any production staff job, you need to master whatever technical crafts are required by taking classes and working on student or nonunion films. You also must have the kind of personality that does well in a team atmosphere. You have to be fun to have around at 3:00 A.M. in a rainstorm in the jungles of Peru. And you must learn to shmooze with other crew members on the set and between jobs, because that's where your next gig may come from. You'll also need tons of physical energy, because the demands are enormous.

UPM (Unit Production Manager): the person in charge of the crew, under the line producer (sometimes the same person does both jobs). The job involves hiring crew, setting the deals for all crew and vendors, overseeing all work done, and maintaining the budget and the schedule. If you are organized, fairly extroverted, with good team leadership, project management, and administrative skills, you might enjoy being a professional production manager.

Stage Manager (theater, tape): the UPM/assistant director of the stage and TV world.

Location Manager: finds locations and arranges their availability.

Location Scout: works under the location manager.

Script Supervisor: a vital, little-understood position. Helps the director with continuity issues by keeping track of all the details of each scene and take. Which color hat was the actor wearing on that shot three weeks ago, which we have to match now? Which hand picked up the fork at which line? To do this job well you must be extremely organized and observant of details. A major link to editing.

Production Coordinator: liaison between producer, UPM, AD, crew, and actors. Also in charge of the production office. Makes arrangements and distributes call sheets and all other materials.

Production Accountant/Auditor: keeps track of the money. Pays the bills; reports back to the studio (or whoever is financing the film) on how things are going. An accounting background is obviously necessary. This job is now done on computer, so computer skills would be valuable. A good job for an organized, efficient, detail-minded person. May involve location travel. This job is becoming more and more important.

Production Secretary: sometimes entry-level and an outstanding way to break in the door and meet key industry creative talent. Works directly for the coordinator.

Production Assistant: The P.A. does whatever needs to be done that no one else has time for. This is the classic gopher or "gofer" (go for this, go for that) entry-level job. It's an excellent first job for anyone interested in understanding what goes on on a film or TV set.

CAREER TRACK: The senior production jobs are skilled positions, requiring knowledge gained by many hours of working on the set. These are the people who know what must be done before, during, and after a shoot, and they are responsible for ensuring that it gets done, on time and on budget. They are on the managerial rung just below the director and producer. The other production jobs, and the entry-level positions, are the gateway to a production career and offer the opportunity to learn about all aspects of motion picture and television production.

__ **CAMERA** (film or tape). Camera people (cinematographers or videographers) capture images on film or videotape to tell a story. Positions in camera are both creatively and technically demanding.

Director of Photography: works hand in hand with the director; the DP creates the visual look of the film; supervises the lighting and the selection of lenses and filters; and helps to design camera movements.

Camera Operator: physically operates the camera. In countries other than the United States, the director of photography is also the operator.

Assistant Cameraperson (focus puller): helps manipulate the camera during shooting by adjusting focus. Responsible for the camera.

Camera Loader (second assistant cameraperson): changes film magazines during shoot. Does the slate; keeps camera reports.

Specialist: in aerial cinematography, Steadicam, computer-operated camera, underwater, and other specialized areas.

Lighting Director: works with the director of photography and the director to obtain the "look" of the film.

Still Photographer: takes on-set production stills for publicity purposes. Some industry still photographers specialize in doing performers' head shots.

CAREER TRACK: Take classes at film schools or elsewhere to learn the basics. Develop your craft. Shoot things on your own to develop a reel. Shoot student projects. Work on nonunion projects. Try to get on a crew as an apprentice or intern. The union offers training programs but newcomers have to work hard to be accepted. Persistence is the key. Try to get both film and video experience and see which you prefer.

__ ELECTRICAL. These jobs involve the lighting of a film set. Ultimately, the gaffer and his assistants carry out the orders of the director of photography, helping him or her to fulfill lighting requirements. These are highly technical jobs, controlled by unions.

Gaffer (chief electrician): supervises all lighting and electrical personnel on the set. Works closely with the director of photography.

Best Boy (second electrician): responsible for ordering and maintaining equipment.

Third Electrician

Lamp Operators

CAREER TRACK: Experience is the key. Take classes. Work on student projects and nonunion films. Meet people.

__ **GRIP.** Grips are the laborers of the team, moving equipment to and from sets and locations (including camera dollies, cranes, and booms). They move, erect, and strike the various scaffolding and at times assist other crew departments with equipment and materials. The key grip is the foreperson, directly responsible to and works intimately with the director of photography and gaffer. A grip can fix or mount anything, anywhere. Grips have a reputation for a salty attitude, wild clothes, beer drinking, and off-color jokes. But they work long, hard hours on most movies, and magically pull out just the right tool in a crisis to improvise solutions to anything. With hair and wardrobe people, they are usually the first to arrive and the last to leave.

Key Grip

Best Boy Grip: first assistant.

Dolly Grip: pushes camera dollies during shots.

Company Grips: "hammers," rigging.

CAREER TRACK: Since the unions control the grip department, best entry is through nonunion films. But meet as many union people as possible who may help you make the transition. Once you've reached the level of key grip, advancement could be toward second-unit directing.

__ **PROPS.** The prop crew is responsible for the rental, purchase (including scouring of flea markets and antique shops), and construction of all props indicated in the shooting script. Each time a prop is used or altered, it must be restored to its original condition, or continuity will be affected. If a bowl of soup is full at the beginning of a scene, and the actor spoons a bit into his mouth as part of the action, then for each retake the soup bowl must again be full. This is a key job of the prop crew.

Property Master

Assistant Property Master

CAREER TRACK: Start by doing props for theater productions, student projects, nonunion films, and TV projects. If you're a visually sensitive person, observant of detail, an experienced shopper, and reasonably organized, this may be for you. Ability to do research and be accurate are also important.

__ **PRODUCTION SOUND.** The sound of a film—what is heard—is an important part of the emotional and dramatic impact of every motion picture and television program.

Sound Mixer: responsible to the director for the recording of all production sound. Can protest a take where he or she deems sound to be faulty. Chooses the boom operator and whatever assistants are necessary.

Boom Operator: a strong-armed person who maneuvers the long "fishpole" mike, keeping it in range of the actors but out of the shot.

Location Sound Assistant (cable person): sets up sound equipment, puts mikes on actors.

Playback Operator: plays back prerecorded music, lip sync.

CAREER TRACK: Here one starts as an assistant, moves up to boom operator, and eventually to mixer and into postproduction (sound editor's domain). Learn the craft by taking classes or working on student films and nonunion projects. Meet people who can help you move up.

__ **WARDROBE.** The wardrobe department on a movie or TV set designs, creates, or acquires and maintains the costumes actors wear for a production. The director, cinematographer, and production designer work with the costume designer to achieve a look that satisfies any historical considerations as well as achieves the artistic look desired.

Costume Designer: head of the wardrobe department. Researches and designs the costumes for the actors on motion picture and TV programs. Works closely with the director, production designer, and cinematographer.

Costume Supervisor: prepares the wardrobe budget. In charge of fittings, acquisition, inventory, and care of costumes. Also responsible for hiring wardrobe staff.

Costumer/Stylist: part of the "shopping bag brigade," along with set dressers and continuity. Finds whatever is needed.

Tailor/Seamstress: sews the costumes.

Wardrobe Attendant: takes care of costume maintenance and alteration.

Dresser: "dresses" the star.

CAREER TRACK: Although the wardrobe unions offer lectures in wardrobe design, the way to begin a career in the wardrobe business is to work for a costume house, where you learn the business from the ground up. Alternatively one can work in the theater, probably for no pay, and apprentice in that way. Whatever the road, these are predominantly union positions, and you would be well advised to begin making contacts in the business as soon as possible.

__ **MAKEUP.** The makeup department deals with the actors before anyone else each morning on the set. Makeup people help actors to create their characters and perform an overall supportive role for the "talent" of a movie or TV shoot. Working from the script, and in consultation with the director, the makeup artist collaborates with each actor as a fellow artist. The makeup artist can also work in more mundane settings, such as a TV news department, where the hours tend to be more reasonable and the task less creative.

Makeup Artist: head of the makeup department; coordinates makeup schedule and hairstylists.

Assistants: apply "regular" (non-special-effects) makeup.

Body Makeup Artists

CAREER TRACK: You can apprentice to a makeup artist, if he or she will have you. There are also schools that teach the art. Getting a job then entails finding an entry-level position, working as an assistant at a local TV station or on nonunion films until you develop the skills necessary and make the contacts to help you move up.

___ **HAIRSTYLIST.** Besides shaping and coloring hair, the hairstylist carries around a substantial collection of toupees, mustaches, eyelashes, and so on, to accomplish whatever effect the production designer requires.

CAREER TRACK: First one must be a state-licensed hairstylist. Start by working on student and nonunion projects. Then you may want to apply to the hairstylists' union for permission to work as an auxiliary on the set. This means that you can work when no union stylists are available. You must thereafter accumulate 120 hours of work on the set in a period of eighteen months. This entitles you to take the two-day union examination, leading to membership, albeit at the bottom rung of the profession. Sound like an obstacle course? It is, one meant to keep the average hairdresser out of the business.

___ **SPECIAL EFFECTS/VISUAL EFFECTS.** The difference between special effects and visual effects is that the former are shot with the production camera, whereas the latter are shot with a special camera and employ the techniques of mattes (painted backgrounds that are combined with live action footage), animation, and miniatures. Special effects include fog, rain, and snow, shot by the camera operator working on the set. Visual effects are shot in a high-tech environment, in another location, normally not involving actors. In both cases, the job is to make an audience believe it is seeing what it is not really seeing.

Visual Effects Producer: the DP of visual effects; a first cameraperson with a specialty.

Special Effects Makeup Artist (also "FX artist"): creates creatures and monsters; an artist in polyester resin.

Explosives Specialist: produces the explosives called for, including the small charges that create the illusion of bullet wounds.

Model Maker/Miniatures: involved in the visual effects department.

Matte Painter: designs and paints backgrounds for matte shots, which are combined with live footage.

Computer Graphics/Animation Specialist: creates computer graphics and animation; the special effects and visual effects field of the future.

CAREER TRACK: The way into these creative fields is to have a passion for a particular form and then find a job with one of the companies specializing in that kind of work. Passion is the key.

__ SET OPERATIONS.

Craft Services: provides on-set snacks, treats, drinks, and so on. Actual meals are provided by a catering service, which may have only a half hour to feed an entire crew, up to a thousand people, sometimes in a jungle a million miles from nowhere.

CAREER TRACK: Work for a caterer, learn to cook, and learn the needs of the set and how to communicate with the 2nd AD (second assistant director).

__ SET DESIGN. One of the artistic departments. Along with the director, cinematographer, and design group and under the control of the production designer, set design people create the look of the film.

Production Designer/Art Director: in conjunction with the director, creates the visual design of a film. Chooses colors, textures, and materials that set the emotional tone. Supervises location hunt, set building, and dressing and coordinates all that pertains to artistic design, including props, costumes, hair, and makeup.

Set Designer: executes plans for construction of sets, draws blueprints from the drawings and designs of the production designer, and oversees construction.

CAREER TRACK: Learn excellent drawing technique, especially architectural drawing. Know history of architecture and design and enjoy doing research in period looks, including the future (spaceships). This is an area that requires a long apprenticeship in artistic fields. Attend art school or get a degree in theater arts (study to be a director).

___ GRAPHIC DESIGNER/ARTIST. The art department does everything from providing drawings as the director plans the production (months and even years before the actual shoot) to supplying titles for TV credits on the evening news.

Illustrator: helps the director and production designer visualize the look of the film. Literally puts their ideas on paper. The ultimate tool for visually planning the film is a fine illustrator. The illustrator has a talent for figure drawing and perspective.

Storyboard Artist: Overlaps with the illustrator, who often must create storyboards for the director. Storyboards depict the action and conception of a feature film, TV commercial, or animated cartoon.

Matte Painter: (see Visual Effects).

Title Designer: working with the editor, producer, director, and an optical effects/titles company, designs the type style, color, and over-all concept of the titles.

Animator: creates visual effects that move, either through tradi-tional cel (a sheet of clear plastic celluloid on which a single frame of animation has been hand-painted), stop-motion, or computer ani-mation techniques.

CAREER TRACK: Art school, computer design training, and drawing expertise are musts. Long apprenticeships are common. Get to know production artists of all kinds and eventually they will hire you.

___ SET CONSTRUCTION.

Construction Coordinator: oversees construction of a production's sets; prepares and updates the construction budget; hires the crew. The construction coordinator acts as liaison between the production designer and production manager.

Set Crew: construction foreperson, labor foreperson, paint foreper-son.

Construction Labor, Carpenters

Standby Painters

CAREER TRACK: Do construction on a union or nonunion film. Watch the foreperson and the coordinator. Learn. The union rules allow a worker, technically, to become a construction coordinator after thirty days of work on a union set.

___ SET DRESSING.

Set Decorator: designs, plans, and supervises the dressing of a set, be it a living room or a doctor's office. Works closely with production designer and director.

Set Dressing Crew: comprises a *Lead Person* and the people he or she supervises, the *Swing Gang.* They are the actual movers and placers of all set dressing.

Greens Person: the landscaper and gardener on the set.

CAREER TRACK: The set decorator is an interior designer. He or she must have the confidence of the production designer to work in films or TV. Many set decorators are interior designers by profession.

___ TRANSPORTATION.

Transportation Captain: runs the set and the transportation department.

Transportation Coordinator: responsible for providing, maintaining, and operating every vehicle needed for a production, from antique cars to honey wagons and the camera truck. Works with Teamsters Union officials.

Drivers: the Teamsters who move the vehicles.

CAREER TRACK: Learn to drive a truck. Make friends with the crew captains in the transportation department. Let the union know you're interested in movie/TV work. The hours are long, but the pay is good.

___ ANIMAL HANDLERS.

Animal Specialist/Trainer: handles and trains animals, often the trainer's own, and often in less than ideal conditions. Deals with both trained and dangerous animals.

Wrangler: usually deals with horses, cows, and livestock.

CAREER TRACK: Assist a handler or wrangler to learn the ropes and make contacts.

__ **ON-SET MEDICAL.** Although a doctor is not always hired for a production, a first-aid specialist (usually a highly skilled nurse) is required.

Doctor

First Aid Specialist: performs routine medical care, plus any emergency situations that may arise, requiring ability to deal with ambulances and hospitals far from the location.

CAREER TRACK: For a nurse looking to work in the movies, the best advice is to get to know production people who can help you break into the business. Experience in an emergency room or paramedic situation would be a plus.

__ **ON-SET TEACHER.**

Studio Teacher: required by law for all school-age minors working on a production. Must teach curriculum appropriate for each minor for a minimum of three hours a day and ensure their overall welfare.

CAREER TRACK: Must be a state-certified teacher. Jobs go through local Board of Education. Also make Hollywood contacts.

__ **SET SECURITY.**

Local Police

Local Fire Fighter

Security Guard and Security Consultant: guards sets, stars, celebrities.

Watchman

Janitor

__ **POSTPRODUCTION.** When the shooting stops, the cutting begins.

A. PICTURE EDITING

In my opinion, the editor is one of the most important creative talents on any project, making as vital a contribution as the writer or director in many instances. But this is a difficult job. You need good technical skills, plus a filmmaker's vision, a musician's sense of timing and rhythm, and the skills of a diplomat (you're dealing with creative egos at their most fragile moments). A slightly introverted personality would be a plus, although you must be able to get along with people in a high-stress work environment. And you need to be comfortable spending long hours in a dark room poring over shots, piecing together the puzzle. Not for everyone, but if this is your special talent, you'll spend many rewarding, quite lucrative years making films and TV shows emerge from rolls of celluloid or reels of tape.

Film Editor: assembles the film according to the director's vision. Responsible for opticals and matte shots and for synchronizing voice and sound tracks. A very creative job. Sometimes the editor is the real "filmmaker" on a project. Some editors are known as "doctors" who can create a viable film from a pile of seemingly hopeless dailies. Some of these "doctors" design additional material to shoot to solve the problem, and may even go out and direct second unit to get the material they need.

Videotape Editor: *a. off-line*—The off-line editor makes creative choices with the director about what should be in the show. Analogous to the film editor.
b. on-line—The on-line editor functions as the postproduction technical director. Using sophisticated electronic equipment, he or she executes the final edits from the edit list prepared by the off-line editor.

Assistant Editor/Videotape Operator: prepares tapes for editing, assembles the rough cuts, and assists with the on-line edit.

Apprentice Editor

CAREER TRACK: Take classes in film school or elsewhere to learn the craft. Then find a job as an apprentice, somehow, somewhere. You need to accumulate material for a demo reel to show people your work.

B. SOUND EDITING

Sound Editor: creates the sound track for a film (other than music). Task is to pull the audience into the film by a combination of mood and atmosphere. The sound editor supervises all aspects of this process, working with the film editor and director.

ADR (automatic dialogue replacement) Technician: records in-studio line readings, both synchronized ("looping") and nonsynchronized ("walla").

Foley Artist: physically re-creates sounds (e.g., footsteps, rain, street sounds, wind) in a foley sound studio.

Recording Mixer (Audio Sweetener, videotape): mixes production, post-production, and music tracks onto one composite sound track. Working at a mixing console, in sessions with the director and editor, modifies and adds music and sound effects to the sound track of the film/TV show.

CAREER TRACK: Do class work in film school, music school; then apprentice. Get a job at entry level, doing anything, with a sound department in film or TV. As in many of the film/TV professions, most of the important material can be learned only in the workplace.

C. MUSIC

Composer: creates the musical score for a film or TV show, based on the ideas of the director.

Arranger-Orchestrator

Copyist

Conductor

Musician

Music Supervisor: studio job. Keeps track of all the music on a film, clears rights, and may organize scoring session. On any one film the music supervisor may be dealing with songs from many record companies plus the original score, so this can be complex. An administrative/quasi-legal/librarian type job that requires an extensive knowledge of the music business.

Music Editor: in feature films, generally hired by the composer. Assists the composer technically and finally cuts the music into music tracks for final mixing. Selects and edits nonoriginal music for film and TV.

Engineer/Mixer: supervises the recording of live and synthesized music for a production.

Lyricist/Songwriter

Librarian: maintains a music library.

Music Clearance: When music is used, the legal rights to use it must be "cleared." This involves research and administrative skills, plus some legal knowledge.

CAREER TRACK: The potential employers in the music department of a production are the composer, the music editor, the scoring mixer, and the librarian. The musicians' union (American Federation of Musicians; see Resources) should be contacted as a starting place for musicians. The more education and experience in music one brings to the job search, the better.

D. OTHER POSTPRODUCTION FUNCTIONS

Negative Cutter: matches the editor's final cut with a pristine uncut original and carefully edits it to match, creating the master negative from which all prints will be struck. Requires precision, attention to detail, patience—and clean white gloves! Steadily being replaced by video-editing techniques.

Lab Technician: develops film and creates special film effects per the editor's instructions.

Postproduction Supervisor: an administrative job. Coordinates all administrative aspects of postproduction, sets sound mix, and supervises lab work deliveries and schedule. The "UPM of postproduction." On smaller projects, the editor or assistant editor may handle these tasks.

Librarian: in charge of film library, maintained by labs, for storage of final negatives. Also catalogs stock footage for rental and in-house uses.

CAREER TRACK: Apply at film laboratories and postproduction houses.

__ **INSURANCE.** Insuring every aspect of a film's production is a complicated business. Specialists in this field are important to every production. Financing is impossible without comprehensive production insurance. A background in general insurance would be helpful, plus knowledge of production. Apply to companies listed in the *Hollywood Reporter Blu-Book Directory* under "Insurance."

__ **PUBLICITY.** During the filming and even during the creation of a production, frequently the media will be enlisted (hyped) to whet the public's appetite for a major release or new series.

Unit Publicist: responsible for the publicity campaign on a particular film. Often goes on-location. A production's liaison with the press.

Studio Publicist

Independent Publicity Firm: works on a contract or retainer basis, providing publicity for, among other items, a film's release, a premiere, a charity event, or a star.

CAREER TRACK: Since the demise of the old studio system in the 1950s, no apprenticeship programs exist for publicists. However, there are a number of independent public relations firms that hire entry-level employees, and major independent TV stations maintain in-house public relations departments that handle all media relations. If you are fairly extroverted, write well, communicate well on the phone and in person, and have creative ideas about how to interest the public in projects and personalities, this might be a good field for you. A degree (or work experience) in journalism is a plus.

__ **LEGAL.** Lawyers are important players in Hollywood. The amounts of money at stake are so large and so difficult to control that relations between the various production entities (producer, director, actors, financing) need to be carefully defined and redefined. Also, there are the endless maneuverings after the fact, resulting in a flood of lawsuits that have become normal in the entertainment business.

Legal Department Attorney: at production company or studio.

Entertainment Attorney: lawyer who attends to legal issues either independently or with a large law firm.

Paralegal/Legal Secretary: specializes in entertainment law.

CAREER TRACK: Many more lawyers are drawn to the entertainment industry than there are positions for them. But the most determined and aggressive do find work in Hollywood, as attorneys and also as agents, managers, and business affairs or studio executives, and even in creative capacities. A specialization in entertainment law is, of course, important. You can work in the entertainment law department of a firm or in the legal affairs department of a studio or production company. Private practice is risky.

— EXECUTIVE.

A. CREATIVE EXECUTIVE AT STUDIO OR PRODUCTION COMPANY

These are the men and women who decide whether to pursue a particular project—the "hit-pickers." At the lower levels, they can say no but cannot say yes, requiring their bosses' approval to move a project forward. Some supervise the making of the film or TV show from a business or creative point of view. At the highest levels, these executives deal with both creative and corporate concerns—watching box office results and Neilson ratings, maximizing profits, keeping the stock price high. Creative executives' careers are on the line each time a film or TV show is presented to the public. Few remain in this field their whole careers. Most go into creative producing or other areas of the industry, such as agenting or writing.

These jobs are extremely demanding, requiring long hours of meetings and phone calls during the week and extensive weekend reading of screenplays. Also, creative executives need to view films and television shows produced by their own and other companies. These positions are also very political in nature. An extroverted personality is a plus. Titles are different in different arenas; check the detailed "Executive Roster" section of the *Hollywood Reporter Blu-Book Directory* for more detail on specific titles.

Studio Chief: the CEO, the chairperson, the final decision maker.

President of Worldwide Production: oversees the selection, development, production, and distribution of a studio's products. Plans film release patterns (e.g., spring, summer, Christmas films); develops corporate strategy. It is this individual's vision that a studio relies on for the films and TV shows that appear under its production logo.

VP Creative Affairs/VP Production: seeks out and develops projects and oversees production from both a creative and a story point of view and as an executive. Maintains good relationships with agents, writers, and other creative talent. Two criteria for getting these jobs: taste and access to creative talent—writers, directors, stars. Your relationships with members of the community are an important part of why you're hired. Involves a great deal of shmoozing plus reading scripts during nonwork hours, especially on weekends.

VP, Director, or Manager of Development: similar to VP creative affairs/production but narrower scope. Must be able to work with writers to improve the script. Less involvement with actual production.

Creative Executive: lower-level version of VP of development.

Programming Executive (TV): an executive who supervises the acquisition, development, casting, and scheduling of television programs. May hold a president, VP, director, or manager title.

Acquisitions: acquires completed or nearly completed projects for a distributor or network.

Story Editor: head of the story department. Supervises readers, who are responsible for recommending yes or no on a script, book, or play. May do story notes.

Story Analyst/Reader: entry-level position. Synopsizes and evaluates material for film or TV projects. Staff or free-lance. At the studios, readers can be union members.

Development Assistant: assistant to a development executive or story department. Also reads scripts. Entry-level position. Involves clerical work.

CAREER TRACK: Story analyst/reader or assistant are the most common entry-level jobs for this area. An agency background is also looked upon favorably.

B. ADMINISTRATIVE AND BUSINESS EXECUTIVE AT STUDIO OR PRODUCTION COMPANY

Business Affairs Executive: negotiates contracts. This job is often held by lawyers.

Financial Affairs/Accounting: in charge of guiding and tracking the financial status of the company.

Legal Affairs Executive: (see Legal).

Distribution/Syndication: sells the product to exhibitors or independent TV stations.

Marketing

Market Research: predominantly in TV. Does market research, focus groups, track ratings, demographics. This information is needed by the programming and advertising sales departments.

Standards and Practices: network TV censors.

Advertising Sales: sells advertising time on TV.

Advertising/Publicity/Promotion

Consumer Products/Merchandising: licensing of characters or logos to manufacturers of toys, apparel, consumer goods. The millions of Teenage Mutant Ninja Turtles dolls, Mickey Mouse T-shirts, and Batman cups are the result of this activity.

Information Systems Executive: manages computer systems and information resources for the company.

Human Resources/Personnel

___ **GUILD/UNION EXECUTIVE.** A legal, administrative, labor relations, or union background is a plus for this position. Some positions are similar to any other media arts organization job (see below).

___ **MEDIA ARTS ORGANIZATION EXECUTIVE/EMPLOYEE.** Media arts organizations (e.g., the Academy of Motion Picture Arts and Sciences and the

Academy of Television Arts and Sciences) preserve and promote the product of the industry and celebrate the achievements of the creators of that product. To find a list of possible employers, look in the "Associations" section of the *Hollywood Reporter Blu-Book Directory.* The available positions and job titles are similar to those in any nonindustry, nonprofit organization. These tend to be fairly low-paying jobs except in the most established organizations.

Executive Director

Fund-raiser/Development

Special Event Producer/Coordinator

Convention/Festival Organizer, Programmer

Publications Editor

Librarian/Archivist

CAREER TRACK: A degree in film plus an M.B.A. in nonprofit management would be an excellent background for top positions. Background in journalism, publicity, or sales would also be a plus.

__ RESEARCHER.

Script Researcher: does background research for writers and producers.

Market Researcher: (see Administrative Executives above).

Film Researcher: searches out and negotiates licensing of footage for films and TV shows. A specialized skill. Involves some legal knowledge.

__ EXHIBITOR.

Theater Owner

Buyer: rents films.

Projectionist

Usher

Concession Attendant

__ **FILM COMMISSIONER.** Most countries and states now have film commissions to entice Hollywood filmmakers to shoot in their locale. Requires an intimate knowledge of the area in question, familiarity with production requirements, and a sales personality. Background as a location manager would be a plus.

__ **ADMINISTRATIVE PERSONNEL.** As in every business, administrative professionals are needed to keep things running smoothly. (See Chapter 13, on entry-level jobs.)

Office Manager

Executive Assistant

Personal Assistant: assistant to mogul or celebrity. May involve personal and social arrangements, travel, and nonstandard hours.

Secretary

Receptionist

Gopher/Runner

Mail Room Person

Temp: holds temporary administrative positions, such as word processor, secretary, clerk.

Intern

__ **AGENT.** Agents represent talent and collect approximately 10 percent of the client's paycheck for performing this service. (See Chapter 15 on agents.)

__ **CASTING DIRECTOR.** The casting director advises the director and producer on casting choices. Some casting directors concentrate on speaking parts, others on extras. Some specialize in theatrical films, some in TV, others in commercials. Casting directors may become casting executives at studios, production companies, and networks.

Talent Coordinator: books celebrities and other talent onto talk shows or specials.

CAREER TRACK: Many casting directors are former actors. If you have a good nose for acting talent, an excellent memory for names and faces, and an intuitive sense of who would be right for what, you may want to consider this high-pressure, long-hours career. You'll be attending performances and films constantly, assessing new talent. The only way to start is as an assistant to a casting person. You learn the craft by doing it. Talent coordinators often start out in lower-level production jobs on shows.

__ **PRODUCER'S REPRESENTATIVE.** This is a relatively new job category. The producer's rep is an entrepreneur who obtains distribution for independent producers and advises them on some of the business aspects of production.

__ **MANAGER.** Managers advise and guide their clients (usually actors, but, more recently, writers and directors as well) on career moves and business decisions. Managers are paid on a percentage basis, typically 15 percent of a client's earnings for a personal manager, less for a business manager.

Personal Manager

Business Manager: handles client's business affairs.

CAREER TRACK: Many actors' managers are former actors themselves. Others are well-connected former agents or executives.

__ **COMPUTER PROFESSIONAL.** As in every other industry, computers are assuming an increasingly important role. The application of computer technology to the entertainment business is still in its formative stages. New entertainment industry software and services are being created all the time.

Information Systems Executive: (see Administrative Executive).

Systems Analyst: in-house or free-lance.

Programmer: in-house or free-lance.

Computer Graphics Specialist: (see Special Effects).

Computer Consultant: free-lance or may work at a store that specializes in serving the entertainment industry.

Database Librarian: works for companies like Baseline and Casting Call, which provide access to a large library of information on such things as credits and casting.

Data Entry Clerk: enters data into large databases at a database library, agency, or studio.

__ **CONSULTANT.** Free-lance consultants provide information and support to studios, productions, and entertainment industry people in a growing number of areas:

Technical Consultant/Adviser: knowledgeable about an area no one at the studio or on the production has data about—medical, legal, martial arts, fine art, whatever is needed.

Security Consultant: (see Set Security).

Script Consultant: free-lance "script doctor."

Management or Information Consultant: provides advice or information to companies or individuals on business issues, background information, credits, etc. (Also see Researcher, Database Librarian.)

Environmental Consultant: a new category. A number of top Hollywood people who are concerned about environmental issues are hiring such consultants.

Career Consultant: a relatively new position in the entertainment business.

Computer Consultant: (see Computer Professionals).

Financial Consultant: advises producers on sources of financing (see Producer's Representative).

__ **COACH.**

Dialogue Coach

Acting Coach

Physical Fitness Trainer

Martial Arts Trainer

Vocal Coach

Dancing Coach

___ EDUCATOR.

College Professor: teaches film/TV course work.

Instructor/Lecturer/Seminar Leader: for institution or free-lance.

On-Set Teacher: for child performers (see above).

___ MEDICAL.

Physical or Mental Health Professional: specializes in helping entertainment industry people with health or other personal problems.

First Aid Specialist: (see On-Set Medical).

___ BANKER. Specializes in entertainment industry financing.

___ STOCKBROKER. Specializes in entertainment industry stocks.

___ ENTERTAINMENT INDUSTRY JOURNALIST (TV or print). In recent years, a number of journalists who cover the entertainment industry have been able to cross over into creative executive positions at production companies and studios, based on their in-depth knowledge and the contacts they made while reporting on the industry.

Editor

Reporter

Writer

Producer

Film Critic

Anchor

Moderator, On-Camera Host: (see Performer).

___ ACCOUNTANT.

Financial Affairs Executive/Accountant: at production company or studio (see Administrative and Business Executive).

Accountant: at accounting firm specializing in helping entertainment industry clients.

Business Manager: (see Manager).

MY TOP FIVE INDUSTRY JOBS

Here are the five industry jobs that interest me the most:

1. _____
2. _____
3. _____
4. _____
5. _____

6

☆

Target the Niche
That's Right for You

★　★　★　★　★　★　★　★　★　★　★　★　★　★

This is a wonderful business to waste time in. If you don't know
what you're doing you can wander around Hollywood for years,
like a dog that's lost the scent, until you get clued in to what it is
you have to do.

—Former Literary Agent/Pitching Coach
DAVID DWORSKI

ADD IT ALL UP: TARGET YOUR SPECIFIC GOAL

Now you're ready to add it all up and target a specific niche within
the entertainment industry where your unique gifts (your passion,
talent, temperament, skills) and the industry's needs come together.
X marks the spot! X is the place where you'll have the best chance
of career success and creative satisfaction in show business. But
you'll need to be specific. For example, it's not enough to want to be
a director. What kind of director? A director who specializes in getting great performances from actors in intense dramatic material? A
director who's known for technical expertise, special effects wizardry,
and a unique visual style? A director of television sitcoms who specializes in working with difficult series actors? A director of commercials whose specialty is hot action sequences with great stunts? A
producer-director of hard-hitting documentaries? A writer-director of
small, independent personal films on man–woman relationships? A
director of major-studio star vehicle comedies?

WHY DO I NEED TO BE SO SPECIFIC? WON'T IT LIMIT MY OPTIONS?

Sometimes my clients resist the idea of targeting their goals in such detail. They worry that they'll be boxed in, limited, typecast. Why not just say, "I want to be a director," and see what develops?

While I agree that it's great to stay flexible and open to opportunity (even after you've targeted your niche), I've found that people who avoid getting specific about their goals and are unable to describe their target niche in vivid detail have a harder time selling themselves to the industry and being as successful as they could be. After all, how can you run a race flat out if you're uncertain of where the goal line is? The shortest distance between two points is a straight line, not a zigzag path or a meandering wave. I have seen too many people in my counseling office whose résumés are "a little of this, a little of that" and who have spent the last ten years wandering around Hollywood not getting where they'd really like to go because they weren't sure where the target was!

Believe me, even with a clearly focused goal, you'll do some wandering around, responding to opportunities that present themselves to you. Why make it worse by not knowing exactly where you're aiming?

There's a terrific selling advantage in being very focused about your goal. "Well, I thought I might like to direct . . ." is a real turn-off. It just tells potential employers that you haven't done your homework by thoroughly investigating your own talent, learning about the industry's niches, and pinpointing your goals. Also, by targeting a specific niche you'll stand out from the crowd. You're not just one more standard, plain-vanilla director, you're a director with a special knack and a specific vision of where you're going. That's a big plus.

BEWARE THE OBVIOUS CHOICES

A number of areas are already grossly overcrowded. Sometimes it seems that *everyone* on the planet wants to direct. Blame it on Steven Spielberg, I guess. T-shirts that say "But I really want to direct . . ." are hot sellers in Los Angeles. Hollywood crew members can often be seen wearing them on studio sets—as a joke.

As you work at targeting your niche, try to avoid the already-crowded niches that most people think of when they first get involved in show business and that are often the toughest to break into, such as directing major-studio feature films. Hollywood turns out a couple of hundred feature films every year. That's approximately 200 directing jobs. When you figure in all the already-experienced, hot directors who work regularly, the writers who can demand to direct their own screenplays, and the millions of wannabes out there (including all those crew members wearing "But I really want to direct . . ." T-shirts), we're talking some serious competition here, folks!

I don't mean to imply that if this is your deep-down dream you shouldn't pursue it. If everything in the last five chapters leads you to believe this is the one right niche for you—go for it! But please do me and yourself a big favor: at least consider the alternative areas—television, cable, commercials, independent films, documentaries. People have created some very successful and exciting careers in those areas. And, amazingly, sometimes directing success in other niches actually *does* result in your getting to direct a major-studio feature.

DON'T LET THE HOLLYWOOD PECKING ORDER LIMIT YOUR CHOICES

Because of the Hollywood pecking order, sometimes people are afraid to target niches that aren't the top creative categories, like directing, producing, acting, or writing. Even if they would be perfectly happy as, say, an editor or cinematographer or assistant director or hairstylist or secretary or makeup artist or special effects wizard or distribution salesperson or technician, they feel they should aim for an "above-the-line" (nontechnical) career goal. Nothing could be further from the truth.

Some of the most productive, creative, and happy Hollywood people I know are those who have created excellent, well-paying careers for themselves in the less-glamorous areas. Why should they drive themselves crazy trying to be someone they're not, butting heads with the endless crops of new geniuses who arrive in town every day? A behind-the-scenes person with a solid track record and good reputation often has a better chance of a long, lucrative entertainment industry career than those on the creative front lines.

NICHES TO CONSIDER

Let's get down to specifics. Here are some niches—some hypothetical, some based on people currently working in the industry—that are specially tailored to showcase the talents and interests of the person involved.

★ An agent trainee, not just a garden-variety type, but one of part-Latino heritage specializing in Hispanic literary talent who is on the board of directors of the Latino Writers Association.

★ A colorful, larger-than-life character who creatively masterminds and aggressively produces large, studio feature films, mostly action pix. He's known in the industry to be a wizard in postproduction.

★ A creative supercutter known for exciting montages and an even-tempered ability to get along with erratic, tempestuous directors and producers.

★ A director of action films with a strong stunt background and superb command of the technical side of filmmaking.

★ A production consultant specializing in liaison with Moscow who performs such tasks as translation, casting, and location work.

★ A development executive with a great sense of story structure who specializes in the solution of intractable script problems. He has a mainstream studio movie sensibility, is married to a hot young agent, and is well connected around town.

★ A former Ivy League university linguistics professor who has developed a special system to help actors lose their accents or gain new ones. A "dialect doctor."

★ A producer of visually startling commercials who has teamed up with an exciting, new director to form a highly successful commercial production company that is now crossing over into features.

★ A segment director for "reality" TV shows whose skillful re-creations using nonactors keep her constantly employed.

MY TARGETED NICHE

So what's right for you? Fill in the blanks below. This is your written goal.

I'd like to work in the _____ area doing _____ _____ and to be known for _____ _____ .

In the next chapter we'll take this information and craft it into your Hollywood Pitch.

A NICHE MAY NOT BE FOREVER

Those of you who don't like to be pinned down or locked in may be experiencing just a touch of claustrophobia right about now. But don't let it stop you from filling in the blanks above. Just remind yourself that whatever goal you choose today isn't forever. Goals can change as you gain experience and achieve success. You may be working toward one goal and fall in love with a new niche. You may be presented with a wonderful opportunity you decide not to refuse. Or you may achieve success in one area and decide to take on a new challenge. No problem. Just adjust your targeted niche definition and rewrite your paragraph.

WRITTEN GOALS, VISUALIZATION, AND CAREER COLLAGES

It's important to write goals down (some people like to do five- and one-year goals). There's something magical about it that I don't quite understand. Putting your dream in black and white seems to act as a signal to your unconscious that you're really serious about this: you actually intend to do it. (I know this is true because I've watched it work in my own life. Last year I wrote in my yearly goals list that I wanted to really explore the possibility of writing a book proposal, getting an agent, selling a book, and writing the book. When I updated my yearly goals list in January of this year, I was astonished to find that I had accomplished the first three and was well on my way to achieving number four!)

Another powerful way to let your unconscious mind know that you're seriously intending to be what you say you want to be is to find a quiet place, let yourself relax with deep breathing, meditation, or self-hypnosis, and imagine your life in vivid detail as you successfully work in your targeted niche. Engage all your senses and emotions. What do you see? What do you hear? What do you touch? What do you smell? What do you feel?

You may also want to create a career collage. As you read magazines, tear out pictures of people doing what you'd like to be doing and living the life you plan on leading. On a bulletin board, pin up these photos, if possible adding snapshots of your face for their faces. Hang the bulletin board over your desk where it can inspire you as you make your calls and work on your career.

DO SOME HOMEWORK ON WHAT IT TAKES TO MAKE IT IN YOUR TARGETED AREA

Once you've begun to narrow down your area of interest, you'll be amazed at how easy it is to find information about it. Now that your eyes are peeled, you find yourself stumbling across all kinds of interesting stuff.

For example, let's say you've decided that you want to be a TV director on three-camera sitcoms, which you've loved since you were a kid. You still watch them all the time, and now you notice the names of directors. You've started to keep a list of them. Just last week you caught an interview on the E! cable channel with one of these directors. She was talking about how she got started. You took notes!

You subscribe to industry publications and pay careful attention to bios of successful directors. What tracks did they follow to get where they are? You order a couple of books from the Samuel French catalog for more info, and decide to go to L.A. to visit the industry libraries and bookstores to pursue things further (see Chapter 8 for sources of information). You strike up a friendship with a reference librarian, who suggests some additional resources and contacts, and you call your brother's cousin-in-law in Burbank to see if he has any useful contacts. Amazingly, after a few calls you track down a director who is willing to talk to you, and he gives you the inside scoop on a number of different avenues into sitcom directing. You also find out about a UCLA Extension class where you can hear and meet some of the top TV comedy directors in person.

HOW DO I ACQUIRE THE INDUSTRY-SPECIFIC SKILLS I'LL NEED TO SUCCEED IN MY TARGETED NICHE?

Your targeted career niche may require industry-specific skills that you can't fake. If you're aiming for a career as a documentary cameraperson, for example, there's no way around understanding lights, F-stops, and 16-millimeter and video technology. If you're focusing on sitcom writing, you need to know about three-camera shows.

At this point the dreaded question arises: SHOULD I GO TO FILM SCHOOL?

THE PROS AND CONS OF FILM SCHOOL

First, the pros.

★ A good film school will give you an overall understanding of film or television that's extremely helpful. You'll watch and critique a lot of films and TV shows, developing your critical eye and taste.

★ Film school will teach you some fundamental directing, writing, and production skills, which you'll be able to practice on student productions. Anyone who wants to work in the business in any capacity will benefit from the experience of developing a product and working on the "factory floor" as it's manufactured.

★ The hot film schools, many of them in Los Angeles or New York, provide you with a built-in network of contacts with students, former students, faculty, and guest speakers that can jump-start your career. Many people think this is the major benefit of going to a good film school. This can be particularly helpful for people with no previous entertainment industry contacts, including many minority students. Of course, film schools in the boonies may not offer much in this regard.

★ Some film schools arrange internships for their students with prestigious production companies and studios.

★ You can use your student film as a showcase for your talents. The better film schools hold industry screenings and help students get their projects into festivals. Top students get "discovered" and can become successful very quickly. The Academy of Motion Picture Arts and Sciences gives Oscars each year for the best student films, and some student fims have also won in the documentary and short subject categories, competing against professional films.

★ The prestige film schools have a certain cachet on your résumé.

Now, the cons.

★ There are other ways of learning about film besides going to film school. You've already spent years absorbing thousands of films and TV shows. To hone your critical skills even further, rent tapes, read books, create discussion groups.

★ There are other ways of learning the specific production, writing, directing, or performing skills you need for your targeted niche besides going to film school.

1. Take classes. Go to Los Angeles, get a job (preferably in the industry), and take some of the many classes available around town in everything from acting to cinematography to distribution to entertainment law. They're usually taught by savvy insiders with a glittering list of industry panelists who may be able to give you more current information than some of the professors at non-industry-connected film schools around the country. The American Film Institute public programs division and UCLA Extension have some great classes. (AFI and UCLA also have excellent film schools.) UCLA Extension even offers a certificate program if you take enough of their showbiz classes. But even that may not be necessary. Just take the classes you really need and put together your own "program." One nice thing about extension classes is that there are few restrictions or requirements. You can often just sign up, pay the fee, and show up. In class, you can make excellent contacts with other students, the teacher, and guest speakers.

2. Make your own film. Some film schools don't let all students make their films, so even if you pay your tuition and pass your courses you could get stuck just crewing some other genius's project and graduate without a showcase film. Some people believe that it's a better investment to take the money you would have spent on film school, skip the bullshit, and just make your film.

3. Volunteer or intern. To learn, get experience, and gain all-important credits and contacts, you may want to volunteer to work on someone else's student film (they're paying tuition, you're not!) or work on a low-budget production. You may also be able to arrange an internship where you volunteer your services in return for learning the ropes.

4. Get a job in the industry. Cynics would ask: why pay a school for the privilege of doing dog work on a school production? Why not just go to Hollywood and get paid to do dog work on a real production? Talk someone into letting you apprentice with them. In the entertainment industry, sometimes the best education is on-the-job training.

★ If your interests lie outside the usual directing/writing/production spectrum, you may find film school doesn't address your special needs. You may not find out much about how to be, for example, an agent or a distributor or a network market researcher or an exhibitor or a casting director or a showbiz computer consultant or a star bodyguard or a business affairs executive in film school.

★ Film school is expensive (as much as $100,000) and takes up valuable years of your life. For some people it makes more sense just to get a job in Hollywood and start working your way up the ladder. Few industry employers really care if you've been to film school or not—they just want to know if you've got the talent and the skills to do the job.

★ An expensive film school education is no guarantee of a paying job in Hollywood. Most film schools don't teach you the skills in this book: how to actually find work in the industry. According to Dezso Magyar, director of the American Film Institute's Center for Advanced Film and Television Studies, only 5–10 percent of the 26,000 students who graduate from film study programs each year actually find their way into the industry.

OK, WHAT DO I REALLY THINK?

Here's my advice: if you're young (or fairly young), and have the time and the money, the right film school can be a great way to start your career. You'll learn a number of useful skills and make some good contacts. Film school may not allow you to focus narrowly on your specific area of interest, but it will give you a great overview of the filmmaking process as a whole. This can be very helpful to you later in your career.

If your goal is to work in Hollywood, try to get into one of the hot schools in L.A. or New York. However, if you're a midcareer person who's feeling time nipping at your heels . . . or you're crossing over into show business from another field . . . or you're in tight financial circumstances . . . I think that it can sometimes be preferable to just go to Hollywood and learn as you work. Really focus on the specific skills you need for your targeted job. You may not need the broader overview that film school can provide. Full-time film school could slow you down. Try the get-a-job-and-take-classes-on-the-side route. Or just make your film and let the industry see your work. It's faster and cheaper.

But don't take this as a hard-and-fast rule. There are some excellent programs that you might want to pursue. The American Film Institute, for instance, offers a program for women directors, which a number of midcareer women have used to showcase their talent.

Another program to be aware of is the highly regarded Assistant Directors Training Program at the Directors Guild of America, which presents a great opportunity for outsiders without Hollywood connections—especially women and minorities—to break into behind-the-scenes Hollywood. The program trains second assistant directors to work in movies and TV. Star alumni include directors Walter Hill *(48 HRS)* and Alan Rudolph *(Choose Me)*; producers Howard Kazanjian *(Return of the Jedi)* and Richard Hashimoto *(Beetlejuice);* and TV director-producers Win Phelps ("L.A. Law") and Philip Parslow ("Dynasty"). But the training program is tough to get into: each year it accepts only 8 to 15 people from more than 1,000 applicants.

THE MOMENT OF TRUTH: ARE YOU WILLING TO PAY THE PRICE?

> Bunker Hunt, the Texas oil billionaire, was asked once if he had any one piece of advice he could give people on how to succeed. He said that success is simple. First, you decide what you want specifically; and second, you decide you're willing to pay the price to make it happen—and then pay that price.
>
> —ANTHONY ROBBINS
> *Unlimited Power: The New Science
> of Personal Achievement*

You've targeted your specific goal. You've looked at the price tag (you may be in sticker shock). Now comes the moment of truth: are you willing to pay the price of success in Hollywood?

It's important not to be naive about all of this. Most things really worth fighting for involve a certain amount of dues-paying and pain. That's just the way the world is. No pain, no gain.

Sometimes the news is grim. You've read everything and you've done "information interviews" with at least twenty people and they all tell you it's going to involve some things you absolutely don't want to do. Don't let yourself be discouraged until you're totally sure there's no way around the difficulties, but if you become convinced that this is wrong for you, by all means let go and find another niche that's more comfortable.

But the more probable scenario is that, after careful consideration, you'll realize that nothing else excites you like this particular career goal and you're willing to do whatever it takes to achieve it.

What's the next step? Learning to pitch yourself into the niche you desire.

PART IV

ALL THE
RIGHT MOVES

7

☆

Pitching and Hustling

★ ★ ★ ★ ★ ★ ★ ★ ★ ★ ★ ★ ★ ★

A WAY OF LIFE

Life's a pitch!
—Former Literary Agent/Pitching Coach DAVID DWORSKI

Sometimes in Hollywood it really *does* seem as though life is just one long pitch. In the day-and-night showbiz bazaar, everyone's hustling something: talent, services, projects. Hype is everywhere.

If you're a natural salesperson, you'll be in your element. This is your town. As long as you take things with a boulder of salt, you'll do fine.

But what if you're a creative person who has trouble selling yourself to others? What if you hate hustling and are allergic to hyperbole?

SALES SKILLS FOR PEOPLE WHO HATE TO SELL

Being able to market yourself successfully doesn't involve becoming a sleazy used-car salesperson or a high-pressure hustler. It involves taking the information you've discovered about yourself in the last few chapters and presenting it clearly and enthusiastically to other people. *In show business, sales is the art of sharing your passion and enthusiasm*—for what you do and for the stories you love.

Keep in mind the basic definition of a sale; it's the point at which what you have to offer and your buyer's current needs meet. Your buyer has a need or a problem. You have (or are) the solution. It's as simple as that.

"HOW I'M SPECIAL"—DEVELOPING YOUR HOLLYWOOD PITCH

You must be clear about what you're selling: your unique combination of special strengths, talents, passions, and experience.

In show business, it's not enough to be good—you've got to be special in some way. In a field as competitive as this one, good enough just doesn't cut it. There are too many other people who are good enough, too.

Focus on your strongest skills, as you've outlined them in previous chapters. For maximum career success, go with your best and most enjoyable gifts—your strong suit.

Once you have a clear sense of (1) who you are, (2) what your special strengths are, (3) your chosen niche, and (4) your targeted goals, you're ready to transform this into your "How I'm Special" statement—your Hollywood Pitch.

THE HOLLYWOOD PITCH

This is the pitch you'll give to hundreds of people—friends, strangers at parties, people on the phone, prospective employers. Be ready to give it anytime, anyplace. If I were to wake you up at 3:00 A.M., you should be able to immediately give me a coherent Hollywood Pitch!

This is your ad for yourself. (Some people also think of it as an entertaining oral presentation of the highlights of your resume.) It will give people the information they need to hire you or get involved with you and your projects.

The Hollywood Pitch is, by definition, brief. People in this industry have notoriously short attention spans. The basic pitch should take no more than ninety seconds; this means you've got to lead with your best stuff. If your prospect still looks interested, you can add further detail and embellishment.

Update your Hollywood Pitch at regular intervals, as your career progresses and you have interesting new things to talk about.

To develop your own personal Hollywood Pitch, first fill in the form below and then adapt it until it flows naturally. Don't worry if it seems a little stilted at first. Take the time to work on it—make it great. Put it in your own words, your own style, so it comes off your tongue smoothly and easily. If you need help, ask a writer or publicist to work on it with you. Practice it in front of a mirror or with friends. Try it out in acting class or pitching class. Or videotape yourself delivering the pitch, changing it until you're happy with the results.

Don't forget that this is show business. Your pitch should be interesting—perhaps even entertaining—and be presented with a little style. Remember the two industry sins—don't be dull and don't be desperate.

The pitch should be upbeat, positive, enthusiastic. Show you're passionate about the business and what you bring to it. A little wit or humor adds spice to a pitch and makes it fun to listen to.

I. I am a . . .

_____

(writer, editor, director, production assistant, makeup person, accountant, etc.)

who specializes in . . .

_____

(situation comedy, theater, action pictures, working with actors, keeping budgets under control.)

2. My special strengths and skills include . . .

_____

_____

(Now is the time to toot your own horn about the special gifts and skills that might be useful to whomever you're pitching to: terrific follow-through, a fabulous German accent, a great eye for detail, an uncanny ear for dialogue, a knack for numbers, computer wizardry, encyclopedic knowledge of old films, sex appeal, good story sense.)

3. I'm passionate about . . .

_____

_____

(This is another way of telling people what you're great at. Share your enthusiasm for whatever areas of the industry you've targeted: working with story, *film noir* lighting, doing your own stunts, getting rights to esoteric Jim Thompson novels, composing film scores, organizing chaos, working with child actors. You may also want to mention the kinds of people and projects you're passionate about getting involved with.)

4. I've worked on . . . with . . .

_____

_____

(Think of this section as a news bulletin. Think NEW and HOT. Start with your most recent, most exciting credit—hopefully they're one and the same. Without being obnoxious, let people know about what you've achieved and accomplished. Be specific and colorful. A good reporter mentions who, what, where, when, and why.)

Speaking of who, don't forget to name-drop. Talking about how you just saved Joe Dante's backside in post-production on his new film _Gremlins 12_ at Warners is a lot more interesting than saying you've been a film editor for four years. Describe the train model you just built for George Lucas's new project; the story structure class you just took from Robert McKee; the wild and wonderful year you spent working as Mike Ovitz's assistant (with a few choice anecdotes illustrating your best strengths); the day-and-night, two-week, page-one rewrite you did on _Megahit 3_ for Marvin Mogul; or the David L. Wolper Student Film Award you recently won from the International Documentary Association for your film on Laotian immigrants in Los Angeles, which Carol Burnett executive-produced and narrated. Two important rules about war stories and anecdotes: keep them positive and don't trash anyone. Just talk about challenges and achievements, showing how you used your special talents to create success.

5. Don't-be-dull tidbits:

_____

_____

(Add interesting and entertaining tidbits or anecdotes about your personal history and non-film-related skills and interests. For example: "I was born in the Soviet Union and escaped to the West in 1968." "I speak fluent Swahili." "George S. Kaufman was my grandfather." "I grew up on a Navajo reservation." "Last year I was the hang-gliding champion of Malibu." "I'm a former CIA hit man" (don't laugh, an action screenwriter told me that as he was pitching me a particularly devious and gory spy thriller). Without making stuff up, be creative here. These fun tidbits wake up your listeners and make them remember you when you call the next day. ("Hi, Joan. This is Phyllis. We met at the screening last night. I'm the one who collects miniature horses.") It's also a great way to bond with people quickly.

QUESTIONS PEOPLE OFTEN ASK ABOUT THE HOLLYWOOD PITCH

Q: Can I describe myself as a writer, editor, director, producer, or such if I'm just starting out or if I'm earning my living some other way?

A: In general, the sooner you start identifying yourself with your target career, the better. If you've written a screenplay, you're a writer. Don't pretend to be more experienced than you are (the Hollywood bullshit artists all have great noses for other people's BS, so don't try it!) but let people know that writing is where your heart and commitment lie.

There are, however, two important exceptions to this rule. (1) When you're applying for a specific job with a title that's different from your usual self-identification, call yourself by the job title at hand. If someone is looking for a production assistant, identifying yourself as a writer isn't going to get you the job. Describe yourself as a production assistant who has all the skills required for that job, plus a special interest and background in writing. (2) If your chosen skill is directing, be cautious about identifying yourself as a director before you've earned the title. It's extremely difficult to become a director in Hollywood, and if you say you're a director before you have some way of proving it, people won't take you seriously. But if you're actually directing—theater, commercials, industrials, TV magazine segments, a student film—you're a director. As soon as you qualify to say it, say it!

Q: Do I need a different pitch for every job?

A: You need to be completely comfortable with your *true* basic pitch. Then, like your resume, you can adapt it to suit the circumstances and job opportunities that present themselves to you. A little creative writing is not unheard of in a Hollywood Pitch.

SAMPLE HOLLYWOOD PITCHES

JERRY THE ANIMAL TAMER

Jerry is a theater director from New York who came to Hollywood last year and got hired to direct a couple of episodes on a new TV series with a difficult star. His passion is working with actors on dramatic, character-driven material. Here's how he could adapt his Hollywood Pitch in an interview with the producers of another series.

TV SERIES EXECUTIVE PRODUCER

Hi, Jerry. Glad you could come in on such short notice. Joyce [Jerry's agent] has filled us in a little on what you've been doing, but maybe you could tell us a little bit about yourself.

(Note: they don't mean your life story! The request to "tell us about yourself" is a common one in an entertainment industry interview. It's your cue to go into your Hollywood Pitch.)

JERRY

Well, I'm the kind of director who seems to get called in when the star is driving everyone crazy.

Everyone laughs knowingly.

(Note: This is the *kicker,* a little joke or clever statement that leads into the pitch. It also happens to be a good reason for these producers to hire Jerry.)

JERRY

Actually, my specialty is working with actors—that's my passion. I directed theater in New York before I came to L.A. to do television, and I think it's given me a special feel for character-driven material. Last year I did a couple of episodes of "TV Series X" for Columbia and I think we did some nice things for Nancy Neurotic's character. . .

At this point our director has deftly introduced a number of salable elements into his Hollywood Pitch: he knows from doing his homework that this executive producer's TV series is in trouble because of a difficult star's temper tantrums. He's tailored his pitch to appeal to his buyer's needs, plus he's introduced four elements of the Hollywood Pitch: he's a director who specializes in working with (difficult) actors and has a passion for character-driven (as opposed to plot-driven) dramatic material. He's name-dropped about a series and star he worked with last season.

JOY'S HORROR SCRIPT PARTY PITCH

BOB
(munching an hors d'oeuvre)

Hi, Joy. Great to see you. What've you been up to?

(This question strikes terror into the hearts of many people in show business. Especially if they're currently unemployed. Be prepared with a good Hollywood Pitch.)

JOY

Oh, I'm really focusing on my writing now. I took John Truby's story structure course in June and now I'm so deep into the second act of my horror script that I'm even scaring myself! I didn't know I had such a calling for blood and guts. What're you doing, Bob? Are you still free-lance reading?

(She throws the ball back into Bob's court.)

> BOB

Well, I'm doing development at New Line.

(He may be a secretary in the development department or a reader, but what the heck—it's nice to have a contact at New Line, especially if you're a screenwriter.)

LEE'S INDUSTRY SCREENING PITCH

Jake and Lee are attending the cast-and-crew screening of a new studio release—a time-travel thriller set in New York in the 1840s, 1940s, and 2040.

> JAKE
> (approaching the empty seat next to Susan)

Is this seat taken?

> LEE

No, it's yours if you can crawl in.

> JAKE

Thanks. Hi, I'm Jake.

> LEE

Lee. Did you work on the film?

> JAKE

Well, indirectly. I work at the studio. What about you?

(Note the classic Hollywood euphemism, "I work at the studio." What does that mean? Jake could be anything from studio security to a production executive. Showbiz people are often creatively vague about exact jobs and credits ["I work with Marty Scorsese" or "I work in production"].)

LEE

I wish. I'm a costume designer. I hear the costumes are fabulous in this picture. I'm doing the new play about Martha Mitchell at the Odyssey, and I'm having a ball rummaging around for Nixon-era ballgowns for Actress X. I'm nuts about period stuff. I'd love to work on a film like this, a real period piece.

SOME ADDITIONAL "HOW I'M SPECIAL" HOLLYWOOD PITCHES

At my seminars I ask participants to develop their own pitches and sell the rest of the audience on their special qualities. Here are some typical (fictional) pitches:

★ Heather is a Hollywood literary agent who specializes in new writing talent. She's particularly knowledgeable about playwrights who may be crossing over into screenwriting, and attends new plays at least twice a week. She is also on the board of the Independent Feature Project/West, where she hears about up-and-coming talent. She discovered Jane Doe, author of the new $1.2 million spec script *Bidding War*, which Tom Trendy flipped for at Columbia. Her strengths include persistence, persuasiveness, and a passion for writers and good writing. She has a degree in theater from a prestigious East Coast school and is the granddaughter of a well-known New York playwright.

★ Shirley is a cinematographer who specializes in music videos and commercials. She just finished a new Sinead O'Connor video that's now playing on MTV. Originally a high-fashion photographer based in downtown New York, she brings a unique sense of off-beat style to all her projects. Before she became a photographer, Shirley was a Soho painter noted for the moody lighting in her portraits. Her unconventional eye is her trademark and people call her when they need a fresh or unusual look. She now wants to bring this vision to the field of independent features à la *sex, lies and videotape* or *Metropolitan.*

★ Marty is an assistant film and tape editor who specializes in compilation films. He's a wizard at creating clever tracking systems so that the thousands of feet of film pulled for the project don't get lost. He has an incredibly organized mind, plus an intuitive sense of what constitutes a great clip. He's a former rock 'n' roll drummer, so his feel for rhythm and pacing is also superb. Last year he had a great time working on a network TV special about great movie love scenes where he watched and logged over 100,000 feet of film!

★ Cody is a comedy writer whose goal is to be on staff on a TV sitcom. A former stand-up comic, his specialty is the wacky one-liner. He's the guy to call if dialogue just lays there like a lox, he says. He's written spec scripts for "Roseanne," "Murphy Brown," and "Golden Girls" and a full-length comedy screenplay called *Tough Tooties* and is also writing gags for a comedy team appearing at the Comedy Store and on HBO. His agent, Sammy Slick, is really excited about his work and has arranged a meeting with the executive producers at "The Simpsons" next week.

HERE'S YOUR PITCH:

_____

_____

_____

_____

PITCHING YOUR PROJECTS

Have a great ninety seconds to give me, then have the goods to back it up.

—JOSH DONEN
Senior VP Production, Universal

Now that you're ready to pitch yourself, what about your film or TV project?

Tens of thousands of projects are registered at the Writers Guild of America each year and hundreds of thousands of pitches are made to studio or network executives and producers. To stand out from the crowd, follow some of the basic rules of pitching.

I. Keep it short. Just as with your personal Hollywood Pitch, ninety seconds is a good length for your project pitch. That minute and a half should describe the concept—the one-sentence *TV Guide* logline that summarizes the premise. Usually this sentence presents the set-up for the film, describing the main character's dilemma that must be solved in the film. Spielberg has said that almost every good film is about someone losing control of his or her life in act 1 and spending acts 2 and 3 trying to regain that control.

A word here about "high concept." High concept movie ideas lend themselves to snappy one-liners and appealing movie posters, ads, and trailers. There is often a "gimmick" set-up that immediately attracts the moviegoer, making the film easy to market. It may be expressed as a "What if . . . ," as in "What if a young boy found himself in an adult man's body?" or "What if a young boy was left home alone by his parents when they went on a trip to Europe?"

The downside of high concept is that the rest of the story may not deliver on the promise of the premise or may be superficial. Hollywood people are somewhat suspicious of the glib high concept premise, putting a renewed emphasis on character and well-thought-out stories. In fact, many excellent stories don't lend themselves to the high concept treatment. This can be especially true of European-style slice-of-life films, art films, character-driven dramas, or complex tales.

But even if your project doesn't fit into the high concept format, you still must be able to describe it in a brief, evocative sentence or two. If you're having trouble boiling your project down to an appealing one-liner, try imagining the movie poster. See the visual image that would capture the essence of your project and would create a "want to see" attitude in the audience. Think about the short "teaser" phrases that would appear on the poster. This should get you moving in the right direction. For example, *Twins* was marketed with a poster showing Arnold Schwarzenegger and Danny De Vito in identical outfits. The line: "TWINS . . . Only their mother can tell them apart." Take a good look at the movie ads in the newspapers for further inspiration.

2. If it's appropriate to your project, add some glitz: stars' names, a snappy title, an evocative Movie Cross. Some people like to include stars' names in their pitches, to give an idea of the possible casting. This is sometimes done in high concept pitching. It's a sort of shorthand way of giving the listener the idea of what your film will look like. "Alec Baldwin is a private detective who discovers that his mother isn't really his mother." "Roseanne Barr-Arnold and Kevin Costner find themselves thrown together on a Blind Date from Hell."

Screenwriting teacher Rick Pamplin has also recommended that you add a snappy title and a "Movie Cross" to your pitch. A Movie Cross involves the use of two film titles that are already familiar to the listener. For example, "This film is *Double Indemnity* meets *Attack of the Killer Tomatoes*" or "*Ghost* meets *Home Alone*." (Pitchers love to use current high-grossing blockbusters in their Movie Crosses to lure bottom-line-loving studio execs.)

3. Be prepared to describe the rest of the story in detail if asked. A good, short pitch is a come-on: it should intrigue the buyers and make them want to know more.

Just as with the personal pitch, if your prospect likes the ninety-second version, continue. But don't tell the whole story, blow by blow. Simply give an entertaining description of the set-up and describe the "inciting incident" that propels us into act 2. What is the hero's basic predicament?

Work out the story problems *before* the pitch. Hollywood has heard too many overly flip high concept pitches that have no developed story to back them up.

4. Always be ready for an informal pitch. If you run into a potential buyer at Gelson's market or at a Lakers' game, be ready to tell him or her what you're up to now and how excited you are about your new project or idea. Sometimes the best pitches are casual ones. This is why socializing is such an important part of the Hollywood game.

5. Only pitch projects and genres you're passionate about. If you love what you're pitching, you'll naturally express enthusiasm and confidence. Don't pitch a TV movie if you never watch TV. Don't pitch a detective thriller if you're bored by whodunits. You'll need all the enthusiasm you can muster to keep pitching over many months or years until you sell the project, so pick something you know and love.

6. Understand the genre in which you're pitching. Know the important films or TV shows in the genre. Be able to tell the buyer how your project is different and special. It's a Hollywood truism that "there are no new stories." What you're offering is a fresh twist on a tale, a new take on an old subject or theme.

7. Know the appropriate medium for your pitch. Don't pitch an obvious TV movie to a feature development person unless it is in some way special enough to justify big-screen treatment. Small, emotional dramas or melodramas; true-life tales of the ordinary person who rises to a challenge; disease-of-the-week sagas—all tend to be seen as TV movies. An exception is made when truly outstanding elements are added to the project. For example, *Rainman* was a small, poignant story of two brothers that could have been a terrific TV movie, but the presence of Dustin Hoffman and Tom Cruise made it important enough to be a theatrical feature film "event." Staying up on what sells to whom will give you a good sense of what to pitch where.

8. Don't embarrass yourself by pitching something that your credits don't support. For example, TV networks will seldom buy a TV series idea from a writer or producer who hasn't already done a lot of work on other peoples' TV series. Focus on areas that are open to newcomers: spec scripts for existing series, features, or TV movies. Or pair up with an established writer whose credits will support the pitch.

9. Rehearse your pitch with friends. If the pitch is good but your presentation is dull, rehearse with friends or take an acting class to learn to project enthusiasm and passion in your voice and body language. Remember, the people you're pitching to aren't just listening to your story. They're also watching you to see if you're the kind of person they'd like to do business with. They have to like what they see.

10. Be prepared to move on to your next idea or project if they don't bite on your initial pitch. Busy Hollywood people don't have a lot of time to waste on ideas they're not interested in. "It's not our cup of tea" or "It's similar to something we already have in development" will end all discussion. Be ready to move on to your next idea or project. Some agents suggest that you have at least five projects ready to pitch when you take a pitch meeting.

11. Deliver the written treatment or screenplay a day or two after the pitch. This allows you to make adjustments based on the buyer's response to your story. It also gives you a good excuse to stop by personally to drop it off, reinforcing the sale and the relationship.

12. Keep in mind that every good pitch is a win. Even if your prospect doesn't respond to any of the items you pitched, you've still succeeded because you've started a good working relationship with someone to whom you can bring your next project. Unless the buyer thought you were a total idiot, he or she will probably be glad to hear about anything new you develop. Also, some Hollywood people have discovered that making the rounds with projects is a clever way of job hunting. Producers are often much more willing to meet with you when you have a project than if you ask for a job interview. Even if they say no to your ideas and scripts, perhaps you've impressed them with your cleverness and talent. Let them know you'd love to work with them.

13. Read books and take classes on the art of Hollywood pitching. Robert Kosberg, known as the industry's King of Pitch and the best "idea man" in Hollywood, has written *How to Sell Your Idea to Hollywood*, an excellent guide to the dos and don'ts of pitching your projects. In Los Angeles there are also numerous classes and seminars on this arcane art for those who want to sell ideas or scripts to the entertainment industry. You'll read about them in the trades.

14. Match your pitching style to your temperament. If you're quiet and intense, give a low-key, intense pitch. If you're funny and charming, make your buyer laugh. Use your best stuff. Lead with your strong suit.

15. Be creative. Rules are made to be broken. In the end, all that matters in pitching yourself or your projects is that you don't commit the two Hollywood sins: being dull or desperate. Let your passion and your creativity be your guide as to how best to tell your story. If you're inspired to do so, you may want to act out roles, bring in visual aids, do shtik, try something different. People who listen to boring pitches all day are dying to hear new and special stories that really excite them.

A PITCH AT THE IVY: DO THE DANCE

Here's a typical scenario. You (the producer) have scheduled a meeting for lunch at the Ivy with Margie, the studio executive, and Sidney, your writer. The steps in this dance would go something like this:

After the usual kiss-kiss and the ordering of drinks, you'd focus on small talk to connect with Margie and Sidney on a personal level. You might talk babies, airplanes—whatever you have in common. You're trying for some bonding here. Keep it light, fun.

After the food has come and everyone's suitably relaxed, you might ease into the "Producer's Preface." You turn to Margie and warm her up for the pitch. You may tell her how you came to discover this project or how excited you are about Sidney's past work and how much you've been wanting to work with him. Or you might tell a personal story that leads into the subject matter of the project. The story would tell Margie that you're personally passionate about the content of this film.

Then you'd turn the meeting over to Sidney for the actual pitch. Or, if the writer isn't present, you'd make the pitch yourself. (If you're the writer and no producer is present, you'd do some of the above yourself before launching into the pitch.)

Watch carefully for Margie's reaction to your pitch. If she doesn't reject the idea out of hand, continue the pitch, a few sentences at a time, carefully building the story until Margie is as excited as you are about making this film or TV show.

If this sounds like seduction—it is. Remember the first time you put an arm around a potential lover, and then moved on to a hand-hold, a light kiss. . . . Same idea.

8

☆

Targeting Your Buyer

★ ★ ★ ★ ★ ★ ★ ★ ★ ★ ★ ★ ★ ★ ★

HOW TO GET ACCESS TO PUBLIC, PRIVATE, AND SECRET HOLLYWOOD INFORMATION

> The control of knowledge is the crux of tomorrow's worldwide struggle for power in every human institution.
>
> —Futurist ALVIN TOFFLER
> *Powershift*

If the idea of pitching terrifies you, try focusing less on the first part of the selling equation (what you have to offer) and more on the second: your buyer. Even people who hate hustling can effectively sell their talents and projects—if they target the right buyer who really needs what they have to offer.

The key skills for success here are research, detective work, organization, persistence, and empathy. Because even the best pitch is useless if it's directed at the wrong person.

Who needs what you've got? Who's in a position to hire you or buy your projects? You'll need names, titles, companies, addresses, and phone and fax numbers. You'll need background information. You'll need the inside scoop on what they're *really* looking for.

How can you get this important information if you're not yet a Hollywood insider? A little homework will help you target exactly the right prospects for your pitching campaign.

THE INFORMATION ADVANTAGE

In Hollywood, information is power. To make it in the entertainment industry in the nineties and beyond, you'll have to know what's happening—to whom, where, when, how, and why. On a global basis.

Smart Hollywood players collect this information the way David L. Wolper collected Picassos. The more knowledge you possess, the better your chances for success. The more well informed you are, the more valuable you are as an employee or partner. Your knowledge and your contacts, built up over time, are assets you bring with you to any project or job. They are truly "intellectual capital."

For those of us who weren't born into Hollywood royalty, futurist Alvin Toffler assures us that, fortunately, "knowledge is the most democratic source of power." Anyone who systematically and conscientiously becomes a collector of knowledge about the entertainment industry can easily amass a fortune in valuable information.

There are three types of information you have to get your hands on: public, private, and secret.

PUBLIC INFORMATION

Just a few years ago, it was almost impossible to find up-to-date, accurate lists of studio heads, development people, studio development deals, creative people, below-the-line technical talent, agents. Now you can call the specialized industry bookstores and order many excellent directories and Who's Whos.

Invest in the latest versions of the directories covering the areas you're interested in. These books will save you months of work. With these invaluable Who's Whos at your side, you're an instant Hollywood insider.

Also, keep a copy of *Premiere* magazine's annual "Power in Hollywood" survey close by. It lists players, their current rank, their rank last year, pending projects, strengths, and weaknesses in frank, get-right-down-to-it language. Isn't it important to know that Paramount's Stanley Jaffee is a "hothead" who "figures to kick butt," that Creative Artists Agency's Jack Rapke is a "great hand-holder," or that superlawyer Peter Dekom is both a "compulsive punner" and "too smart, by half—you don't want to sit across from him at a bargaining table"? You never know when such information will come in handy. Besides, everyone in town reads the survey to see how their friends and enemies fared this year. This list will give you a jump-start on your Power Rolodex (see Chapter 9) and if you're new to the business and take a phone-answering job, you'll know who not to put on hold.

ENTERTAINMENT INDUSTRY LIBRARIES AND BOOKSTORES

A visit to the Academy of Motion Picture Arts and Sciences famed Margaret Herrick Library at the Center for Motion Picture Study in Beverly Hills is an almost mystical experience for true film lovers. The center has clipping files on 60,000 films and 50,000 people, plus thousands of books, periodicals, scripts, stills, and films. Knowledgeable reference librarians will be able to help you survey this gold mine, and you will undoubtedly do so many times during your entertainment industry career. If you need background information on any Hollywood player, this library should be able to provide it or at least point you in the right direction.

Other good libraries to know about include the Academy of Television Arts and Sciences Library, the American Film Institute's library, the UCLA Theatre Arts Library, the USC Cinema-TV Library and the Lincoln Center Performing Arts Library in New York City.

The Hollywood bookstores are irresistible. If you love show business, you'll get hooked on Larry Edmunds Bookstore, Samuel French's Theatre & Film Bookshop, and Elliot M. Katt's Books on the Performing Arts.

THE TRADES

If you don't read the two Hollywood trades, you're not in the business. So take a deep breath and order at least one of them: *Daily Variety* or the *Hollywood Reporter*. Each will cost you approximately $120 a year but without them you're still in cement or insurance.

Reading the trades is a fine art. The arcane lingo in *Daily Variety* (e.g., "Stix Nix Pix") has been cleaned up a lot, so that's no longer a problem. The real trick, according to producer Lynda Obst *(The*

Fisher King), is knowing what to read. Obst told *Premiere* she recommends taking a quick look at the headlines, the grosses ("you spin the numbers to endorse your latest movie idea"), and the gossip. She likes Army Archerd's legendary column on the second page of *Daily Variety* and Robert Osborne's "Rambling Reporter" in the front of the *Hollywood Reporter* plus George Christy's "Great Life" column in the back.

Obst also cautions readers to beware of public relations "plants" placed by people who are desperate for a job or whose deals are expiring. The truth about such "autospin," she says, is "you can buy it." (A reliable friend recently confided in me that his production company had been approached by a trade paper reporter who wanted round-trip tickets to Hawaii. The company, according to this friend, gladly wrote the reporter a $1,000 check, assuring the firm an excellent story on its current slate of projects.)

If you don't believe everything you read, you'll get a lot of useful information from the trades. Especially helpful are the regularly updated listings of TV and film projects in production or going into production, and stories on projects in development (even if they are puff, they reveal general trends in the town's thinking).

Some of what you'll read in the trades isn't very timely. The *Daily Variety* announcement of my employment at Stormy Weathers Productions, for example, appeared many weeks after I had started work.

But that doesn't mean there's no valuable information in the trades. Once you start reading them daily (which you definitely should do!) you'll begin to read between the lines. As you regularly track companies, productions, and employees, you'll begin to develop a sixth sense about when things are liable to open up at a particular company or on a project.

HELP-WANTED ADS IN THE TRADES

You may also want to check out the ads, but keep in mind that the best Hollywood jobs usually don't show up in the "Help-Wanted" sections of the trades. If they did, employers would be overwhelmed with responses and resumes from outsiders and wannabes.

But don't hesitate to respond to an ad you find interesting, however. What do you have to lose? One key to getting a response to your letter is to describe yourself in exactly the terms specified in the ad. If they're looking for an "aggressive go-getter," say you're an "aggressive go-getter" (assuming you can live with that label).

WHAT ABOUT PLACING A "POSITION-WANTED" AD?

My advice: save your money. Few people in Hollywood would be likely to hire a person who hasn't been recommended to them by someone they trust. For all they know, you could be a lunatic fan or a *National Enquirer* reporter!

Besides, putting a "Position-Wanted" ad in the trades makes you look desperate—one of the two Hollywood sins. It also makes you look like a naive Hollywood outsider.

OTHER PUBLICATIONS TO READ

Other trade publications to check out: *Weekly Variety, Screen International, Drama-Logue* (actors), *Billboard* (music biz), *Millimeter* (production), *On Location* (production), and *Cinefex* or *Cinefantastique* (science fiction, fantasy, special effects).

Industry insiders also read *Premiere* magazine, *American Film, Movieline, Entertainment Weekly*, the "Risky Business" column by Anne Thompson in the *L.A. Weekly*, and the "Celia Brady" column in *Spy* magazine. They read the "Calendar" section of the *Los Angeles Times* and the magazine, book, and arts sections of the *New York Times*. And they regularly watch "Entertainment Tonight" and the E! entertainment cable network.

You may also want to read the newsletters from the various guilds and associations in the entertainment industry, so that you'll know about upcoming events you may want to attend. The industry libraries will carry these important publications and you may also be able to order them from the organizations themselves.

LET YOUR FINGERS DO THE WALKING: ENTERTAINMENT INDUSTRY DATABASES

You can also use your computer or your phone to contact entertainment industry databases that are chock full of strategically important info. But be aware that these services often charge substantial fees.

BASELINE calls itself "the largest central source of information ever developed for the entertainment industry, and the only online [computer] service designed specifically to meet the needs of film and television professionals." It's a research and information service that can answer your questions in print, over the phone, or online (it has a number of large computer databases). It has info on people and their credits (and how to reach them), products (who made what features, pilots, TV specials, and series, plus who's working on what right now), numbers (box office, demographics, showbiz stocks), news, release schedules, screening dates, electronic mail. If you're job hunting you might want to find out more about BASELINE's Inpro database, which lists projects by whether they're in development, in preproduction, shooting, wrapped, or on hold. BASELINE also publishes books like *Who's Who in American Film Now: All the People Who Make Movies*, which lists over 11,000 creative and technical personnel.

Celebrity Service International, established in 1937, is a low-key, discreet service that provides up-to-date information on the biographies, contact people, and current whereabouts of celebrities and major Hollywood players. The bad news is that Celebrity Service won't accept you as a subscriber unless you're able to convince them that you're an established entertainment industry person with a known firm or project.

Entertainment Data provides its subscribers with overnight box office grosses, plus information on scheduled releases, including title, stars, major credits, and story synopses. Entertainment Data also prepares reports from its historical database comparing genres in the marketplace, release patterns, release dates, and market share.

Another oft-quoted source of information on the entertainment industry is consultant Paul Kagan of Carmel, California. He and his associates keep tabs on the industry, publishing a number of newsletters.

If you're a member of the Writers Guild of America, you can use your computer modem to dial into the guild's popular electronic bulletin board, where you can pick the brains of other procrastinating writers. The bulletin board offers a popular Research forum. An added benefit: the opportunity to shmooze at a "writer's table" not unlike those that each studio used to maintain in its commissary.

SEMINARS, CLASSES, AND SPEECHES

For the price of admission, you can attend public seminars, classes, and speeches where industry insiders share information on an amazing variety of show business topics. Not only will you gain valuable knowledge that directly applies to your targeted career niche, but you'll make excellent contacts, meeting people who might otherwise be inaccessible to you. How do you find out about upcoming events? Simple. Read the trades.

ENTERTAINMENT INDUSTRY CONVENTIONS AND FILM FESTIVALS

Every industry has its conventions, and the entertainment business is no exception. By attending seminars and walking the convention floor you'll pick up a lot of information and you may also meet new people who can be helpful to your career.

Showbiz Expo is held in the springtime in Los Angeles and in the fall on the east coast. It presents seminars and products of interest to both above- and below-the-line people.

You may also want to gather more information by attending a few of the important film markets and festivals each year. A reference librarian at any of the show business libraries can help you put together a list of the events of most interest to you.

PRIVATE INFORMATION: YOUR OWN PERSONAL DATA BANK

The public information mentioned above is available to anyone who is (or wants to be) in the industry—if they're willing to do the legwork or pay the fees. But the information that will prove to be most valuable to your career is the private—and even secret—knowledge that only you possess. Gaining both private and secret information is the result of carefully cultivated personal relationships. Private information is information that you won't get by pursuing any of the public methods listed above. This is personal stuff that people share with each other in small groups or one-on-one.

Start meeting regularly with anyone you know who has anything to do with the industry. Share information. Soon you'll be hearing the buzz and getting a sense of how the collective Hollywood mind is thinking about the areas you're interested in. You may not agree with Hollywood Conventional Wisdom, but you'll be plugged in. When you make your pitch, it will be a knowledgeable pitch, based on your private information about what the industry and your specific buyer are looking for.

SECRET INFORMATION: BUILDING YOUR OWN PERSONAL SPY NETWORK

The line between private and secret information can sometimes get a little fuzzy. Everyone in town knows that Marvin Mogul is a graduate of the Betty Ford Center—so is that private or secret data?

I usually define secret information as information that someone would rather you didn't know. If Marvin trumpeted his victory over drugs on "Oprah," it's public; if he jokes about it in the Warners commissary, it's private; if only his doctor, secretary, and mistress are in the know, it's definitely secret.

Players hoard secret information carefully, holding it close to the chest, sharing it only with close friends or trading it for favors.

Secret information includes extremely personal facts about important industry people; confidential lists of who's considered "in" and "out" by various networks and studios; lists of projects in development all over town; titles of scripts that will go into "turnaround" (be available for repurchase) next week; details about who's to be promoted or fired (which may mean a job opening for you); agency client lists; real production budgets and accounting figures; copies of closely held scripts (Spielberg's next film or this week's hot spec script); early word on important deals; or scuttlebutt from the set.

How can you get access to this kind of inside information? Industry insiders rely on their well-positioned friends to help them keep up on secret information. Some even have their own "spy networks" of pals in high and low places at the various studios, agencies, and production companies around town. In addition to keeping their buddies updated on the latest confidential developments, these "spies" may slip them copies of internal correspondence, memos, lists, reports, or hot scripts that are under wraps.

I'm not suggesting that you do anything illegal, but if you'd like to develop your own sources of information, it isn't difficult. Befriend someone—a secretary, mail room person, or production assistant would be fine—at every major company that interests you. Cultivate that person. Have lunch regularly, and chat on the phone. Sooner or later, you'll begin to hear about what's *really* going on and who's doing what to whom. This information will come in handy when you're going in for an interview or are pitching a project.

THE BREAKDOWNS: PUBLIC TO SOME, SECRET TO OTHERS

If you're a talent agent or a personal manager, you can subscribe to the "breakdowns" from Breakdown Services, a company that obtains and "breaks down" scripts that are currently being cast. Each morning these descriptions of available roles are delivered to subscribers' offices, saving agents and managers the hassle of getting and reading scripts themselves.

The problem: Breakdown Services is not available to actors. So only for agents and managers, this information is public information (if they pay the fee). For actors, it's very desirable secret info that they can use when they call their agent ("A friend told me there's a role on 'Roseanne' I think I'd be perfect for. Will you put me up for it?") or to try to talk their way into an audition even without representation.

It's not strictly kosher, of course, but a number of actors have been known to gain secret access to the breakdowns. Sometimes they share this information with friends, sometimes they don't.

PLUG INTO THE INFORMATION SYSTEM BY WORKING FOR AN AGENT

Agents—the information brokers of the entertainment industry—have become more and more powerful in Hollywood as a direct result of their excellent grasp of public, private, and secret information. This data, plus their vast network of contacts, allows them to set up projects, put together packages, and exert power behind the scenes.

If you'd like to plug into this vast store of information, put in a few months as a temp, secretary, assistant, or receptionist at an agency like Creative Artists (CAA), International Creative Management (ICM), William Morris, or Triad Artists. You'll find yourself at the center of an enormous, whirling tornado of data on people and projects. Absorb as much as you can. You'll never regret this unique (and sometimes exhausting) experience. A bonus: the relationships that you form with other employees will provide you with a well-informed group of contacts for your Power Rolodex.

THE ACCELERATION OF THE HOLLYWOOD INFORMATION EXPLOSION

> Nothing is hidden; there are no secrets.
>
> —*Spy* magazine

Hollywood used to be the ultimate insider's town. Few people knew—or cared—about the inner workings of the movie manufacturing mechanism. There were millions of fans who loved the stars and the shows, but they weren't interested in the behind-the-scenes hustles or technicalities. A few thousand players, mostly invisible to everyone but other players and knowledgeable wannabes, went about their business in relative obscurity.

But the ever-accelerating information revolution has changed all that. More and more previously obscure filmland facts are being gobbled up by an increasingly hungry general public. Every night, over 7 million viewers watch Paramount's "Entertainment Tonight" on 165 TV stations around the country. Millions catch CNN's reports on show business and the E! entertainment cable channel. Over 2 million people regularly read the twenty-eight entertainment industry publications listed in *Standard Rates & Data Service*. Mainstream publications like the *Wall Street Journal*, the *New York Times*, and *Fortune* do savvy analytical pieces on the business.

The trip from secret to private to public is getting shorter and faster. Dirt that was dished surreptitiously between consenting adults just yesterday is burning up the phone lines today and will be openly gossiped about at Morton's next week, only to appear in *Premiere* next month.

What does this mean for you? If you plug into the Hollywood information revolution, you may be able to take advantage of the long-awaited opening up of the previously closed shop. It means that even if you don't know any Hollywood insiders right now, you can quickly learn the game, know the players, and understand what insiders are looking for.

DEMASSIFICATION OF THE MASS MEDIA

Another trend that can work in your favor is the move away from broad-based mass media (current blockbusters notwithstanding) to audience-specific, focused "narrowcasting." The slow shriveling of the three television networks (the ultimate mass media) and the rise of multichannel cable are just the tips of the iceberg. In the media's New World Order, the magic words will be "personalized" and "interactive." Product will be targeted to specific audiences and responsive to their desires. There will be more niche marketing and specialized shows of all types in addition to the large, globally popular films.

The old industrial-age power pyramids are flattening. People and products at the top or bottom levels may thrive, but those in the middle are being squeezed. The major studios will become ever-more-powerful global entertainment behemoths and the little person will also have increasing chances to create a product and deliver it to particular audiences who might enjoy it—around the globe.

GLOBALIZATION

Another megatrend you'll want to keep track of in your ongoing entertainment industry information search is the increasing globalization of the industry. Hollywood is no longer just a tacky town in southern California. It's now an international business environment.

When you target your potential employers or partners, don't limit yourself to Los Angeles or even the United States. Even though the Hollywood diamond is still the center of the action, opportunities for entertainment industry success are becoming increasingly global.

Successful independent producers need to keep track of hundreds of potential coproduction partners, attractive locations, and buyers on their databases. Complex, multipartner, ad hoc alliances will be created and dissolved with each project. If you become knowledgeable about the best (and cheapest) sources of financing, literary properties, talent, locations, services, and distribution around the world, you'll be way ahead of the pack and well prepared for the entertainment industry of tomorrow.

9
☆

Building Your Power Rolodex and Hit List

★　★　★　★　★　★　★　★　★　★　★　★　★　★　★

Now that you're plugging in to the sources of public, private, and even secret Hollywood information, how on earth can you keep track of it all?

It's important to develop a good memory for names and faces in this business, but sooner or later your brain will overload. There's no substitute for a Power Rolodex, on which you'll track all of your industry contacts. And if you're serious about building this Power Rolodex, eventually you'll need a computer database to file and sort all this information.

But for those of you who haven't yet discovered the joys of bits and bytes, the old-fashioned, cheaper paper systems still work. Some people use 3″ × 5″ index cards, which are fun to color-code and are easily portable. Others use large Rolodex cards (large enough to carry a lot of information plus pictures clipped out of the trades). Still others like three-ring binders.

On these cards or sheets of paper, list the name, title, company, address, and phone and fax numbers of your contact. Also leave room for personal information—hobbies, spouse—and credits. List the assistant's name and info. Note who referred you to this person. Leave room for dated entries of calls, contacts, cards, and presents sent, plus "tickle dates" when you should recontact.

ADD COMPUTER POWER TO YOUR POWER ROLODEX

When you realize how much information needs to go on each "card" of your Power Rolodex it becomes clear that sooner or later a computer will become a necessity for a successful Hollywood career.

You don't need a complicated database program. I consider myself a computer nudnik, but even I can use a simple database program like PFS Professional File. And there are many others on the market. Ask your friendly neighborhood computer consultant to prescribe one for your needs. Or contact the Writers' Computer Store in West Los Angeles, which caters to the industry.

Once you have one of these gems, design a form to track your information. Here's one suggestion:

ELECTRONIC POWER ROLODEX CARD

Last Name: **First Name:**
Title:
Company:
Work Address:
City: **State:**
Country: **Zip:**
Work Phone(s):
Work Fax:
Car Phone: **Car Fax:**
Home Address:
City/State: **Zip:**
Home Phone: **Home Fax:**
Vacation Home Phone/Fax:
Assistants' Names:
Assistant Info:
Colleagues: (Who works closely with this person? Who does this person know that they might introduce you to?)
Agent/Manager:
Lawyer:
Other Advisers: (Pr, etc.)
Major Credits:
Current Projects:
Spouse/Significant Other:

Children's Names, Ages:

Personal Info: (hobbies, interests, affiliations, lovers, etc.)

Birthday: (You may want to send a card or call.)

Contact Log: (dates of contact, type of contact, notes on what was discussed, pitched)

To Do Next: (Plan your next "right move.")

Tickle Date: (When do you want to recontact this person or make your next move?)

Contacts Given: (people whom this person suggested you contact)

Will Call On My Behalf? (Will this person make a call to introduce you—a "Godfather Call" or "Godmother Call"?)

Can I Use Name? (Can you use this person's name as the "two magic words" when calling the new contact, as in "Marvin Mogul suggested I call"?)

Rating: (your own personal A, B, and C ratings to determine how "hot" a prospect or contact you think this is)

Priority: (How important is it to pursue this? A 1, 2, or 3?)

Code: (Note: This database feature will allow you to create and print out reports, lists, or mailing labels based on various criteria such as to whom you want to send holiday cards, etc.)

Additional Notes:

You may also want to order the new Power Networking software, designed by entertainment industry computer applications pioneer Jack Smith of DotZero, using my theories about information tracking in Hollywood.

When it's time to start a serious job or pitch campaign, the value of your growing Power Rolodex will become apparent. You'll be able to zip through your cards, targeting both Referral Sources and prospective buyers. A Referral Source is anyone who might be able to refer you to buyers or other Referral Sources. Referral Sources can include friends, relatives, classmates, past or present co-workers, former bosses, agents.

WHO NEEDS YOU? PUT TOGETHER A HIT LIST

Who is your prospective buyer? Who needs your talent, service, or project? Who can say yes to you? Remember, no matter how terrific your pitch, it's unlikely that you can sell anyone a product, idea, or service they have absolutely no need for. Take the time to think about the answer to this question. How successfully you target your prospects can make the difference between a hit-and-miss career and one that's focused.

If you're a good cinematographer, for example, your most important prospects are people who care about the look of their picture or project: directors, producers, and studio executives. They need your good eye. If you're an actor, you need to meet casting directors, agents, and, ultimately, directors. They all need to find the best possible acting talent for the role. If you're a TV producer, you need to meet studio and network executives who can greenlight your projects. They need audience-drawing programming. You'll also want to know talented writers and stars who need a producer like you to bring their work to the studio and the network. And if you're a production manager, you need to know creative producers, directors, and studio executives.

Who do *you* need to know to succeed in Hollywood?

Go through your Power Rolodex and mark or code the cards of prospects and referral sources that could be important to this particular job search or sales campaign. These names are your "Hit List" for this round of pitches. Don't be afraid to include a lot of people on this list. You never know who will know whom. Especially in Los Angeles, it seems that everyone in town knows someone in show business, even if it's a second cousin who works in the Disney copy room.

If you're not happy with the size of this list, you may want to add new names from industry directories: people you don't yet have access to but whom you'd like to add to your Power Rolodex. And if you really want to expand your Hit List to the max, try the Pyramid System.

THE PYRAMID SYSTEM: HOW TO EXPAND YOUR HIT LIST AT A GEOMETRIC RATE

The Pyramid System is a very simple technique that will help you rapidly lengthen your Hit List and fill up your Power Rolodex at a geometric rate. It is both a research method and a sales tool.

Call all the Referral Sources on your Power Rolodex. First, take the time to do a little shmoozing. Ask how they're doing. Pass along any advice, information, or referrals you might have for them. Then, when the time is right, ask for *their* advice, information, and referrals in return. You're looking for the names of people or companies in the market for projects or employees. If this is an important contact, instead of having a quick conversation on the phone, use the call to ask for an in-person get-together, preferably around a meal. If that's not possible, ask for five or ten minutes of their time in the office.

Ask each Referral Source for the names of two or three other people to contact—either prospects or additional Referral Sources—who might be willing to talk with you. Also ask each source if he or she will make a "Godfather Call" or "Godmother Call" (see chapter 10) on your behalf to open the door and prepare the caller for your contact. If they are not willing to do that, ask if you can use their name (the "Two Magic Words") when contacting their referrals.

Hollywood is a small enough industry that if you pursue this Pyramid System conscientiously, you'll soon find yourself getting referred over and over again to the same people. That's great. It means you've done your homework. It's also very impressive to have lots of sources calling one referral on your behalf. If one Godfather Call is good, ten are great!

THE ART OF BUILDING BRIDGES TO PROSPECTS

They say that everyone on the planet is only six people away from everyone else (at maximum). In other words, if you targeted someone in, say, Tibet, you could theoretically call someone who knows someone who knows someone who knows someone who knows someone who knows that Tibetan.

I don't know if this rule holds up in the rest of the world, but it certainly does in a small town like Hollywood. With enough phone calls, you can find someone who knows your prospect, even if he's Mike Ovitz or Steven Spielberg.

This is what I call "bridging": building a bridge of people between you and your targeted buyer. The process is similar to the Pyramid System: call everyone you know and ask them if they know anyone who knows Steven Spielberg. If they say no, ask them for the names of two other people whom you could ask the same question. Eventually you'll find someone who knows the famous director personally. Building a relationship with that final all-important Referral Source may eventually land you the meeting or interview you want.

SALES TIP: TREAT PROSPECTS AS REFERRAL SOURCES—ASK FOR ADVICE, NOT A JOB

Some savvy job hunters and project pitchers approach prospects as if they were Referral Sources, casually asking for advice rather than high-pressuring them for a job. It's a clever move and a subtler sell. Describe your situation (a nice Hollywood Pitch) and ask for advice, ideas, suggestions, referrals, or information rather than a job. You'll probably encounter less resistance with this ploy. When you directly ask for work, people tend to feel put on the spot and get defensive. The easiest thing for them to say at that point is, "We don't need anyone right now." But when you ask for advice, they're often very helpful.

Try approaching your prospect as a potential adviser and mentor. Few people will deny you a couple of minutes of advice. If your prospect has a current need for someone with exactly your qualifications, let it cross her mind that you might be a useful person to have around. (Many Hollywood people like to appropriate all good ideas as *their* ideas.)

The beauty of this tactic is that it puts neither of you on the spot. It creates an opportunity to get to know each other in a nonthreatening way and for you to let a potential employer know what you're looking for, what you feel your strong points are, your passion for your craft, and your eagerness to get started. Later in the conversation, after you've built some rapport and feel that a relationship is in the works, you might let your prospect know that of course your greatest dream would be to work with her, if such a thing were ever possible. Sometimes it works.

THE HIDDEN JOB MARKET

If the most desirable jobs aren't listed in the trades, how do you find out about them? Use your Power Rolodex. The best possible source of job leads is your own carefully cultivated network of friends, advisers, mentors, and Referral Sources. Your Hollywood Buddies who keep their ears to the ground will hear about openings long before an announcement or an ad appears in the trades.

I got my job at Columbia Pictures Television as vice president of development for actor Carl Weathers's Stormy Weathers Productions, for example, because my friend Sandy, a terrific TV producer, had heard through her grapevine of friends that Mr. Weathers was looking for someone. I immediately called both my agent and another friend who worked on the Columbia lot. My agent made a Godmother Call to Mr. Weathers's manager on my behalf, and my friend on the lot, a well-known and well-respected producer, casually dropped by Mr. Weathers's office and put in a good word for me. I got an interview and landed the job.

If it hadn't been for my friends, I would never even have known that the position existed.

DOING YOUR HOMEWORK LETS YOU PITCH TO THOSE WHO CAN SAY YES

As you're doing your research, try to qualify your potential buyer. Target people who really have the power to hire you or buy your project. This isn't always possible, of course. Busy Hollywood players hire underlings to meet with people and listen to pitches. These sidekicks have the power to say no, but not the power to say yes by themselves. Because it's their only power, some of these nay-sayers get carried away with saying no. They love to flex their muscles by turning you down. But don't underestimate them; if they become passionate about you or your project, they can pitch you enthusiastically to their boss, who may then see you personally.

Doing your homework and checking out your spy system will save you from the time-wasting frustration of pitching to the wrong person. If Executive X is on the way out, it may not make sense to meet with her till she lands a new job. (On the other hand, a truly Machiavellian career strategist might decide that this is the *perfect* time to meet with her—she has lots of time and needs friends, which may stand you in good stead once she's made her move.)

GET THE INSIDE SCOOP ON YOUR PROSPECTS BEFORE YOU PITCH THEM

What are the prospects on your hit list looking for? What problems do they face? Do your homework to discover your buyers' needs and you'll be way ahead of the competition. Before you call or meet with anyone, find out all you can about them.

Start with the public sources we've already mentioned. Next, pick up the phone. Call your network of friends and referral sources. Tell them you're trying to find out some information about Producer X who has a deal on the lot. Do they know anyone who works for Producer X? How would they suggest that you go about finding out more about Producer X's current projects and needs?

You'll make a lot of telephone friends doing this kind of research, and it's important to thank them properly and tuck them away in your Power Rolodex for future reference. These contacts will be a valuable asset to you in years to come.

Once you have a lead into Producer X's office, by all means call (using your two magic words once again) and ask questions directly. Some people may not want to talk with you, but it's surprising how often you'll find an assistant, development person, or reader who will take the time to fill you in on what's going on at the company. People like to talk about themselves and their activities. If you're a good interviewer, they'll relax and chat. Any information you find out about the buyer's company, situation, hobbies, or special interests is pure gold.

NEVER ASSUME YOU KNOW WHAT THE BUYER'S NEEDS ARE

When I worked with actor Carl Weathers, who became an international star as boxer Apollo Creed in the first four *Rocky* movies (and who starred in Joel Silver's *Action Jackson* and costarred with Arnold Schwarzenegger in *Predator*), one of the first things he told me was that at least for the present he hoped to avoid boxing roles. (After all, how could he top the indomitable Apollo?) As his development person, I contacted as many Hollywood agents, producers, and writers as I could to fill them in on what we were and weren't looking for. But of course we couldn't get the word out to everyone.

In spite of our efforts, we continued to be approached with occasional boxing projects. What was the problem? A number of people weren't bothering to do their homework. A simple call to our offices would have saved them (and us!) a lot of wasted effort. I was more than happy to talk with anyone who was thinking of submitting material to us and to tell them about our current focus. The winners called. The novices and self-sabotagers didn't bother, setting themselves up for disappointment.

So before you submit anything to anyone—call and find out what kind of material they are or aren't currently interested in.

GET YOUR PROSPECTS' CREDITS AND LOOK AT THEIR OLD FILMS

Nothing is more annoying or insulting to a Hollywood player than your ignorance of his work. Go to the entertainment industry libraries and to the video store before you approach any important prospect.

BE A GOOD INTERVIEWER

Here's good news for those of you who get a little shy or anxious in a selling situation: it's more important to listen than to talk. If you're doing all the talking, something's wrong.

Relieve some of your anxiety by empathically focusing on the buyer and her needs rather than on yourself and your nervousness. I try to do this whenever I give speeches. If I concentrated on all the people out there watching me or on my own good or bad performance, I'd freeze up. Instead, I move my attention off of myself and onto the audience and ask questions at the beginning of every lecture. I get so involved with their stories and problems that I forget all about being nervous and can concentrate on creative ways of meeting their needs in my seminar. I relax, and so do they.

In pitch meetings or interviews, break the ice by asking your prospect a few intelligent, informed, and perhaps unexpected questions (based on your background research, of course). Right away, you separate yourself from your competitors by showing that you're smart, plugged in, and have done your homework.

People love to talk about themselves and their activities, and Hollywood players are no exception. If you get a director chatting about the unusual crane shot at the end of one of her early pictures . . . or a business affairs executive discussing the news in today's trades about the Tri-Star deal . . . or a producer describing a project he's in love with . . . you're off on the right foot.

A production executive I know used to love to shock and impress potential employers during interviews by asking questions based on secret information about their activities. I don't recommend this ploy for novices, but my friend found it a powerful way to demonstrate his ability to keep on top of everything that was going on in Hollywood.

As your prospect is answering your questions, listen very carefully for information about her current needs or projects. Watch for an opening. When you hear about a need that you can fill, ease into your pitch. "You know, that makes me think about a story I've been working on recently . . ." or "Yeah, I love wrestling too—in fact, I shot some film of last summer's tournament if you'd like to take a look at it . . ."

Having a great pitch is one thing. Knowing enough about your prospect to pitch it at the right time in the right way is quite another. A person who's empathic and does her homework has an important edge over the competition.

WHAT ARE YOUR BUYER'S HOT BUTTONS?

As you research and question your prospects, you may discover what motivates them. Once you understand their "hot buttons," you can adjust your pitch to appeal to these motivations.

Some typical Hollywood motivations and how to take advantage of them:

★ **Greed.** "This project's a sure money maker."

★ **Altruism and Meaning.** Many Hollywood people feel vaguely guilty about the luxurious life-styles they enjoy. So they get involved with good causes and occasionally like to do projects they perceive as "meaningful." Point out the impact that your project could have on peoples' lives.

★ **Insecurity.** Hollywood executives and creative people are notoriously insecure about losing their jobs or being out of work. It's incredibly difficult to pick the hits, and people are always looking for reassuring guarantees of success (like well-known talent) that make a project a supposedly "sure thing." Focus on the "low-risk" aspects of getting involved with you or your project. Emphasize your proven track record, the surefire elements, the financial appeal of the deal. Hopefully these comforting factors will give your listener the courage to hire you or pitch you to their boss.

★ **Fame and Glory.** A lot of Hollywood people thrive on public recognition. Emphasize that your prospect's discovery of you and your project could lead to a boss's approval, audience delight, even an Academy Award.

★ **Freedom from Overwork and Worry.** Many Hollywood people are grossly overworked. You could be the answer to their prayers. Encourage them to have confidence in you. With you on board, they can relax—you'll take care of everything.

READY FOR ACTION

Now that you're systematically tracking all of your prospects and Referral Sources—and the important background and transaction information about each one of them—on your ever-growing Power Rolodex, you're ready to move into high gear on a Hollywood sales campaign.

10

☆

Just Do It!

★　★　★　★　★　★　★　★　★　★　★　★　★　★

THE ACTION LOG, SALES SCALE, AND RHINO SKIN

The biggest selling mistake people make is not taking action. You need to do whatever it takes to get "belly-to-belly" with lots of prospects so you'll land a job or make a sale.

Keep track of all the steps you're taking toward your goal. Some people like to keep a daily "Action Log," listing the things they've done, big and small, so that they can reward themselves for positive action. It's also interesting to keep track of your feelings as you take these steps. You may surprise yourself by finding out that you can take effective action even when you're not feeling your best. In fact, the simple act of making a call or writing a letter will often improve your mood. People who give themselves excuses for not taking action often blame it on their feelings. "I'm so depressed this morning. I shouldn't call until I feel better." Keeping an Action Log helps you keep moving.

THE ACTION LOG			
Date	**Action Taken**	**Feelings**	**Ratings***
5/02/92	Call to Mr. Mogul	Nervous	★ ★ ★ ★ ★
" "	Lunch w/ agent	Relaxed	★ ★ ★ ★ ★ ★
TOTAL:			11 stars

★ THE SALES SCALE RATING SYSTEM

★★★★★★ THE SIX-STAR, BELLY-TO-BELLY MEETING.

An in-person, face-to-face meeting between you and your potential buyer or between your representative (agent, "godfather," friend) and a buyer earns you six stars. An in-person meeting with a Referral Source (someone who might refer you to a job or buyer) earns you five stars. Give yourself an extra star if the meeting is over food or drink, which is a superb, relaxing selling environment.

★★★★★ THE FIVE-STAR PHONE CALL.

The purpose of a phone call is to get a belly-to-belly meeting if possible. Pitch on the phone only if you can't get a personal meeting. But give yourself five stars for a phone call—it's an audio meeting between you and your buyer. Also give yourself five stars for a call to your buyer from an agent or friend pitching/recommending you (see Godfather/Godmother Calls below). Four stars for a phone call with a Referral Source.

GODFATHER/GODMOTHER CALLS: THE SAVVY HOLLYWOOD JOB HUNTER'S SECRET WEAPON

It's hard to overemphasize the importance of Godfather Calls in getting hired in today's Hollywood—especially for higher-level jobs. It really is "who you know" well enough to ask them to call on your behalf that makes the difference in who gets the job.

Here's how Hollywood Godfather Calls work: Jim, Janie, and Joe are up for a Director of Development job at Fox. All three have very nice backgrounds and credentials. Toni has to decide which one she will hire. Jim worked for a prominent director and when Toni called her, she said nice things about Jim. Janie had worked at Hollywood Pictures and an executive there said he'd been pleased with her work.

But Joe got the job.

Why? Because not only did his former bosses say nice things about him, they also took the time (at Joe's request) to call Toni before she called them. Also Joe called in every favor he had around town. Superagent Sammy Slick rang in from his plane en route to Hawaii to rave about what a great guy Joe was. Toni's old friend Marvin Mogul called her about Joe. Newly hot junior agent Maria Money left a message for Toni about how great Joe was. Million-dollar writer Paul Pen dropped her a line telling her how much he had enjoyed working with Joe on his last script. Toni's boss, Fred, got Godfather and Godmother Calls about Joe too, as well as nudges from people at his exclusive gym who said Joe would be a great guy to have on the Fox team. Fred asked Toni who this guy Joe was that everybody was raving about. Everywhere she turned, Toni kept hearing Joe's name.

How could Toni *not* have hired Joe? She would have had to justify her actions to a disappointed Fred, Sammy, Marvin, Maria, and Paul who had put themselves out on Joe's behalf. Not a smart career move.

BUDDY CALLS

But what if you can't get Mike Ovitz to call on your behalf?

Godfather Calls can be effective even if the callers aren't industry heavyweights with mucho clout. Low-level agents, newly hot talents, or just friends of the employer or her assistant can make an impact. Sometimes it's just the volume of calls that the employer gets on your behalf that do the trick. "Buddy Calls" are friendly references, showing that you're a known quantity around town, a friend of a friend.

I advise my clients to always use Godfather or Buddy Calls on every job campaign or project pitch. Even if you just have the assistant's yoga teacher call on your behalf to say what a nice person you are and how glad she is that the assistant and his boss will be meeting with you—it all helps. Without friends and mentors, you're just another Hollywood wannabe.

HOW TO GET THROUGH TO PEOPLE ON THE PHONE

Speaking of the importance of assistants, charming them is the key to getting through to people. That's why it's important to make sure a few Buddy Calls are sent in their direction. It's important to learn how to romance them and turn them into allies or friends. Yes, they can be grumpy, but use your empathy: it's not easy working for a high-strung, temperamental, insecure, possibly abusive player. Every day the assistant is bombarded with many more calls than the boss can possibly answer. If you're dull or nervous or irritable, why should the assistant waste time on you?

Here, as everywhere else in Hollywood, you have to be special to win. Following are a few suggestions about how to get through to people.

★ **Find out the assistant's name and use it!** Some callers like to start a conversation with an immediate question. For example:

> STEVE
> (Irritable)

Donna Development's office.

> LEE
> (Pleasant tone)

Who am I speaking with, please?

> STEVE
> (Curt)

Steve.

LEE
(As if they've been friends forever)

Hi, Steve. This is Lee Jones, the writer. I think Marvin Mogul spoke to you and Donna this morning about my project. Is she available?

★ **Use a Godmother or Buddy Call to pave the way for your call.** Lee knew that Marvin had called that morning because he had stayed in close contact with Marvin's long-time assistant Susan, who told him when Marvin had actually reached Donna. In a town where information overload and short-term memory loss are epidemic problems, timing is everything. By the next day, both Steve and Donna might have forgotten all about Marvin's call.

And don't forget to thank Marvin and Susan for their help in reaching Donna. You may want to write a handwritten note or send flowers or an imaginative gift. Keep them up to date on your progress. And stay in touch—you may need their help again.

★ **Use the two magic words.** Even if Marvin Mogul hasn't made a Godfather Call to pave the way for your call, drop the first and last name of the person who referred you to Donna. Hopefully it's a name with some clout. But even if it's the name of Donna's son's riding teacher, it helps. The two magic words will separate you from the hordes of wannabes who call every day.

★ **Send a letter or fax first so you can refer to it when you call.** "Hi, Susan. This is Jane Meyer, the costume designer. I'm following up on the letter I sent Marvin last week at Joe Dante's suggestion. . . ." Susan may be so frazzled that she doesn't remember the letter in question, has forgotten its contents, or can't think where it might have gotten to. But now you have her on the defensive. She certainly knows who Joe Dante is, so she just might let you talk to Marvin. It's worth a try.

★ **Give good phone.** There is an art to charming people over the phone.

Experts on cold calling say that the success of a phone call is 10 percent content, 40 percent tone of voice, and 50 percent facial and body expression—the smile on your face and in your voice. Practice into a tape recorder if you have trouble using your voice to convey positive emotion.

If you're nervous about the call, prepare notes or a little script of what you're going to say. You may want to include elements of your Hollywood pitch in the script.

★ **Be a nice nudge.** Be pleasant but be persistent. Hollywood respects persistence. One TV producer I worked with never takes phone calls from people he doesn't know unless they call at least ten times. He figures if they're not aggressive enough to call ten times, they aren't aggressive enough to be in this business.

My clients often resist this advice. They worry about annoying people and making them mad. They usually call too few times rather than too many. Ask yourself: how did your buyer get where she is? Was she a shrinking violet? Most successful Hollywood players completely understand the need for a newcomer to be persistent.

The trick is being *nice* about it. Especially with the weary assistant. Be friendly and understanding. "Hi Susan, it's Paul again. Sounds like you're having a rough day. . . ." (Marvin is screaming in the background.) Or "Hi, Josh, it's Stan the cameraman once more. Any way you can put me on her callback list today?"

If you're charming and fun for the assistant to talk with on the phone, she really may make an effort to see if Marvin will take or return your call. In the best of all possible worlds, you strike up a real phone relationship. And at a certain point, just drop in to say hi to the assistant and "put a face to the voice."

★ **Call at odd hours.** Peak phone times in Hollywood are 10:00 A.M. to noon and 3:00 to 5:30 P.M. Most people are at their desks during those hours.

Of course that also means that everybody else is calling during those time slots, so your call is competing with the calls from heavyweights and important colleagues.

Find out as much about Marvin's normal schedule as Susan will tell you. If he's an early bird, try calling before 10:00 A.M. when Susan gets in. If he works late, try calling after 6:00 P.M. when he may be returning calls and answering his own phone. This is well known in Hollywood as the best time to reach agents.

★★★★ FOUR-STAR IMPACT: REELS, HEAD SHOTS, AND GIFTS

Audiovisual aids are an important part of making a sales impression in Hollywood. There's no better demonstration of your talent than a tape or reel showcasing your efforts. Even when you can't land an interview or score a phone call, you may be able to get a potential employer or buyer to watch your reel or listen to your music in the car. Or you may want to put your pitch onto video or audio tape. Because this is an audiovisual business, people are used to communicating in pictures and sound, so there's sometimes less resistance to watching or hearing a tape than to reading a resume or taking a call or meeting.

Even a still picture is worth a thousand words. Performers need to put their head shots into the hands of as many people who can hire them as possible. Pitchers sometimes create a mock movie poster, complete with a log line, or storyboard drawings to add visual impact to their oral presentation.

And don't underestimate the impact of a little three-dimensional theater.

SAY IT WITH FLOWERS, FORTUNE COOKIES, BALLOONS, AFTERNOON TEA . . .

In Hollywood they say, "Show me, don't tell me." Entertainment industry people often respond better to a visual or physical demonstration than to the written or even the spoken word. The grand or clever or emotional gesture is appreciated, as long as it's not an act of desperation.

Hundreds of stores and companies benefit from this show business predilection. Hollywood people love to exchange gifts and can respond with delight to a bouquet of flowers, a plant, a zany gift or toy that relates to the project or the producer's hobby, a "cookie bouquet," a popcorn pizza, balloons with a cute saying or sales pitch on them.

This might seem a little childish to people who work in banking or insurance, but remember that in Hollywood, unlike most other industries, it's OK to indulge the little kid in you. That's part of the fun of working there. But keep in mind that many industry people are used to the best. The gift doesn't have to be very expensive, but it must be clever or fun. After all, this is the entertainment business and it's your job to be entertaining.

For example, fortune cookies can carry sales messages to your prospect. Let your fingers do the walking in your yellow pages until you find a company willing to insert your pitch or quip into the cookies.

These gestures can be amazingly effective. An actor client of mine landed a face-to-face get-together with a difficult-to-reach talent agent by sending her flowers every day until she agreed to meet with him.

ADD A LITTLE 3-D IMPACT

Many savvy Hollywood job hunters include a little 3-D pizzazz in their sales strategies.

After an interview with a prospective boss for a distribution position, one of my clients followed up by having afternoon tea delivered to the boss's office from Trumps, complete with tuxedoed waiter. While the surprised and delighted boss was enjoying the tea and scones, a giant "action" slate was delivered, carrying the message: "For serious sales action, hire Jim." The boss, amused and impressed, called Jim to thank him. They set up a second meeting.

A student of mine was up for an on-air talk show host position. Instead of just sending her picture in, like everyone else, she had a large blow-up made of her head shot, put it on heavy cardboard backing so it could stand on its own, and had a messenger deliver it. She attached a bright red, bow-tie-shaped note to the bottom of the picture, saying "To see the rest of me, call . . ." The producer, who had a sense of humor, was delighted. He called her in just to meet the woman who had the guts to send such an outrageous picture. He liked her spunk and she got the job.

According to Hollywood legend, a variation on this "right move" was used by a hot young actor who was up for the part of a seductive stud in "Hollywood Wives," based on the Jackie Collins novel. The novel described how the stud had attracted Hollywood's top female agent by sending in a life-size shot of himself in tight jeans and no shirt. The actor decided to have a similar life-sized shot done of himself and had it delivered to the casting offices at Aaron Spelling

Productions. Everyone got a big kick out of his clever sales tactic. He probably would have been cast in the part anyway, but it didn't hurt to add a little humor and fun to the pitch.

Give yourself four stars on the Action Log when you make audio-visual impact.

★★★ THREE STARS FOR WRITTEN CONTACT: RESUMES, CARDS, AND LETTERS

Many of my clients and students get overly hung up on the written word—especially the cover letter and resume. Don't worry, we'll deal with them both, but bear in mind that Hollywood is a talking town, not a reading town. You're lucky if people read the first few sentences of anything you send them. If you're fairly confident and extroverted, I would recommend that you just go ahead and call before putting any paperwork in front of your prospect. Paperwork makes Hollywood people nervous. It reminds them of legal contracts and the piles of reading matter they're already avoiding. But if you're introverted and sending a letter makes you feel more secure, do so.

THANK-YOU NOTES, BIRTHDAY CARDS, AND POSTCARDS FROM THE EDGE

These are the exceptions to the "nobody in Hollywood reads" dictum. People *will* read a nice handwritten thank-you note (if it's brief) or a clever card, even if they don't really know you very well. Everybody, no matter how well known, likes strokes. As long as your offering is in good taste, it will probably be appreciated. Some industry folks make a point of remembering birthdays and holidays and sending congratulations and humorous good wishes.

Postcards are also popular. If your work is now appearing on TV, film, or in the theater, toot your horn! Let everyone in your Power Rolodex know about your achievement. Using your computerized database, you can quickly code the people you want to send cards to and your printer will spit out a mailing list or mailing labels. Now you can even get mailing labels printed in fancy script or calligraphy if you want a handwritten look.

A typical entertainment industry postcard is slightly oversized, with a great photograph or visual on one side and an announcement on the other. The image should illustrate your work. It might be a still from your film or play, a shot of you directing the cameraperson and star, a close-up of the star wearing your special effects makeup. Performers sometimes have postcards made from their head shot. They leave the Announcement section blank so they can send notes to casting directors, directors, and others who might hire them. For actors, the secret of success is being seen. An actor's face is his best visual aid. When he can't get in to see someone in person or when he wants to jog a casting person's memory, a postcard may do the trick.

Postcards also work as clever (and inexpensive) holiday cards. For instance, a grip could send out a yearly shot of himself decked out in a silly Santa suit lugging cables on the set of his latest project. The greeting would be printed on the announcement side of the card: GET A GRIP ON THE HOLIDAYS THIS YEAR!

BUSINESS CARDS AND ROLODEX CARDS

Everyone in Hollywood needs a card. A plain card with your name and contact information will be fine. You can also include your occupation. When you meet people, jot a note on your card reminding them where and when you met (and possibly the subject of your discussion), so when they go through their wallet or purse a week later, they'll remember you. (Also, don't forget to get their cards so you can call them and put them into your Power Rolodex.)

Rolodex cards make nice alternatives to ordinary business cards and offer opportunities for you to show your creativity. Gary, a clever grip I know, had a wonderful business card shaped like a rolodex card with "GRIP" written in large letters on the tab. But he didn't stop there. On the left side of the card was a humorous line drawing of Gary—emphasizing his trademark nose—by *Los Angeles Times* cartoonist Conrad (Gary is a talented shmoozer and had met Conrad on a shoot). The cartoon showed Gary holding a dolly and a key (symbolizing his work as both a key grip and dolly grip). This unique card with its sly, insider humor made an indelible impression on everyone who saw it. Let's put it this way: once you met Gary and put his card in your Rolodex, you didn't forget him.

But be careful about being too gimmicky. In general, this kind of shtik is considered less appropriate for above-the-line talent than for such people as crew and extras.

FUSCHIA ENVELOPES AND ANAGRAMS

Industry job hunters are always looking for new ways of separating themselves from the competition. One client of mine swears by the tactic of always putting letters in brightly colored envelopes, to assure that they will be opened first. Another client told me about a friend who likes to send anagram letters, as in:

M is for the money you'll make if you hire me . . .
A is for the artist that I am . . .
R
V
I
N

M
O
G
U
L

Well, I'm not sure about that one . . . but I think it illustrates how far many people are willing to go to stand out from the pack. The creativity some Hollywood job seekers put into their marketing strategies can be impressive. These tactics may sound outrageous, but the outrageous is seldom out of place in Hollywood, the town of "don't be dull" and "try a little chutzpah."

Give yourself three stars on your Action Log for every written contact with a prospect, and add an extra half star for written contact that includes a special visual component (postcards, Rolodex cards with your picture on them, etc.).

★★ TWO STARS FOR GOOD PUBLIC RELATIONS

A story by or about you and your activities (in the trades, other publications, on TV) can be a nice boost for your career. For a day or two you'll be able to get through to people who otherwise wouldn't take your calls.

I experienced this extra career boost twice during my entertainment industry career. In 1982 I founded the International Documentary Association, a nonprofit professional organization for nonfiction film and TV program makers. On 27 January 1983, the very day that I had an interview for a program development job at an important television company, *Daily Variety* ran a story about me and the new group, mentioning that important television producers like David L. Wolper and Jack Haley, Jr., were involved. As I entered my interviewer's office, I was delighted to see a copy of *Daily Variety* on his desk; when I was pitching my accomplishments and skills during our meeting I casually picked it up and pointed out the story. He was definitely impressed.

A few years later I was the beneficiary of some even more powerful public relations. As luck would have it, when I went to work for Carl Weathers he was having a disagreement with his publicity firm about the poor placement of a previous story in the trades on Mr. Weathers's company. To patch up the rift, the firm promised front-page placement of his next story—which happened to be about me being hired to do development for his company! Apparently they pulled out all the stops and called in all their favors, because my picture and a brief story made the front page of *Variety*. I was Flavor of the Day on Thursday, 24 July 1986. It was amazing how rapidly my calls were returned that day (and for the rest of the week) and how many calls I got from people I hadn't heard from in years.

The moral of the public relations story: carpe diem (seize the day). In just a few weeks, my newfound celebrity had faded into yesterday's news. However, that brief burst of publicity had its intended effect: people around town were aware of our company and its activities when I called them even months later.

On your Action Log, give yourself two stars for good public relations. And milk it for all it's worth before it fades.

★ ONE-STAR TOOTS OF THE HORN: TAKING OUT ADS

Taking out a full-page ad in the trades congratulating yourself for an award or achievement may make you feel good, but it's not a substitute for belly-to-belly selling. Ads do have their uses, however. A full-page ad (a back-cover or center-page placement is considered to be most desirable) in both of the trades has marked the launching of a number of important careers. This is an especially valuable tactic for an actor who has just landed his or her first plum role. Each ad will cost you approximately $2,000—and you have to place the ad in both trades, or one may be offended and could withhold future editorial coverage, publicists say.

Ads can help you build name recognition by introducing you to the industry or reinforcing a positive impression. And even though self-serving ads are less impressive to players than news stories, when your name comes up at a later time, they may remember they have heard of you but not recall that it was in an ad rather than a news story.

So go ahead and place ads when it seems appropriate, but don't be disappointed if the phone doesn't immediately ring off the hook. Ads are usually a long-term investment in becoming better known in the industry rather than an immediate source of work.

As mentioned earlier, "Position-Wanted" ads are seldom used by industry pros, who feel they are almost useless.

RUN AN HONEST JOB CAMPAIGN: ADD UP YOUR DAILY STARS

Using your Action Log, add up your total stars each day. This will keep you honest about whether you're really selling yourself or just kidding yourself.

Also, you may want to set daily goals (e.g., a ten-star Tuesday) and shoot for them. Come up with a reward you'll give yourself if you hit the targeted number of stars.

The key is to *stay in touch* with your prospects and Referral Sources, using every contact medium at your command. Some experienced Hollywood job hunters believe in rotating their methods (a call, a fax, a note, a gift, then another call, etc.) and in shifting their focus back and forth among different people in a targeted office (the head person, the deputy, the assistant, etc.) for maximum impact.

RHINO SKIN: LEARNING TO LOVE NO

According to director Elia Kazan, to succeed in Hollywood you need "a very thick skin. A very sensitive soul. Simultaneously."

It takes a lot of nos to get to yes. It can take 300 letter-and-resume pitches or 50 phone pitches to land an interview . . . 75 pitches to get an agent . . . 100 pitches to land a job . . . 300 to sell a movie. If you quit after the first 10, 20, or 50, you may never get there. Selling is a numbers game. The odds are as impersonal as the slot machines in Las Vegas. You just have to keep pulling on the arm of the one-armed bandit.

There's a story that sales trainers love to tell about the young real estate salesman who discovered the value of no. He was going door-to-door, trying to get people to list their houses with him, and he was getting doors slammed in his face. He got discouraged and was thinking about choosing another line of work. Then he asked a more experienced real estate salesman how many doors he would have to knock on to get one listing. The veteran thought for a minute and then answered, "Well, probably around a hundred." The young man then asked, "How much commission would I stand to make from that listing?" The answer: "Oh, say $5,000 in this neighborhood." "Hmmm," said the young agent. "That's fifty bucks a no!" He went back to work with new enthusiasm. Every time a homeowner slammed the door in his face he yelled "Thank you!" and patted himself on the back for earning $50. Feeling better and better, he kept collecting his nos, and soon he got a yes and made his $5,000.

The moral of the story: just keep knocking on those doors.

IF YOU'RE NOT COLLECTING LOTS OF NOS, YOU'RE NOT DOING YOUR JOB!

Keep track of the number of nos you collect each day and each week. Reward yourself for collecting lots of nos. A high score means that you're out there pitching. A low score means you're not going up to bat often enough, which lowers the chances of hitting that home run. Hiding out in your apartment won't get you a new job or a movie deal.

NO DOESN'T MEAN YOU'RE NO GOOD

Don't interpret a no as a personal rejection. NO ONLY MEANS THAT WHAT YOU ARE OFFERING DOESN'T MEET YOUR BUYER'S NEEDS *AT THIS TIME*—but in the future it may! Don't interpret the no as a rejection of you or a confirmation of your worst fears about your own worth.

Sometimes at a TV network, no just means "We don't currently owe you a deal." Networks have been known to encourage and reward valued suppliers by giving them periodic yeses and commitments even when there are more deserving projects from less favored producers on the table. This system hasn't always led to impressive results on the tube, of course. But even if you're selling to a network that follows this unfortunate policy, you can still get a yes by being persistent. Once you've pitched a number of good projects, they may feel obligated to you too, and the no may turn into a yes.

NO CAN BE A VALUABLE SOURCE OF INFORMATION

Even a sales pro can sometimes be tempted to avoid no.

Recently an agent friend of mine was thinking about not calling a TV producer who he was sure would pass on one of his writers. He *knew* the answer would be no. But, being a pro, he called anyway. He just wanted to tidy up the books and collect his no.

When the producer came on the line, the agent kidded her, saying he was calling to collect his no. The producer did indeed say no, and explained why. She gave the agent good feedback on why she felt the writer in question wasn't right for her current project, plus some valuable information about exactly what she was looking for. The two kept chatting, building the relationship. By the end of the conversation, the producer had confided that she needed another director to do a show at the end of the season. Did the agent happen to have any appropriate directors? He did indeed.

Never avoid no. Every no is a valuable piece of information. It gives you feedback and tells you something about the buyer's current needs and what it will take to fill them. It also allows you to complete one transaction with the buyer and open the door for future dealings.

EVERY SALES CONTACT IS A WIN

Even if you don't land the immediate job or sell the project today, you can come away from every sales contact a winner. The prize? A valuable new relationship with an important entertainment industry contact.

Take the long view of your career. You're going to be in the business for many years. The person you've met today may turn out to be a valuable ally, client, employer, or colleague in the years to come. Just focus on thanking him or her for the meeting and making sure the door is left open for future contacts and pitches. Most people will agree to that because "you never know . . ."

THE HOLLYWOOD YES—WHICH MEANS YES, NO, OR MAYBE

The "you never know" factor also shows up in The Hollywood Yes. Because you never know when today's lowly pitcher will be tomorrow's hot commodity, insecure Hollywood people are often afraid to say no openly and directly. What if this project turns out to be the next *E.T.* or *Home Alone*? (Everyone in town knows the names of the people who turned down those blockbusters!)

So these insecure types hedge their bets. They say, "I love it. Yeah, it's great. Call me tomorrow and we'll make a picture." Or "Old Joe referred you? Sure, call me Monday and I'll see what I can do for you." Then they don't take your calls, despite your best phone shmoozing efforts with the assistant.

What happened? Did you do something wrong?

People can agonize over these situations, but rest assured that it isn't you. It happens all the time. It's just the Hollywood Yes—which may mean yes, no, or maybe. (A close relative of the Hollywood Yes is Letshavelunch, not to be confused with Let's Have Lunch!)

The only way to find out what a Hollywood Yes really means is to try to close the sale (or have your agent or lawyer try to make a deal). If, despite your best, most persistent efforts and nice nudging, it just won't close—it's a no.

Some Hollywood insiders believe that a true yes will close quickly and that with each passing day, it is less likely a Hollywood Yes (or a nonanswer) will turn into a deal. But the "You Never Know" rule can also apply. Sometimes even a long, drawn-out Hollywood Yes will turn into a film or a job if you're persistent.

As film critic Pauline Kael so accurately observed, Hollywood is a town where you could die from encouragement.

THE DEAL THAT WON'T CLOSE

A nasty variant on The Hollywood Yes is the Deal That Isn't. The executive gushes over the project and says what appears to be a clear yes. Not just, "I love it and let's make the picture," but "Have your agent call and let's make a deal" or "We'll call your lawyer on Monday." You're thrilled and blow the month's rent on a celebration dinner at Morton's. Wrong. In Hollywood, a deal may not be a deal until the first day of shooting—and maybe not even then. Sometimes even a signed contract can't prevent people from weaseling out of making your picture or giving you the job.

THE TINY WINDOWS OF OPPORTUNITY

The trick is to realize that when an executive or producer says yes, the clock starts ticking. You or your representative must attempt to close the deal at once, because with every passing moment the heat can cool. The idea is not to let the buyers have time for second thoughts to set in, but to get them sufficiently "pregnant" that they can't back out without severe embarrassment or penalties.

There are two other tiny windows of opportunity to be aware of. First, the "grace period" when you're new to the industry. You're "fresh meat," and many people will agree to meet with you or read your script to check you out. This lasts about three to six months, after which you're no longer new merchandise in the bazaar. Second, there is a magic time between when you're hired to work on a project and the time the project comes out. For that period, you're ultradesirable. Strike while you're hot. After the film or show plays or after you're out of work, things often cool down considerably unless the project is a major hit. Even if you're ultrabusy working on your project, don't forget to take time to water your contacts and hustle for your next job.

GET MAD AND THEN GET OVER IT

Sometimes, even with your best efforts and the efforts of your godfathers, godmothers, agents, and lawyers, you may not be able to turn a Hollywood Yes into a deal. You feel ripped off, lied to, cheated out of a good opportunity.

There are only two things to do if you get one of these nasty nos. Get mad and get over it.

Get your anger out by sharing it with trusted personal friends or loved ones—not industry contacts who could repeat it to the offender. ("That SOB didn't even have the guts to say no to my face!") Then deal with it like any other no. Don't take offense. Don't get bitter. And keep up the relationship in spite of the nasty no. You'll probably be surprised to find out that the person who gave you this indirect no isn't angry at you. In fact, she may be happy to continue a dialogue with you about the progress of the project and will probably want to hear about your next project or activity.

People sometimes find this hard to believe, but it's true. The experienced players know that this is a small town and go out of their way not to give overt offense. That's why many of them lack the courage to say no directly. They expect you to understand that a Hollywood Yes (No) isn't any more personal than any other no. It's just business.

THE PSEUDORAVE: "I LOVE IT"

A close relative of the Hollywood Yes, the Pseudorave is another way industry people protect themselves from the possible downside consequences of an honest but negative response to anyone or anything. As they see it, there's no percentage in criticizing someone's work or giving unsolicited advice about how it could have been better. The offended artist will never forget the bad review and even if you believe the artist has no talent and will never make it, the "you never know" rule may come up and hit you in the face if he or she actually succeeds.

Savvy industry players are amazingly creative about digging out the one or two positive points about any script or film so that they can give a believable Pseudorave to the filmmaker. This is especially important when one attends frequent screenings. "Interesting" just doesn't cut it anymore. Everyone knows it's an insult. "I loved the scene where you shot the bad guy with that nifty airgun," "The score is fabulous," or "It's a definite E-ticket ride" are less likely to offend fragile egos. True cowards slip out before the lights come up so they don't have to face the hapless filmmaker.

Once you've been around Hollywood for a while, you may be surprised to find yourself learning this arcane art out of necessity. Unless you're actually working on a project and your honest input has been solicited, it makes little career sense to put down others' work.

THE HOLLYWOOD SNIFFING RITUAL

The Hollywood Sniffing Ritual isn't some bizarre new cocaine trip, it's a rite of passage you'll be subjected to when you begin to sell yourself or your projects in the entertainment industry.

For example, let's say that you've just completed a fantastic showcase film. You did everything right. You planned a series of gala screenings at a prestigious screening room in Los Angeles. You hired a publicist and put together excellent press materials and classy brochures and invitations. You had everyone involved with the project working the phones, using the Pyramid System—inviting agents and players around town. You used the two magic words and dropped names galore.

The response was terrific. The right people showed up and made the right noises. They loved the film. They love you. Could you possibly come to see them in their offices?

A few of these approaches were really Hollywood Yeses or Pseudo-raves, but you got an amazing number of good meetings at which more nice noises were made. The agents were heavy breathing on you. They covered themselves by saying they wanted you and would pitch you to their colleagues who, of course, would have to agree before any new client could be signed (the Hollywood pack mentality as excuse). But they love you!

Get out your rhino skin and be prepared. You're being sniffed over by the town, and it's unusual for someone to get a yes on the first sniff.

A client of mine who went through this ritual was devastated when all the courting didn't immediately result in an agent or a deal or a job. He began to doubt himself and his film. I reassured him that neither of these was the problem. He's an extremely talented guy and his film is terrific. In fact, there *wasn't* a problem. He had made all the right moves and was just going through the normal Hollywood Sniffing Ritual. The town was sniffing him over before deciding whether saying yes to him would be a defensible move.

IT TAKES TIME FOR SNIFFS TO BECOME YESES

So what does it take to turn sniffs into yeses?

Sometimes it just takes time. By the third or fourth or tenth sniff (meeting), a yes may be in the works. As director Sam Raimi commented about a friend's showcase film premiere: "I think this guy is gonna wonder why he didn't get an offer [as a direct result of his screening]. In six months, he'll think 'But everyone told me it was so good, I don't understand.' He has to go through a little more suffering. And then, if he's still there in two years, he'll be a filmmaker."

But it *still* may not happen, and then you need to grow your double-thick winter coat of rhino skin and keep trudging forward.

SUMMARY OF THE TEN POINTS TO KEEP IN MIND AS YOU'RE PITCHING

You may want to put this list up over your desk to remind you of the ten important points to keep in mind during any contact or conversation.

★ **Godfather/Godmother Calls or Buddy Calls.** Let these calls open the door for you before you contact a new prospect or Referral Source.

★ **The Two Magic Words.** Open the conversation with the name of your Referral Source.

★ **Bond and Shmooze.** Find something in common. Take a little time to chat.

★ **Info.** Gather information both before and during your conversation. Learn about your prospect and the marketplace. Ask questions. Listen.

★ **Hollywood Pitch.** Slip it into the conversation as subtly and graciously as you can. If you can, close—get your prospect to agree to take some action, which you'll follow up on after the meeting.

★ **Advice and Referrals.** Ask for them if appropriate.

★ **Keep in Touch.** Follow up. Ask, "When would it be good to call again?" Do so.

★ **Thank Yous.** Notes and gifts reinforce the good impression you have made and leave the door open to future contact.

★ **Rhino Skin.** Stay positive. Nos are steps toward yes. Focus on the "wins" in every contact. You're building your Power Rolodex and opening doors for future sales.

★ **Stay in Action.**

11

☆

Don't Be Dull!

★　★　★　★　★　★　★　★　★　★　★　★　★　★　★

THE CHUTZPAH FACTOR

BEING BORING IS A HOLLYWOOD SIN

As you know, there are only two sins in Hollywood: to be dull and to be desperate. It's always amazing to me how many of my clients forget that this is the *entertainment* industry—Hollywood people want to be entertained, to have fun. If they didn't love to be around creative, interesting, passionate, charming, attractive, dramatic people who have exciting ideas, they would have gone into banking or insurance.

Many folks assume that as long as they're not actors, the above adjectives need not apply to them. Big mistake. Whether you're a film editor or a studio executive or a secretary, you need to sprinkle a little tinsel on your image to make it in Hollywood. Even the accountants in this business are just a little more interesting and fun to be with than the accountants in any other industry.

This doesn't mean that you can't be yourself in Hollywood. It just means that you need to identify what's unique and special about you—and accentuate the positive. Without becoming phony, try turning up the volume just a notch. If you're a good storyteller, learn to spin a tale even more colorfully. If you're a redhead, wear colors that show off your crowning glory. If you're a baseball fan, take it to the max. If you're funny, let that side of you blossom even more. If you're quiet and intense, be even more dramatically taciturn and obsessed.

Develop your own personal style and make it work for you.

CREATE YOUR OWN UNIQUE LOOK

While it's important that you pay attention to the accepted "uniform" of the top people in your chosen target niche, it's also helpful to develop a look that's all your own, which helps people remember you and lets you stand out from the crowd. If you need help with this, there are personal image consultants who can advise you—but make sure you hire someone familiar with the entertainment industry. Costume designers, for instance, often help friends and clients put together a look that's both personal and industry-savvy.

Hollywood is incredibly looks-conscious, which is not surprising since this is an industry that manufactures visual imagery. The town can be as fashion-sensitive as Seventh Avenue and as quick to pass comment as a high school clique. Rightly or wrongly, Hollywood people may judge you by how you look, so it's best to present yourself carefully, the way you want to be seen.

GOLD CHAINS ARE OUT—ANTIQUE FORTIES TIES ARE IN (THIS WEEK)

Over the years Hollywood has entertained itself with a succession of amusing looks, which change as rapidly as the seasons. The legendary producer decked out in gold chains and hairy bare chest is long gone, but the zoot-suited development executive with big-shouldered, subtly-patterned jackets, baggy pants, and hip antique ties is still with us. We've been through down vests, owlish horn-rimmed glasses, ponytails for men, Spielberg beards, "Miami Vice"/George Michael two-day stubble, moussed hair, politically correct brown and green earth tones. Who knows what's next?

Every segment of the industry has its dress code. Male studio executives on the creative side tend to favor expensive Italian shoes and double-breasted, slouchy-shouldered suits. Female development execs might favor Calvin Klein jackets and Romeo Gigli slacks. Both women and men in powerful positions seem to like Armani. Directors look more "rough and ready," with baseball caps, shirts, and jackets being popular. Their casual outfits can sometimes confuse newcomers to the set, who mistake them for grips. Writers are renowned for their slightly collegiate look, complete with script-laden over-the-shoulder bags that look as though they've been from here to Tibet. Sport shoes like Converse sneakers, Reeboks, and Nikes are worn by many creative types.

The only thing you can count on with these endlessly changing looks is that they will be out soon after they're in. Be aware of the trends, but don't be afraid to buck them. A studio exec who graduated from Harvard affects an understated but immaculate Ivy League look, no matter what's in. He feels it makes a statement about his pedigree that does him no harm in status-conscious Hollywood.

ANIMAL EARRINGS AND NEW YORK BLACK

A New York writer I worked with had also developed her own personal style—one that accentuated both her hip downtown sensibilities and quirky sense of humor. She wore the obligatory New York black, highlighted by a radical, asymmetrical haircut and a wonderful collection of brightly colored, animal-shaped earrings she picked up at flea markets around the world. The earrings were always a conversation starter and no one who met her forgot her!

A top music industry mogul is well known for dressing all in white. His pristine Armani jackets, white jeans, and tennis shoes are his personal trademark.

Be creative. You might decide that hats will be your thing, for example. Put together an interesting collection that can hang on an antique coat rack in your office. Soon people will be telling you about wonderful hats they've seen at swap meets or, better yet, they'll start bringing you presents of wild and wacky headgear.

Some folks around town collect production jackets with show logos on them, or production-logoed baseball caps. The chic thing is to wear paraphernalia from some offbeat, campy, long-departed picture, not the current blockbuster you're working on.

TOYS FOR THE BOYS AND GIRLS

Since we're on the subject of collections, a number of people around town collect expensive toys for their homes and offices. Fifties pinball machines and jukeboxes have been popular, as well as old movie posters. In Hollywood it's a point of honor never to have grown up.

If collecting toys sounds like fun to you, think back to your childhood. What did you love? Beach blanket movies? Day-Glo posters? Beatles records? Barbie paraphernalia? Surfing? Japanese baseball? Whatever it was, bring it back into your life and entertain your Hollywood friends by sharing your passion with them.

TURN YOUR OFFICE INTO A SHMOOZY HANGOUT

When Paul was a business affairs executive at a large TV production company, he discovered the value of turning his office into a fun place to hang out. To help him relax in a very stressful job, he bought a large, soothing aquarium and stocked it with colorful, entertaining fish (plus a few lovable, acrobatic aquatic frogs). Paul was surprised when more and more people from every department of the company began dropping in to see how the office mascots were doing. His visitors included top producers and executives as well as their assistants.

Paul soon gained public, private, and even secret information about important activities and politics going on at every level of his company, thanks to Freddie the Frog and his friends.

Other industry people have also discovered the benefits of creating an entertaining environment in their work space. Some do it with nostalgic movie posters or animation cels from favorite films. Others have popcorn machines or cappucino makers or pinball machines to attract their colleagues. I always enjoyed visiting producer Joel Silver's offices because he is an astute collector of fascinating, very comfortable furniture from the thirties to the fifties, and his suite is always full of fun "toys" to entertain his employees and visitors. He had a great "rec room" where his talented buddies could hang out with him as they created new movies.

PICK UP SOME TRICKS FROM ACTORS

Taking an acting class is always a good idea for anyone in show business, no matter what your target niche may be. In a good class you'll get feedback on how you come across and on your unconscious, nonverbal communication style. Some teachers also use videotape to help you see yourself as others see you.

Acting classes can also help you learn how to project your voice and presence. There is an art to the impactful gesture, the subtle movement, the tone and speed of speech, the facial expression. You can learn how to enter a room with aplomb, exude confidence as you take a meeting, and exit with style. You'll learn how to take what you have and use it to communicate most effectively.

You also need to develop your own brand of charm. Every successful person in Hollywood—no matter how arrogant or abrasive he may be to people he feels no need to impress—must have the ability to be charming when he needs to be.

THE OPPOSITE OF DULL: PASSIONATE

In Hollywood, passion for your craft and your projects is the most charming trait of all. It is the opposite of dull. Expressing your joy and love for what you do is always a right move. It's even OK to occasionally go a little overboard with enthusiasm for the work and eagerness for the job. If you err, let it be on the side of chutzpah.

Barry was a dancer who came to L.A. to take acting lessons and break into Hollywood. He heard people talk about how hard it was to get a Screen Actors Guild (SAG) card or an acting job, but didn't let that discourage him.

One day he went to Richard Simmons's exercise studio in Beverly Hills, where his wife worked as an aerobics teacher. At the time there was a SAG strike against the commercial producers. One of Barry's wife's students was a woman in her late forties who happened to be a commercial agent.

After the class, as Barry, his wife, and the agent were sitting at a table enjoying their carrot juice, the agent turned to Barry and said, "You know, you could do commercials."

It happened "just like that!" said Barry. "So, I signed with her as an interim client during the SAG strike. She literally sent me on three or four auditions a day for the duration of the strike. Although I was called back many times by casting people, I never got hired.

"When the strike was over, the agent called me and, expressing her regret at my continuing lack of employment, suggested that I at least go on a commercial shoot as an extra, so that I could get a feel for how it all worked. She suggested a Continental Airlines spot that would be shooting the next day.

"The next morning I boarded a bus along with thirty other extras and traveled to Long Beach, where the McDonnell Douglas plant is and where there are mock-ups of DC-10 cabins. I noticed that my fellow extras were all deeply involved in crime magazines, crossword puzzles, and idle chit-chat. Since I thought this was going to be a work day, I'd brought nothing extraneous, and was too intensely curious and excited to speak to anyone.

"Before lunch, seated in the DC-10 mock-up, both the principal actors and the extras rehearsed a song for the commercial. We were coached to sing, 'Well you should see us now, we'd like to take a bow. . . .' The words were continuously projected on a screen at the front of the cabin, and we were left on our own to practice. But I noticed that not a single soul, including the principal actors, was practicing.

"The production and technical staff rushed around madly preparing for the afternoon shoot, but the 'talent' were buried in crossword puzzles and murder mysteries. After lunch, for the hour before the shoot was to begin, the ad agency and the director were deep in conference, standing next to the screen where the words to our song continuously rolled down the screen. I sensed that they were less than thrilled with the lack of enthusiasm by the talent on the set.

"I got out of my seat and began belting out, 'Well, you should see *me* now, *I'd* like to take a bow . . . ,' and did a little soft-shoe in the aisle next to my seat. As if on cue, the ad rep turned to the director and pointed in my direction. The director pulled over the assistant director, whispered something to him, and looked both at the principal actor and then at me.

"To make a long story very short, I was promoted to principal performer status, made nearly $15,000 on that commercial, and I got my SAG card (I was 'Taft-Hartleyed' in). The former principal actor got to finish his crossword puzzle from the quiet and humiliating solitude of a rear window seat."

THE CHUTZPAH FACTOR

Assertive is nice. Aggressive can definitely work. But way beyond both lies pure chutzpah.

Chutzpah is a Yiddish word that can be loosely translated as "outrageousness" or "unmitigated gall." Chutzpah means pushing the edge of the envelope.

Let's be blunt about this: chutzpah sometimes involves doing things that aren't strictly kosher. However, everyone in Hollywood knows people who have succeeded by bending the rules. In fact, I would venture to say that most successful Hollywood players have at one time or another used chutzpah tactics to succeed—and will probably admire your aggressiveness and ambition as long as you don't go over the top or make yourself obnoxious.

Hollywood hairstylist Laurie Fraser tells a wonderful story about her grandfather that perfectly illustrates chutzpah. As a young man, showbiz publicist Jack Oliphant wanted to represent singer Sophie Tucker. Sophie looked at the young man's meager credentials and sniffed, "Why should I let you represent me? You don't know anybody!" Laurie's grandfather knew the situation called for drastic measures. Now was the time for chutzpah.

He came up with a plan. He found out Miss Tucker's normal daily route to the theater. Then he hired an actress to roll a baby buggy with a doll in it in front of Miss Tucker's car. The car came to a screeching stop. Oliphant opened the car door, put a real baby into Miss Tucker's arms and had a photographer snap a picture. The next day the papers ran a front-page story with the picture. The headline read "Sophie Tucker Saves Baby!"

Miss Tucker decided that anyone who had that much chutzpah must be a good publicist. Oliphant's passion charmed her. She hired him, and he (with his wife, Julie) went on to a successful career in public relations, representing many important stars, including Ida Lupino, Lena Horne, Gypsy Rose Lee, Nat King Cole, and Dorothy Lamour.

FLORAL CHUTZPAH

In 1976 Gene Narmore co-wrote a screenplay called *Blue Roses*, which he and his writing partner wanted to get to then-superagent Sue Mengers at ICM. Gene was working as a waiter at Joe Allen's restaurant and had no industry contacts, so he felt that chutzpah was his only recourse.

Gene and his partner created a dozen handmade blue roses out of silk ribbon and laid them out beautifully in a florist box—over a copy of *Blue Roses*. Gene's partner donned a delivery man's jacket and bravely marched into ICM, brushing aside receptionists and assistants by saying that he had orders to deliver the flowers to Miss Mengers personally. He swept into her office with great aplomb. When he found himself standing next to Miss Mengers he drew a copy of his screenplay from its hiding place amid the flowers and presented it to her. According to Narmore, she agreed to read it. But not every chutzpah move pays off. In spite of Narmore's creativity and enterprise, *Blue Roses* hasn't yet sold, and Narmore returned home to his native North Carolina, where he owns his own studio—a video store called Video Studios. He still comes up with story ideas in his spare time.

SAY YES

One of the most popular chutzpah tactics in Hollywood is to say yes. Even if you choose not to use it (it isn't exactly honest), be aware that many other aspirants will not be so scrupulous.

Here's how it goes: when people ask you if you can . . . sing . . . dance . . . pull focus . . . ride horses . . . cut tape . . . speak Lakota—SAY YES! And quickly learn how. This isn't a smart move if they're asking if you can do dangerous stunts, of course, but in non-life-threatening situations many show business people live by the "say yes" rule.

Twenty-five-year-old pop star/actor Gerardo ("Rico Suave") reportedly used the "say yes" tactic to break into the entertainment industry. He started out his career by winning dance contests and when he was approached by a casting director who asked him if he had ever acted before, he "lied, of course, and said 'Yeah, I've done lots of acting.' " He landed a small part in a movie, which led to other roles, including one in Dennis Hopper's 1988 movie *Colors.*

In his audition for *Colors* he also used another chutzpah tactic: because he had heard that the director was looking to hire real gang members, "I went to the audition like I was some guy off the street and scared the crap out of them." It worked.

MORE CHUTZPAH MOVES

According to Hollywood legend, a young Steven Spielberg sneaked onto the Universal lot and set up shop in a vacant office, jump-starting his career. A definite chutzpah move.

A friend of mine recommends another chutzpah guerrilla tactic: have lunch at Le Dome or Morton's and leave behind a copy of your script in an envelope with your prospect's name and address marked clearly on the outside. If you're lucky, the maître d' will think Mr. Katzenberg or Mr. Medavoy forgot his lunchtime reading and will forward it to his office.

CRASHING THE PARTY OR AUDITION

Some Hollywood people have turned crashing into a fine art. Clients have told me that by being charming and polite, they have been able to meet people they would otherwise have no way of getting to.

Estelle Harman, founder and director of the Estelle Harman Actors Workshop, has been training actors like Sharon Gless, Michael Landon, Carol Burnett, Tony Curtis, Victoria Principal, and Dennis Weaver over the last thirty-five years. She and her daughter Eden Harman, an acting coach and theater director, told me about a few of the tactics that they have seen some of their more enterprising students use to break into Hollywood.

A young actor they know went way beyond crashing an audition: he found out the time and location of the departure of a bus that was taking the cast of a film out on location. "He just got on the bus and went out there with them," Estelle said. "No one quite knew who he was but he finally found himself cast and working in the film."

Another of Estelle's students heard that a role was being cast on a soap opera. "She didn't even have an agent. She didn't have a reading. She just went to the callback and said that William Morris was her agent. She went at the end of the day when nobody at the agency could be reached. She ended up reading, did a very good job, and, although she wasn't cast in that soap opera, the casting director liked her so much that she ended up confessing the real story and getting an agent out of it." By the way, Hollywood rumor has it that Sylvester Stallone once used a similar tactic, showing up at an audition late in the day and just talking his way into it.

Estelle emphasizes the importance of being able to back up your chutzpah with real talent. If you con your way into an audition and are wonderful, for example, your deception may be considered amusing and forgivable. If, however, you waste everyone's time, you'll have a very annoyed casting director on your hands who can put the bad word out on you. "Don't present yourself before you're ready," Estelle cautions. "Casting directors have memories like elephants."

DROPPING BY PEOPLES' OFFICES UNINVITED

It's a time-honored Tinseltown tactic to drop by unannounced. Some people hate to be interrupted in this way, but others will give you a handshake or a brief chat if you have a believable explanation for your presence. "I just had a meeting with Marvin Mogul down the hall, and thought that while I was here I'd pop in to say hi" or "I'm working on *Hook II* on the lot and was thrilled to see your name on the building directory." The trick here is convincing the assistant with your charm and sincerity.

"When Keenan Ivory Wayans was first getting started in his career," Eden Harman remembers, "he was very good friends with another actor, Eddie Velez, who's doing quite well now. They used to travel around to the casting offices and the agencies and just charm people. They would call each other in the morning and say 'Let's do something today.' And instead of sitting down and griping about how hard the business is, they would go out and meet people. They would walk right onto the lot, right into the offices and end up chatting with people. Both of them got some readings out of that particular tactic. I don't know that everybody is qualified or charming enough to pull that off, but they took the initiative."

"I think what it takes," says Eden, "is a little bit of chutzpah, a little bit of imagination. The same thing that is annoying in one person is the ticket for another. It's just a matter of trying and believing that you have something worthwhile to offer once you get in that door."

But it's not as easy to get in to see people as it used to be. Hollywood players are increasingly security-conscious—with good reason—and the assistants, consultants, and bodyguards who surround them do a good job of protecting their bosses. They take a dim view of people who circumvent their security measures.

CHUTZPAH TO THE MAX: MARTY CREATES A MANAGER

Marty, an actor I know, took chutzpah to the max. He created a mythical manager named Marlon.

He ordered stationery with Marlon's name and address (a post office box). He set up a phone in his house with a special number for Marlon. He created a wonderful voice for Marlon, complete with quirky accent. Then he started sending out letters and making calls touting Marlon's talented client Marty. Marlon sent out Marty's head shot and resume all over town. Whenever a part showed up in the breakdowns that Marlon thought might be right for Marty, Marlon was right on it. How many managers are as devoted to their clients as Marlon was?

Estelle Harman told me that Victoria Principal had at one time started her own and agency—a legitimate one—to help create work for herself. "Her career was sort of limping along," said Estelle, "and she set up an agency and submitted herself for 'Dallas.' That got her career going again." This isn't a tactic I'd necessarily recommend, but it illustrates the lengths entertainment industry people may be willing to go to in order to get work.

CHUTZPAH IS LIKE DYNAMITE: HANDLE WITH EXTREME CARE

There's a very fine line between charming outrageousness and passion to do your work, on the one hand, and obnoxiousness and truly unethical behavior on the other. A little chutzpah goes a long way. A word of caution: serious dishonesty can really backfire. As you know, Hollywood is a small town and news gets around very quickly.

Before you make any chutzpah moves, I recommend that you run them by your Hollywood advisers and friends. How comfortable are you with taking this risk? Are you doing something that goes against your personal value system? Is there a chance that your move could have unforeseen negative consequences?

That said, it's still important to face the fact that, in a high-risk game, cautious souls seldom win. If you don't take any chances, you may lose out on the rewards. It's a risky business, so every once in a while you may decide you need to try a little chutzpah.

12
☆
Resumes, Reels, and Showcase Films

★ ★ ★ ★ ★ ★ ★ ★ ★ ★ ★ ★ ★ ★ ★

FROM NUN TO AGENT: THE CHRISTINE FOSTER STORY

Christine Foster was a nun with the Immaculate Heart order. She was an excellent teaching sister, but she knew that being a nun wasn't her real vocation.

She agonized over her decision, but eventually it became clear to her that she needed to leave her order and pursue something else. I met her when we were both students at UCLA in the Master's program in documentary film.

Some time after we both graduated, Christine drew up her resume. She debated about whether to include her "previous experience" as a nun. Finally she said, "What the heck. It's the truth." It never occurred to her that this "special interest" of hers in God and religion would help her get a great showbiz job.

Her resume landed on the desk of a very successful Hollywood producer who was going through a period of intense religious questioning. He saw her "previous experience" and called her in for an interview. They talked about God for a long time, and then he offered her a terrific job as head of the company's research department.

Christine went on to become a TV network executive, a vice president at a major studio, and, eventually, the highly respected agent she is today. At the Shapiro-Lichtman agency, Christine represents many successful writers, producers, and directors. Which just goes to show you that the old Hollywood maxim "you never know" really *is* true.

The moral of this story is simple. Don't omit anything interesting about yourself and your background from your resume, no matter how far afield it may seem. This is what the "Special Interests and Skills" category is for. At the very least it will help you start an interesting conversation with your potential employer.

THE ENTERTAINMENT INDUSTRY RESUME

Your backup materials (resume, cover letter, and reel) are basically advertisements for you, your talents, and achievements. Their sole purpose is to get you an interview during which you can close the sale and land the job.

Don't get hung up on writing the perfect resume. In Hollywood, your pitching and networking talents (plus some great Godfather and Godmother Calls) are much more likely to get you hired than is your resume writing. Basically, your resume is a piece of creative sales writing that helps you convince your potential employer that you were born to do the job he or she needs done. Remember that people don't hire people because they're terrific—they hire people to do work they either can't or don't want to do themselves. They need help. Your resume should reassure them that your skills and experience make you just the person to take the burden off their shoulders and make their job and life easier.

There are as many opinions on how to write a great resume as there are job seekers and career counselors. Everyone has tricks and tactics. I recommend that you put your resume on a word processor so you can easily change it for every serious job you go after, tailoring it to the specific requirements of that particular position. The entertainment industry is so competitive that employers only bother with resumes that convince them you are *exactly* the perfect person for their needs. A general, one-size-fits-all resume from the printers (you ran off a thousand copies in 1989 and are still sending them out!) is less effective than a customized one. If your employer has to work to figure out the relevance of all that miscellaneous experience to the job offered, it's all over. He doesn't have the time.

DO I REALLY HAVE TO REWRITE MY RESUME FOR EVERY JOB?

Let's put it this way: at the very least, you're going to want to have three to four versions of your resume on your computer so that you can choose which one to send to a particular employer. You may have one that's good for production work, another that emphasizes your development skills, and another for directing or writing. That way you're ready to apply for a variety of jobs in both your A and B categories as you hear about them. Also, having your resume on a computer allows you to adjust it for each pitch, subtly emphasizing different skills and credits that would be especially impressive to the potential employer you're approaching.

Sometimes you'll have the time to make these final adjustments to a resume before you send it out, and sometimes you won't. If for any reason you send out the generic resume, be sure to pay special attention to the cover letter.

DON'T GET CUTE!

Don't get cute on your resume. The place for a little show business razzmatazz or humor is in the cover letter, especially if you're applying for a creative job. The resume should play it straight.

Type or word process it neatly, with no spelling errors, and print or copy it on good paper. I prefer to see resumes on plain white or off-white paper. It's not necessary to jam everything onto one page if it doesn't naturally fit. But try to keep your resume to two pages, three at the most. Put your best stuff up front. In a minute, I'll describe one method of writing an entertainment industry resume. But before I do that, I'd like to emphasize that there are two groups of people for whom this resume would *not* be appropriate: actors and experienced entertainment industry free-lance creative talent with substantial credits.

Actors' resumes are unique. I recommend that you read *Your Film Acting Career,* by M. K. Lewis and Rosemary R. Lewis, for a detailed description of the actor's resume.

The experienced free-lancer's resume, on the other hand, will basically be just a list of credits, starting with the most recent and going back about ten years at maximum, unless a prior credit is an

Oscar/Emmy winner or very exceptional. (Why leave off old credits? Unfortunately the industry doesn't tend to trust credits that are more than ten years old—part of a consistent pattern of age discrimination that artificially shortens many illustrious careers. "Yes, but what has she or he done lately?" is a common reaction to elderly credits.) This listing of credits may run much longer than the usual two-to-three-page resume, but be careful that it doesn't get *too* long—which makes it look as though you've been around Hollywood as long as Vincent Price. The experienced free-lancer's resume will usually be printed on his or her agent's stationery.

Here is an outline of the various categories that can be included in a typical entertainment industry resume. Some of them are optional; feel free to be creative and to adapt this format for your own needs.

★ ★

I.   YOUR NAME
Address
City/ZIP Code
Telephone(s)/Fax/Pager

2. OBJECTIVE: To work at exactly the job that's available, described in exactly the terms used in the ad or exactly the terms you believe the employer would use in describing it.

3. SUMMARY OF EXPERIENCE: This is basically a version of your Hollywood Pitch, adjusted to suit the job you're applying for. Highlight your most important achievements, relevant experience, and special strengths so your employer doesn't have to read the whole resume. You may want to point out how your particular gifts and accomplishments will benefit your employer.

4. EXPERIENCE: List *relevant* experience and credits in this category. For example:

<u>Associate Producer,</u> *Rabbit Romp,* Silver Pictures/Warner Brothers. Joel Silver, Producer; Steven Spielberg, Director; Marvin Mogul, Executive Producer. Tom Hanks, Jessica Toon. (Date is optional).

Organized ... Hired ... Created ... Supervised ... Shot on Location in ... Budgeted ... On Time, On Budget ... Saved the company X dollars ... Made X sales (Note: this is the "toot your own horn" section. Use action verbs to detail your accomplishments. This tells your potential employers what you could do for them.)

<u>Story Analyst</u>, Big Shot Productions/Columbia Pictures. Sonnie Swift, President. Janet Trueblue, Director of Development. Covered more than 200 scripts from all genres with special emphasis on action-adventure and action-comedy.

<u>Production Assistant</u>, Super Student Film. (Note: You can include unpaid work and internships as well as jobs under the "experience" category.)

5. **ADDITIONAL EXPERIENCE:** If necessary, use this section to sum up older jobs/ credits or to add nonindustry experience if you think it would help you sell yourself.

6. **EDUCATION:** Super Seminar on exactly the skill required for this job, the American Film Institute, Los Angeles. Instructor: Syd Sincere. Panelists: Agent X, Creative Executive Y, Super Shmoozer Z.

Master of Fine Arts with a specialty in x, y, z, UCLA, 19——. Magna Cum Laude (if applicable). B.A., Harvard, 19——. Major: Medieval Philosophy. (You're hired! Studios love Harvard grads—gives the outfit class.)

7. **HONORS AND AWARDS:** Oscars, Emmys, film festival awards, student awards, etc.

8. **PROFESSIONAL ORGANIZATIONS:** Women in Film, member.
Crystal Awards, Producer.
Writers Guild of America, member.
USC Cinema/TV Alumni Association, President.
International Documentary Association, member.
American Film Institute, member.

9. **SPECIAL SKILLS:**   Speak and write fluent Chinese. Computer skills: Movie Magic, DotZero. CMX editing: $\frac{1}{2}''$ and $\frac{3}{4}''$ off-line editing; Paint Box; Chyron.

10. **ACTIVITIES AND INTERESTS:**   Earth Communications Office (ECO)
Chess
Championship tennis player

11. **REFERENCES:**   Available upon request.

★ ★

Let's go through this resume step-by-step, addressing each category in more detail.

1. NAME/ADDRESS/PHONE. If possible, list a local address and phone number. Some of my clients who live outside the Hollywood diamond have persuaded an L.A. friend to allow them to use his address and to install a special line and an answering machine in their buddy's house. Others use a mailing service post office box address and answering service. They've found this to be effective because entertainment industry employers are often resistant about calling distant area codes or hiring someone who doesn't seem local. It's also smart to include a fax number (the mailing service company that provides you with the post office box may also offer this service if you don't yet have your own fax machine.) Eager beavers also include their pager number. The idea is to make it easy and appealing for your prospective employer to contact you immediately.

2. OBJECTIVE. This section is optional. Some people prefer to put this information in their cover letter or in the Summary section. The objective is most useful in three situations: (1) when you're applying for an entry-level job; (2) when you're answering a help-wanted ad (you use the exact wording in the ad); or (3) when you're making a crossover move and it's not obvious from your experience that you are seeking a position in a particular area.

Use the objective to tell your employer that you want exactly the job he or she is offering and you want to do the specific tasks connected with that job. Don't list overblown objectives like "produce and direct major-studio feature films" if you're applying for an entry-level position in television! Too many people in the entertainment industry have been burned by employees who really want to be doing something other than the job they've been hired to do. Employers may be reticent about hiring a would-be actor, independent producer, or director to be an assistant editor, production coordinator, or distribution sales rep. They may worry that you'll be bored or distracted or even incompetent at the task they need you to do.

Another way to use the Objective section is to avoid the use of any specific job title but rather to say you're looking for an opportunity to contribute your skills (name them) to an organization or project like your employer's and to gain further experience in production, development, or whatever.

Some examples of objectives: "An entry-level position in marketing or distribution," or simply "Literary agent trainee." More elaborate objectives can include a pitch: "To bring my proven ability to organize and implement large-scale projects into the field of motion picture production," or "To put my extensive background and skills in organizing postproduction departments to work for a company that values timely, cost-effective completion of film and television projects."

3. SUMMARY OF EXPERIENCE. This section can be called "Summary of Experience," "Summary of Achievements," "Summary of Skills," or just plain "Summary." Basically it's a version of your Hollywood pitch, adjusted to the requirements of this particular job. Some people like to put this pitch only in the cover letter, but I think it's good to reinforce it by including it in your resume as well. I also believe it's smart to include a summary because you can never assume that busy Hollywood people will take the time to read your whole resume, line by line, and figure out how it applies to their needs. Make things easy for them: tell them right up front about the specific talents, skills, achievements, and experience that make you the best candidate for this particular job. Show your employers how you can be useful to them. Put the best "spin" on what you have to offer.

This is especially important if you're making a crossover move from one field to another. Spell out your most valuable transferrable skills in the summary. Don't force potential employers to wander around the resume, trying to figure out how your real estate sales career could possibly be relevant to distribution. Tell them in the summary that you're a sales professional with many achievements who is transferring that talent to the sales end of the entertainment business. (If you have a good summary that describes how your background would be perfect for this particular job, you may want to omit the Objective section.)

Incidentally, if you've won any awards, try beginning your summary with phrases like, "John Smith is an award-winning cinematographer" or "Emmy-winning costume designer" or "Oscar-nominated writer." Hollywood loves winners. You may also want to experiment with phrases like "Mary Marvelous is a successful distribution sales executive with a proven track record of achievement at major studios like Columbia, Warner Bros., and 20th Century Fox. Thoroughly versed in _____ _____ and proficient in _____ _____ , she played a major role in accomplishing _____ _____ . Her special strengths include _____ _____ ." Remember to drop names of important companies, players, and talents you've been involved with and what you've done for them.

Here are a few sample summaries that may help get you going:

"Jana Fuentes is an experienced creative affairs executive whose specialty is discovering and developing new screenwriting talent. Among the writers she has discovered while working at Columbia, Fox, and CAA are Joe Genius, Janie Gem, and Samuel Special. Films she has developed include the $98-million-grossing HIGH CONCEPT SPECIAL and Palme d'Or winner INDEPENDENT MASTERPIECE, written and directed by Keith Quirky."

"Joyce Chung is an award-winning documentary film editor who has five years of experience working on projects like 'Hard-Hitting Newsdoc,' 'Portrait of a Celebrity,' and 'Reality Series X' with filmmakers like Bill Moyers, Arnold Shapiro, and Freida Lee Mock for PBS, NBC, HBO, A&E, and the Turner Network. In 1989 she won an Emmy for the 'Jacques Cousteau Special.' "

You can also use bullet icons to make your summary more readable and visually more appealing:

"Bill Cross is an experienced systems analyst who specializes in the application of computer technology to entertainment industry problems:

★ Expert in all word processing software, including Microsoft Word and Scriptor.

★ Experienced in production budgeting and scheduling packages, including DotZero and Movie Magic.

★ Has worked with a wide variety of individual and corporate entertainment industry clients, including Orion, Columbia, and MCA.

★ Good communication and people skills."

4. EXPERIENCE. You'll probably want to start with the title you had on the job. In the entertainment industry, credits are everything.

The next part is pure name-dropping. You pray that your potential employer has heard of the company and the people you worked for and with, because folks in the industry tend to hire people they know—friends or friends of friends. So if you worked on the same set as good old Bruce, you're like a member of the family, right? And if you also happen to have arranged for good old Bruce to make a Godfather Call to your potential employer on your behalf, so much the better. Also, who you know may be a valuable asset to your employer. Your contacts are part of the package you bring with you to your new job.

You can include student work and unpaid work under Experience, as well as paid work. After all, it *is* experience, right? All most Hollywood employers care about is whether you can do the job. The second half of each job description lists exactly what you did for your previous employer. It should consist of action verbs—"organized," "created," "sold," "discovered," "wrote," "directed," "composed." *Boast!* Mention anything special about the job or project (the budget, genre, etc.) and say exactly how you benefited your last employer. Spell it out so your next employer can vividly imagine all the good things you're going to do for her too! This is especially important if your exact job title isn't very impressive and you did much more than it would indicate.

Because you're going to rewrite your resume for every job you're up for, there will be variations in what you emphasize in this section and those that follow. If you're up for a production assistant job and you served as P.A. and makeup on a student film, emphasize the P.A. aspects and downplay the makeup. If you've got a shot at a makeup gig, reverse it.

Usually jobs are listed in reverse chronological order, with the most recent job mentioned first. Dates are optional and are frequently left out if jobs or credits aren't recent or there are embarrassing gaps. If you do include dates, put them at the end of each listing, not in the left margins. Unlike most business organizations, many entertainment industry employers care less about *when* you did things and more about *what* you did and *with whom*.

As you become more experienced, you can shorten or omit the section where you describe what you did on the film or TV project. The credit will speak for itself.

5. ADDITIONAL EXPERIENCE. If you have additional experience that might be interesting to add, put it in this section, on the theory that "you never know" when an employer might find it useful or entertaining. This is where you could put your stint in the Peace Corps, or a fascinating B-job, or an unusual summer job. Just keep it brief.

If you have been around for a while, you can also condense your older experience into this category, to keep your resume short. In that case, you might want to call this section "Previous Experience."

6. EDUCATION. If you've just graduated from a hot film school or Harvard, you might put this section before Experience. Always put your hot stuff up front.

People sometimes ask me if you have to tell the truth about degrees. I know people who've invented sexy educational credentials, but don't try it. Hollywood's a small town and you'll be around a long time. Eventually someone will find out. (Also, don't star in a porn film, as a well-known studio exec did at the start of his career. His enemies delighted in screening his early work.)

Emphasize any special course work that relates directly to the job being offered. (This is yet one more reason why you're going to rewrite your resume for every employer.) If you don't have any course work that's relevant, quickly enroll in some industry seminars or classes and put them on your resume. And don't forget to drop the instructors' and panelists' names.

7. HONORS AND AWARDS. You can list your film festival awards, Oscars, and Emmys here, or you can attach them to your credits lists, with the film itself—which I prefer. Other awards and honors go here. Also, don't forget to list yourself in the summary as "award-winning."

8. PROFESSIONAL ORGANIZATIONS. Belonging to industry organizations makes you an instant insider. And caring enough about show business to be part of these groups shows that you're serious about your career.

9. SPECIAL SKILLS. This is the place to draw attention to unique talents above and beyond those indicated in your credits or job history. I have a friend who got hired straight out of film school as an associate producer on a National Geographic special because she spoke fluent Italian and had lived in Italy. Even if your prospective employer can't use your special skills on this particular job or project, an interesting conversation may result. And she may remember you and your unique talent when she needs it.

Also this helps you avoid the don't-be-dull sin. If you have special skills and interests, your resume—and you—are more appealing.

10. ACTIVITIES AND INTERESTS. Like the section on special skills, this can be a conversation starter. If you share interests, a bond may result.

11. REFERENCES. Usually, "References available upon request" is wisest, unless you want to drop some really big names here. You can also drop big names in your cover letter and, most importantly, have your references make Godfather or Godmother Calls on your behalf. (You can also include letters of recommendation from players or previous Hollywood employers with your cover letter and resume.)

WHAT ABOUT THE FUNCTIONAL RESUME?

Some career counselors and resume writers get very enthusiastic about the functional resume, which lists your experience by category rather than chronologically.

Functional resumes have their pros and cons. On the pro side, if you're crossing over from one field to another, a functional resume can highlight your transferrable skills. On the con side, functional resumes can sometimes be confusing. I've seen entertainment industry resumes that had sections on "producing," "writing," "directing," and "editing," each with its own project or job listings. Sometimes it's hard to figure out what this person is really best at, what direction he's going in, and how these skills would apply to the employer in question.

A lot of employers (and executive recruiters) are positively allergic to functional resumes, figuring that if you didn't have something to hide, you would just list your experience in reverse chronological order. My personal feeling is that you can have the best of both worlds by first using the summary to highlight your most applicable skills and background and then listing your experience in reverse chronological order. I find this both easier to write and easier to read.

SHOULD YOU HIRE A RESUME WRITER TO DO YOUR HOLLYWOOD RESUME?

I've seen resumes written by writers who are not savvy to the entertainment industry, and they are seldom appropriate for Hollywood. If the writer isn't familiar with the correct terms for industry jobs or skills and knowledgeable about what Hollywood does and doesn't value in an employee, the result can be grating or confusing.

Your best bet is to apply the principles listed above and do it yourself. Don't get stressed out about it. Remember that the resume is far less important in getting you the job than personal or phone contacts are.

THE COVER LETTER: START WITH THE TWO MAGIC WORDS

The most important rule: KEEP IT SHORT! Busy Hollywood people don't read long letters. Try to keep it to three paragraphs on one page.

If you're approaching a potential employer for the first time, start the first paragraph of your letter with the two magic words—the name of the person who referred you. And even if you've met or chatted with your potential employer on the phone before, remind her again about the friend you have in common. Do this right up front, because the employer may be thinking, "Who the hell is this person?" You've got to answer that question *fast*, before your letter is deposited in the circular file.

If you're a good writer with a sense of humor and are applying for a creative position, you might want to inject a little comedy shtik into your letter to wake your prospect up and get attention. The trick is to be entertaining without getting corny. If you're not sure which side of that line you're falling on, have a friend read the letter for you.

The second paragraph of a cover letter is usually a version of your Hollywood pitch or the summary from your resume. It's a nutshell description of who you are, your special talents and interests, plus any impressive achievements. It often involves name-dropping.

You may also want to express your enthusiasm for working on the particular job in question for this particular employer. Show your reader that you've done your homework on the company and have thought about how your skills could be useful.

The third paragraph indicates that you're looking forward to talking with or meeting your prospect soon and will call in a few days (make sure you do so!).

GETTING THE RESUME OUT

A terrific resume sitting on your desk will get you nothing. You've got to get it out there into the world. Some eager beavers believe that faxing a cover letter and resume can be more effective than mailing. This is sometimes true, especially when time is of the essence. But don't overdo faxing; it has its disadvantages. Unsolicited fax messages can be annoying. Flimsy fax paper is hard to handle and doesn't give your resume its best presentation. In a large company, fax messages can languish in the mail room for hours or even days. And your letter and resume won't have the privacy of a sealed envelope to protect them from all those mail room spies! Sometimes it's better to mail them or have them hand-delivered.

My advice is to use the "rotate the contact method" tactic. Use faxing as one of many ways in which you get in touch and stay in touch. Many industry directories list fax numbers for studios and producers in addition to phone numbers. You can also just call your prospective employer's office and ask for the fax number.

REELS: SHOW ME, DON'T TELL ME!

A picture is worth a thousand words, they say. That's certainly true in Hollywood. Since showbiz people are by definition more attuned to the visual media than the printed word, they usually prefer to watch your tape (which is still called a "reel," although no one expects you to send film on an actual film reel anymore) than read your resume or cover letter.

Whether you're a performer, director, cameraperson, special effects wizard, stuntperson, hairstylist, costumer, etc., you're probably going to hear "Send me some tape" or "Have you got a reel?" Do whatever it takes to get copies of any work you have done. Sometimes, in the confusion of production, people forget to do this, regretting it later.

If you don't have film or tape on yourself, get some! If you're a director, do a showcase film that demonstrates your talent. If you're an actor and you haven't worked professionally, get tape of yourself in a play or doing a monologue. Some agents will tell you it's worthless because it's not a professional production, but if the tape is well shot and edited and if your performance is fabulous, it's better than nothing.

KEEP YOUR REEL SHORT

A good reel will be short—fifteen to twenty minutes at most, unless it's just a copy of a feature film you've directed or starred in. It will be made up of short clips of your work, starting with your best stuff. Assume the viewer isn't going to have time to watch the whole tape. Assume he'll hit the fast-forward button at the first sign of boredom. Have the reel professionally edited (if you're not an editor yourself) with a nice clean graphic up front featuring your name, occupation, and telephone number. Hollywood people are terrible snobs about the quality of production and editing, so it pays to hire a good editor to put a little professional razzmatazz into your reel. Keep the segments short (two to three minutes should do it) at the beginning, with longer clips at the end. Like resumes, reels should be constantly reedited to suit different purposes. Once you're a pro or have friends who are pros, this isn't too difficult. Some people have two or three different versions of their reel. Perhaps one features your camerawork, another your directing; you pick the right reel for the job being offered, just as you pick the right resume. Don't fall in love with a fancy reel and keep sending it out even after it's no longer applicable. Remember, "one size fits all" doesn't work in Hollywood.

Reels are usually ¾" or ½" tape (VHS). Many executives have ¾" machines in their offices, but it's also handy to have ½" so they can watch it at home. I recommend that you put your stuff on ¾" if possible, and run off a few ¾" copies and a lot of ½" copies off the ¾" master. That way you can ask your potential employer which he'd prefer.

Tapes are expensive, but you need to find a way to pay for them; they're as necessary as resumes or good head shots. Print the title, list of contents, your name, address, and phone number on the tape and on the box the tape is in. That way you've got a fighting chance of getting the tape back; but don't expect to get it unless you call and ask for it or drop by to pick it up. People get so busy that they forget to return tapes or they get cheap about paying to mail, ship, or messenger them back unless you specifically ask them to. The good news it that dropping by to pick up your tape gives you a chance for face-to-face contact with the employer and the employer's assistant.

THE $500, $5,000, $8,500, OR $30,000 SHOWCASE FILM

Sometimes the fastest way to make it in Hollywood is just to make your film and let it speak for you. If you've really got talent, you'll be discovered.

This is what Gordon Eriksen and John O'Brien did. The two Harvard graduates shot *The Big Dis* in black-and-white 16-millimeter film for $8,500. It's the story of a young African-American soldier who heads home on a weekend pass with one thought on his mind: sex. Eriksen and O'Brien made such a charming, witty film that it was booked into a Los Angeles theater and got a rave review in the *Los Angeles Times*, resulting in instant flavor-of-the-month status for the two new filmmakers.

Twenty-three-year-old UCLA film student David Egen also took the fast track. "Hugo and the Blue Whale," a twelve-minute documentary he started as a class project, was shot on a $500 out-of-pocket budget. In his film, David interviewed people on the street about Hugo's Plating, a shabby little building that stands in the shadow of the giant temple of chic decorating, the Pacific Design Center in West Hollywood. The project was shot on an old JVC video camera. It was so creatively done that Egen was able to sell it to PBS as a segment for the "POV" series for $5,000.

There are a few programs that help people put together their showcase films. For example, the Discovery Program (see Resources) helps people who have extensive experience in other areas of moviemaking cross over into directing by financing their twenty-to-thirty-minute 35-millimeter projects.

Industry insiders who don't make it into the Discovery Program or who just want to show their stuff sometimes decide to finance their own showcase projects. If they've made good money in another category (cinematography, editing, etc.) they can afford the $35,000–$50,000 out-of-pocket costs for a professional-level 35-millimeter project, and they often have experienced friends who will volunteer their talents. Some of these projects are truly impressive.

A word of caution: don't hock your house to make your 35-millimeter showcase film until you're really *ready.* You may want to learn your craft—and make your beginner's mistakes—by directing plays or shooting inexpensive video features before you put down serious money on your 35-millimeter calling-card film.

But what if you're not wealthy, not an insider, not in film school, or not eligible for any of the programs?

A friend of mine named Tim came up with an ingenious way to make his showcase film. He wrote a half-hour script that he wanted to direct. Then he approached four friends who wanted a chance to shoot, edit, produce, or act and who needed to showcase their talents in these areas. He proposed a very creative deal: they'd each put up $1,000 to make their film so they'd each have something to show around town. The five friends did exactly that. The project was shot on tape and became a nice showcase for everyone concerned—at a rock-bottom budget.

In 1990, nine actors who worked as waiters at Yanks, a trendy Beverly Hills restaurant, pooled their resources and made an $8,000 film, *The Ticket Outta Here*, about their own efforts to make it in Hollywood. They shot it with a home video camera and transferred it to 16-millimeter film. It premiered at the 1991 American Film Institute's Los Angeles Film Festival and landed twenty-nine-year-old filmmaker/actor Jefferson Davis meetings with CAA and ICM, plus a private screening at Columbia Pictures.

THE BOTTOM LINE: JUST DO IT!

If you want to make movies, then make movies! Do it on super 8, video, or anything you can to show your talent.

—DANIEL WOODRUFF
Curator of Film, Academy of
Motion Picture Arts and Sciences

If your goal is to write, write at least two screenplays or teleplays to demonstrate your talent. If your goal is to direct, shoot, produce, or edit, there's no substitute for making a showcase film. I think that many people avoid this because it's scary to find out whether you really have exceptional talent. Money is often used as the reason not to make your film, but as you can see from the above examples, it's really no longer a valid excuse. As technology becomes less expensive and more accessible, there's no reason for you not to make your film (or two or three—the first one may not do the trick) and find out *now* if you've got something extraordinary to offer or if you should consider another line of work.

People sometimes don't believe me when I tell them that if their film is *really special* it will be discovered. But I promise you that if yours is special, it *will* be discovered, if you just get it into a few good film festivals. Hollywood is full of talent scouts who religiously follow the hot festivals and scout new talent. If your film is fresh, unique, unusual, and distinctive, they'll find you!

Twenty-seven-year-old writer-director Joseph B. Vasquez grew up in the Bronx, raised by his grandmother. He got his hands on a camera at age twelve and shot some homemade movies. He went to City College of New York, became a film editor, and saved some bucks. With those bucks he made a couple of low-budget movies (in the $30,000 range). Then, in a bind for cash, he wrote a script in three days and took it to New Line. Based on his two earlier films, New Line gave Vasquez $2 million to shoot *Hangin' with the Homeboys*. It was the hit of the 1991 Sundance Film Festival. The *Los Angeles Times* loved his tale about four Bronx buddies, calling him "a writer-director with style and compassion in equal amounts." Vasquez became an instant flavor of the month in Hollywood.

Maybe next month it will be your turn. All it takes is a great showcase film.

13
☆

Getting a Foot in the Door
★ ★ ★ ★ ★ ★ ★ ★ ★ ★ ★ ★ ★ ★ ★
ENTRY-LEVEL JOBS

This town loves a virgin.
—ANONYMOUS AGENT

GETTING STARTED: ENTRY-LEVEL JOBS

The good news: it's not as difficult to land an entry-level position in show business—even without prior contacts—as many people think. If you want one, you should be able to get one.

What's the catch?

1. The pay. These jobs usually don't pay well (or at all, in the case of many internships). Because of the level of competition for each job, the pay scale is often below that of other industries. For example, an assistant to a literary agent might be paid much less than an assistant to a manager in a non-entertainment-industry corporation would earn (and would probably work longer hours). It's the law of supply and demand. The "glamour factor" is supposed to compensate you for the lower paycheck.

2. The hours. Entertainment industry employers often want your motto to be "Show Business is My Life." Long hours are expected; they show that you're serious about making it in Hollywood. Industry veterans call this "paying your dues" and they well remember paying theirs.

3. The available jobs. The jobs you'd really like are often the toughest to get. You'd kill to be Steven Spielberg's gopher or a production assistant on Kevin Costner's next picture—but what's actually available may be much less exciting. You may find yourself working as a receptionist at a film equipment rental firm, a phone answerer at a costume house, or an assistant at a small agency.

PAYING YOUR DUES: IS IT WORTH IT?

If you're clear about your career objective, paying your dues in the *right* entry-level Hollywood job will be the smartest thing you've ever done. While working as a long-suffering assistant/gopher at a studio, my friend Rich found himself late one night delivering a repaired TV to a top studio executive's Beverly Hills home. The mogul, returning home exhausted after a business trip to Europe, was surprised to find Rich in his house. They chatted for a while and then the tired traveler asked Rich if he had time to read and "cover" a script for him before tomorrow morning. Rich stayed up all night doing just that—and the rest, as they say, is history. Rich is now a top Hollywood production executive himself. If he had been too proud to do this kind of dog work (delivering TVs), he wouldn't be where he is today.

WHAT KIND OF ENTRY-LEVEL JOB SHOULD I TRY FOR?

"I'll take anything" is the wrong attitude. *Never* say this to a potential employer, personnel officer, employment agency, or recruiter. It tells them that you haven't targeted your specific goal and it opens you up for abuse and exploitation.

THE PERFECT FIRST JOB: BECOME AN ASSISTANT TO YOUR ROLE MODEL

One good strategy is to apply for assistant jobs in your area of direct interest. These jobs may not be easy to land, but they're worth the effort.

If you're aiming to write, become a script word processor or writer's assistant. If you want to creative produce, try to talk a prominent producer into hiring you as an assistant or gopher. If you want to do props, convince a nonunion property master to take you on as an apprentice. If line production is your goal, start as a production assistant or runner. To get into makeup, you might find an experienced makeup artist willing to take you under his or her wing. If you're aiming for development, try to get hired as a script reader or a secretary in the development department. If you want to be a publicist, start out answering phones at a public relations firm.

BUT WON'T I GET TYPECAST AS A SECRETARY?

Just as there are few genuine waiters in Hollywood (they all seem to be out-of-work actors), there are few honest-to-goodness career assistants or secretaries. Everyone seems to be on the way to somewhere else. Hollywood receptionists, clerks, secretaries, and assistants are often really trainees or aspiring, out-of-work creative people. Employers and colleagues will assume that you probably have other goals. In fact, many of them may have worked as secretaries or temps for periods of time to pay the rent.

The double standard being what it is, there's less chance of getting typecast as a secretary if you're male (especially a young male) than if you're a woman. My advice to my female clients who are in this situation is: (1) do a good—not great—job in your secretarial duties and (2) take on one or two tasks above and beyond your normal job—reading scripts, organizing a shoot, doing a budget—that show off your real talents. Work hard and do a *great* job on these tasks. Then, when the time is right, let people know your true aspirations and accomplishments so they can see you in a different light and possibly help you in your career.

By the way, many industry executives, producers, and celebrities would practically *kill* to find a real, live, genuine, dedicated, skilled career secretary. If that's you, you should have no trouble finding an excellent, well-paying job with nice benefits.

TEMPING, ANYONE?

If you're not sure about whether to become a full-time assistant—or if you're having trouble landing the plum assistant gigs—you may want to try temping. Temporary jobs will give you a good all-around education in the industry when you first start out and will help you make those important Hollywood contacts.

Temping is so important in today's Hollywood that *Premiere* magazine's Rob Medich wrote an article on the subject entitled "It's Not Only Temporary: Good-bye, Mail Room; Hello, Temping." Medich claims temping is "a modern-day point of entry for would-be movie executives. With odds running high against a driven cineaste's even landing an interview for a studio secretarial position, temp agencies have become the method of choice for those who want to get a foot in Tinseltown's door."

The entertainment industry temporary agencies will send you around to various show business assignments and you can take it from there. If people like you, they may even hire you on staff. And even if they don't hire you, you can make contacts and get advice and referrals to other potential employers. The people you meet on temp jobs can be the first entries into your Power Rolodex.

More experienced people also use temping as a way to fill in between "real" jobs, a way to meet new industry people, or as a B- or C-skill to pay the bills while they write scripts or sell projects.

There are a few dos and don'ts to know about temping, however.

★ **DON'T** waste your time with non–entertainment-industry temp agencies. They may have a few industry jobs, but they'll try to high-pressure you into taking non-show-business jobs so they can collect their commissions. Focus on the important industry agencies that advertise in the trades: Our Gang, London Temps, All Star, and the Right Connections are perhaps the best known, but there are others.

★ **DON'T** waste the temp agencies' time if you haven't learned some basic typing, word processing, or fast-notes skills that will make you useful to an employer. Typing forty words per minute is considered a minimum. Agencies will often test you—probably on an IBM Selectric. Even if you're quicker on a computer, many agencies won't be sympathetic. So far only a few agencies have bought PCs to test applicants.

★ **FIND OUT** what computer programs are currently in favor in Hollywood—and learn them. As I write this book, the favorite industry word processing program is Microsoft Word. But check with the

Writers Computer Store (the top showbiz computer emporium) or the Association of Entertainment Industry Computer Professionals (see Chapter 14) for news about the latest favorites.

★ **DON'T** approach a temp agency with a resume that emphasizes everything *but* your clerical skills. The relevant facts here are your words per minute, your basic understanding of how the film and TV businesses work, your knowledge of who's who in the industry, your ability to organize, handle phones, juggle tasks, communicate, and get along with people—not your Ph.D. in anthropology, your previous career in sales, or your award-winning experimental films, unless you can directly relate them to the job at hand. A too-dazzling resume can bring up the dreaded "O" word, "Overqualified," which means forget it.

★ **BE COOL** on your temp assignment. Don't immediately pass out your resume or your head shot. Wait till you've created a little rapport with the secretaries or execs and then approach people carefully. If they like you and are pleased with your work, they may be willing to pass along some advice or referrals.

★ **DON'T** get impatient and cop an attitude; don't act like you're above it all because you put in three years at film school. Just do your work well—this is your chance to show that you're a good sport, a great worker, and a fun person to have around. Make friends with other assistants, the receptionist, the mail room folks. They can do you a lot of good if they like you. When things get desperate, remember Rich shlepping the TV to the film exec's house at 11:00 P.M. You never know when opportunity will knock and your big break will walk in.

★ **STAY OPEN** to both temp and permanent assignments. The good agencies have both.

★ **KEEP LOOKING** for a better job while you're temping.

WHAT ABOUT STUDIO PERSONNEL OFFICES?

Many Hollywood job seekers shun personnel departments, feeling that they don't have the power to hire. While it's certainly true that the ultimate hiring and firing decisions don't lie in the human resources department, personnel people can be knowledgeable and friendly. Especially if you're looking for entry-level work, be sure to visit the human resources offices at the major studios and production companies (and call their job hotlines). Meet a personnel specialist if you can, and leave a resume. Check in frequently. Some amazing jobs show up on the job boards. You may still need to use your contacts and Godfather or Godmother Calls to land the job, but if you hadn't dropped by the personnel office that particular day, you might not have known the job was even open!

At a day-long seminar given by the City of West Hollywood last year on how to find jobs in the entertainment industry, a human resources executive from Castle Rock Productions told the story of a young man who found entry-level work at that company through the personnel department and so impressed people with his eagerness and diligence that he was able to become director Rob Reiner's personal assistant on a major film.

ENTERTAINMENT INDUSTRY JOB-SEARCH SERVICES: BUYER BEWARE!

In the last few years, a number of companies have come into existence that claim they will help you find out about entertainment industry jobs or will get your resume or head shot or a synopsis of your script out to potential employers or buyers. Be extremely cautious about dealing with these companies. They often charge substantial fees for their services. Before paying money to anyone, do some background research among your industry friends to see if any of them have found such services helpful. Ask employers if they use these services to find employees or properties. A few of these companies are unscrupulous and prey on unsophisticated Hollywood novices and wannabes without delivering the desired results. Others appear to offer some legitimate assistance. You'll have to be the judge.

MADNESS IN THE MAIL ROOM: WORKING AT AN AGENCY

The agency mail room (read: trainee program) is still considered to be a very desirable entry-level job for anyone interested in a Hollywood career. Outsiders are sometimes baffled by this. What's the point of earning expensive advanced degrees and then taking a low-paying job where all you do is copy scripts and deliver them to players around town? Insiders know that there is no better way to learn the business than to work at an agency. If you want to be an agent, then of course this is *the* logical way to start your career. But it's also a terrific beginning for many other entertainment industry careers as well. If your goal is to be a producer, studio executive, or even a director, writer, or actor, you'll never regret the time spent at an agency. Working at the hub of the business is an instant education in how Hollywood works. The contacts you make and the inside information you pick up will jump-start your career.

The problem? It's tough to land a spot in the coveted agent trainee programs at the top agencies. You'll be competing with relatives and friends of Hollywood players plus graduates of Harvard, Yale, and Stanford. But don't let that stop you. Call the agencies and ask for applications. Emphasize what's unique, interesting, and special about your strengths and background. Do some fancy networking and see whom you can get to make Godfather or Godmother Calls on your behalf.

If you're accepted, work hard, show your stuff, and make yourself useful to the agents and the agents' assistants. You may graduate to assistant in six months to a year. After one to three years as an assistant, you may eventually, if you prove your worth, become an agent.

At any point along this long road, you may decide to take a job at a studio or production company. Your agency background will make you very desirable as an employee because it will be assumed that you're well connected, savvy, and informed about the business.

Even if you don't succeed in getting into a trainee program, there are other agency jobs you may want to apply for: agencies hire receptionists, data entry clerks, secretaries, and assistants (not to mention lawyers and financial people). You can find out about these jobs by signing up with entertainment industry employment agencies or by watching for ads in the trades (although the larger agencies seldom advertise positions). Temping is an excellent way to try out working for the agencies to see how you like it.

If you have a choice, try to work for the biggest, most powerful agencies in town. Positions at smaller agencies are easier to land but may not expose you to the variety of talent and situations available at the major agencies.

ANOTHER WAY IN: BECOME A PAGE

Another time-honored method of breaking into the entertainment industry is to become a page at one of the networks and, in that capacity, meet and impress important people who could help your career. CBS has a page program in Los Angeles; NBC no longer has a page program there but does in New York. Applicants must be at least eighteen years old and have a strong interest in the entertainment industry. College is apparently not required. They currently pay approximately $6 an hour and the hours are irregular. You need to be available full-time.

OR WORK ON LOW-BUDGET, NONUNION FILMS

Many people have broken into Hollywood by talking or networking their way into low-level jobs on low-budget, nonunion films. Producers like Roger Corman, for example, have given wonderful opportunities to newcomers, and many famous actors and directors started out working for peanuts on Corman's films. You'll work long, hard hours, but you'll get an invaluable education and make good contacts. And don't be afraid to do more than you're asked to do. If you do well at your first assignment, you may well find yourself being given additional responsibilities on the next picture or the next. I know a man who started out working for Roger Corman in the editing room. He practically lived at Corman's studio, and worked his way up to head of postproduction. Corman eventually gave him the chance to direct his own films for the company.

INTERNSHIPS AND VOLUNTEER WORK CAN TURN INTO JOBS

If you can't land the paid jobs you covet, you may want to try volunteering your time as an unpaid (or extremely low-paid) intern. As an intern you can often get to work in a prestigious company that might not hire you on a paid basis.

The theory behind this is that by doing an internship you may be able to get a potential employer "a little bit pregnant." He may be so delighted with your services that he won't want to lose you and will offer to keep you on as a paid employee. (Some job seekers routinely volunteer to work for free for a month as a ploy to convince an employer to hire them.) And even if the company doesn't employ you, you'll gain valuable experience and, hopefully, a good reference to put on your resume.

For legal reasons, many employers prefer to arrange internships through film schools, but even if you aren't a student, you may be able to create your own internships. Just approach your targeted companies or employers (preferably through contacts) and volunteer your services. You'll need to sell them on the idea of "hiring" you just as if you were applying for a paying job. They'll want to see a resume, samples of your work, and recommendations from professors or people they trust.

You can also gain valuable experience by volunteering to work on student films in production capacities you're not yet experienced or employable in. And it's a good idea to investigate all the apprenticeship programs available in your targeted niche. A reference librarian at an entertainment industry library can help you do this.

THE ART OF NEGOTIATION: DOING THE DANCE

Let's imagine that you've succeeded in convincing an employer to offer you an honest-to-god paying job. She asks what salary you're looking for or what your rate is. What to do?

Once you've gotten to a certain point in your career, you'll probably want to refer this question to a professional representative: a lawyer or agent who is authorized to negotiate on your behalf. "Susan Smith is representing me on this" is all you'll need to say.

Then your representative will negotiate either with your potential employer or with a professional deal maker (often a former lawyer) in the business affairs department of the production company or studio you'll be working for.

But if you don't yet have a representative, you'll need to handle the negotiation yourself—no easy task in the land of wheelers and dealers! Here are a few tips:

1. Before you go in for an interview, talk to your friends, contacts, and information sources about the going rates for services like yours—especially at the company in question. Know what the low, middle, and high quotes are. The object is to discover your employer's "negotiating spread."

2. Decide what you'll ask for (the top of your negotiating spread) and the rock-bottom price you'll settle for if you have to.

3. Try to get your employer to name a price first. Of course, you may be asked to name a price first.

4. Once a number is on the table, a back-and-forth dialogue ensues. It's a game. Each player has his or her own negotiating spread with high and low numbers. You jockey back and forth trying to find a number that fits both of your spreads: a compromise.

ONCE YOU'VE LANDED THE JOB . . .

There are three important things to remember once you've landed the job:

1. It's show time! You're on. Strut your stuff. Do your dance. Let them see what you've got under the hood. However you say it, it boils down to demonstrating your talent and value to a company and project. Remember: in Hollywood, it's not enough to be good—you've got to be special. Do whatever it takes to stand out from the crowd and impress the powers that be. A good job doesn't cut it—*great* is what you're after. Re-

member, the most powerful marketing moves you can make toward getting hired on your *next* job are to do a superb job and develop an excellent reputation on *this* job.

2. Build lasting relationships with employers and colleagues. If your boss is happy with you, she may hire you again and again over the years, perhaps in higher and higher positions. Also, your buddies on this job may become employers themselves or may be able to refer you to future employers once this job ends.

3. Redo your resume immediately. Job hunting is an ongoing activity in Hollywood. It never stops. Once you've been on the job for a month or so, it may be time to let people know that you're available once this project ends.

ATTACH YOURSELF TO A MENTOR

One of the most effective ways of getting ahead in Hollywood is to attach yourself to an established player or a rising-star player. Sometimes this happens naturally as a result of relationships you've built while working together on a job or volunteer activity. For example, Jeffrey Katzenberg worked for Michael Eisner at Paramount, where they formed a successful working relationship. When Eisner took over Disney, he brought Katzenberg with him.

In other instances, a player will take a novice under his or her wing even though they've never worked together, because they've formed a relationship of some kind. Many different relationship patterns can lead to mentoring: some are positive and some are less desirable.

A healthy mentoring situation usually involves a mutually satisfying relationship between a senior person who enjoys being a godparent/teacher/guru/guide to a novice, who repays the mentor with admiration, learning, and hard work. However, Hollywood people are also aware of a number of not-so-desirable mentorships around town, involving abusive players who like having "whipping boys" or "whipping girls" to vent their frustrations on, insecure players who surround themselves with sycophants and flatterers who boost their fragile egos, or romantic players who promote their latest loves far beyond their talents.

You don't *need* a mentor to make it in Hollywood. Many people have made it entirely on their own steam. If you would like to try this route, however, target a player whose work you admire and try to find a way to meet that player and work to form the right kind of mentoring relationship. Use the same techniques you would use to meet anyone on your Hit List.

THE NEXT CHALLENGE: SUSTAINING A CAREER

Landing an entry-level job in the entertainment industry is (relatively) easy. Turning that job into a long-term career is tough.

The industry can be imagined as a flattened pyramid that looks as though a very large giant sat on it (or, if you have a good visual imagination, a squashed, wide-brimmed hat with a pom-pom on top). The bottom level is capacious; the middle level is much smaller; the tiny top is truly exclusive.

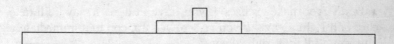

A recent membership survey conducted for the Society of Composers and Lyricists revealed just this pattern. There were approximately 1,000 entry-level composers doing orchestration and other lower-level tasks; 200 middle-level people who compose music for occasional TV episodes and who also do some orchestration; 50–80 composers who earn a good living from their work; and 15–30 people who make top money scoring A-list feature films.

To move from your entry-level job to the midrange, you'll need to make the following "right moves":

★ Pick an entry-level job that gives you an overall understanding of how the industry works or leads directly to your targeted niche.

★ Do a great job. Let employers and colleagues see your exceptional qualities and special strengths.

★ Build a track record and a good reputation.

★ Work hard and work smart.

★ Try to find a powerful mentor.

★ Form lasting relationships.

★ Build up your Power Rolodex.

★ Network and shmooze.

★ Do a superb job of marketing yourself into the next level of job.

★ Keep your eyes and ears open for opportunities.

MORE TIPS FOR SUCCESS IN HOLLYWOOD

Twenty-eight-year-old Lucas Foster is a fast-rising production executive who has spoken at some of the entertainment industry career seminars I teach. Here are some of the tips he has shared with the audience:

★ Be a good listener. That means listen before you talk.

★ Don't ever make excuses. If you haven't done it, say, "I'll take care of it right away." If you've screwed up, cop to it immediately and say, "I'll fix it right away."

★ If you don't know the answer to a question, the right answer is, "I don't know but I'll find out."

★ Do more than you're paid to do. Take on additional responsibilities outside of your job description if you can.

★ Be the best-informed person within a one-mile radius of your job. Read every piece of paper you can get access to—screenplay, book, contract, memo—that will give you a better understanding of how things work. Build your own library of information, scripts, and so on.

★ Don't make assumptions based on partial information. That will get you killed.

★ Be the first to arrive and the last to leave.

★ Do favors and don't ask for anything in return. It will come back to you.

★ If you're in a tough job, try to stick it out but don't let them walk all over you either. Attitude is everything in Hollywood.

★ Find a need within your company and fill it.

★ Be careful about how you treat people. You may be working for them soon.

★ Don't worry about money. As you get better at what you do, it will come. Money is a by-product of good work.

★ Be goal-oriented. Know exactly what you want and work toward it. Work out a specific set of goals—one-year goals, three-year goals, five-year goals. Then work toward them.

★ Don't talk about doing something—do it.

14

☆

The Shmooze Factor

★　★　★　★　★　★　★　★　★　★　★　★　★　★

TRADING INFO HELPS YOUNG PRODUCTION EXECUTIVE SOAR

Twenty-eight-year-old Lucas Foster is a fast-rising Hollywood player. He's now senior vice president of production for Simpson/Bruckheimer Films (*Top Gun*) at Disney Studios. *Lisa*, a film he helped put together for Frank Yablans Productions, where he also served as vice president of production, was released by MGM/UA. While working for Scott Rudin Productions at Paramount, Lucas was instrumental, with Scott, in discovering *The Firm*, a book by John Grisham, Jr., and *Tell Me All About It*, a nonfiction book which will become a movie starring Michael J. Fox.

When Lucas was a twenty-four-year-old executive assistant to MGM studio head Alan Ladd, Jr., he joined a networking group of development executives who met every two weeks at director Ridley Scott's offices at Columbia. The group, started by another enterprising assistant who wanted to move into producing, included well-connected development people who worked for studios, production companies, directors, and actors.

Lucas says that as part of that group, he "basically played an upscale Hollywood version of the kids' game of trading baseball cards"—except he traded information on scripts, writers, agents, and studios with his new friends instead of trading Babe Ruths and Mickey Mantles. (The group shared only nonsensitive information, not competitive information about scripts or writers under serious consideration at their respective companies.) Lucas had created a general list of writers and actors, plus their credits, which he generously shared with the group. Soon people began to repay the favor, calling him at work to tip him off to things happening around town: scripts going into turnaround (available to buy), writers he ought to be aware of, gossip about industry personalities, and lists of projects in development at various studios.

Lucas tracked this ever-growing body of information on his computer, and soon gained a reputation as an important young executive who was especially knowledgeable about new writers and their work. He quickly went from relative obscurity to being well-known and respected as a professional, breaking into into the inner circle of serious people already doing business with each other.

IT'S WHO YOU KNOW

The bad news: who you know counts. The good news: even if you don't know anyone in Hollywood when you arrive, you can shmooze your way to success.

In the entertainment industry it really *is* who you know that counts. But contrary to myth, you don't have to be a player's nephew or lover to get ahead. You just have to master the arts of shmoozing and networking. As Daniel Woodruff, curator of film at the Academy of Motion Picture Arts and Sciences, puts it: "My biggest peeve is when I hear people say that you have to know the right people to make it in the business. I always reply, GO OUT AND MEET THEM!"

Shmoozing is one of those wonderful, semiundefinable Yiddish words that implies a whole world of activity: getting together, chatting, kibitzing (fooling around), sharing gossip and small talk. The way the word is used in Hollywood, it implies all interpersonal activities that create and build useful relationships. For example, the Independent Feature Project/West, an association of independent filmmakers, used to hold periodic "Shmoozers" at the Sugar Shack restaurant in Los Angeles. People wanting to talk film, hang out with industry friends, or build their network of contacts were delighted to attend.

Relationships are so important in Hollywood that people are hired because they have good ones or not hired because they're not well enough connected. At a seminar I moderated at the Directors Guild of America on how to get hired as a director, one of my panelists told the audience to build relationships with important actors. He said that when it comes time to set a director for a picture, the director's relationships (or lack thereof) with star performers is often the deciding factor.

That being so, you won't be surprised at the lengths to which Hollywood people go to add new, important players and friends to their lives and to "water their relationships." Hollywood folks talk of taking "relationship meetings," which are simply get-togethers whose main purpose is to strengthen a relationship (over tennis, on the polo field, at dinner) rather than to discuss business.

POWER EATING: THE SEVEN HOLLYWOOD MEALS A DAY

The power breakfast is now popular in many industries around the world, but perhaps power eating reaches its zenith in Hollywood. Ann, a weary network executive with whom I breakfasted at the Beverly Hills Hotel, says there are seven meals a day for the serious player: breakfast 1 (coffee and fruit); breakfast 2 (toast, muffins, cereal, etc.); lunch; afternoon tea (perhaps at Trumps); drinks; dinner (the most sought-after meal to share with important people); and after-screening bites.

By the way, I was Ann's breakfast 2. And later when I arrived back at the studio, a friend told me, "Your breakfast was my lunch!"—meaning that she had "done" lunch with Ann the same day. It's a wonder everyone in the industry doesn't weigh 200 pounds! But of course they all watch their weight religiously, to the chagrin of frustrated chefs who often find themselves serving endless plates of steamed vegetables and fish to jaded eaters instead of the more elaborate culinary masterpieces worthy of their talent and prices.

HANGING OUT AT THE IN SPOTS: MONDAY NIGHT AT MORTON'S

Every industry subgroup in every city has its favorite meeting and shmoozing spots. Sam, a veteran television writer, told me that whenever he needs to turn up the heat on his career, he eats breakfast at the Bel Air Hotel and the Beverly Hills Hotel (in the Polo Lounge or Loggia Room) on alternate days until he gets hired to write something. He knows that the players who can employ him—producers, network executives—go there regularly. He confided that one should show up around 7:00 A.M. to catch the New York TV network executives who are still on East Coast time, and a little later to see the West Coast execs and producers. Stars, usually late risers, appear later still, often with their managers or agents in tow. Like every successful industry insider I've met, Sam has his shmoozing strategies and his system.

Morton's is the industry clubhouse of the moment, and has been for some time. But you have to go on weekdays, especially Mondays. "You never go on a weekend," says Harris Katleman, president of 20th Century Fox Television. "I've been going to Morton's most of my adult natural life," says Barry Diller, the chairman of 20th Century Fox. Producer Steve Tisch calls it a "high-priced commissary." The "best" tables are reputedly numbers 4 and 6 in front.

SPAGO, THE IVY, HUGO'S, NICKY BLAIR'S, LE DOME . . .

If you read *People* or *Premiere*, you probably know the names of the other top Hollywood hangouts as well. Recent favorites include Wolfgang Puck's Spago and Chinois-on-Main, Trumps, the Ivy on Robertson Blvd., Musso and Franks (since the days of Charlie Chaplin), Hugo's (for breakfast or lunch), Kokomo's at Farmer's Market (writers), Nicky Blair's, Le Dome (especially for music industry people), Citrus, Olive (the young crowd), Chasen's (the older crowd), Asylum, City, the Border Grill, and many more.

Lest you think this a trivial subject, the much-read Calendar section of the *Los Angeles Times* recently devoted a major cover story to the subject of Hollywood "Power Eating," describing the frenzied competition for the precious "right" tables at the dozen or so important Hollywood "power eateries." Calendar named Morton's, Le Dome, the Palm, Spago, Jimmy's, Matteo, the Polo Lounge, the Bistro Garden, La Serre, Maple Drive, Il Giardino, the Grill, and Hugo's as among the lucky in spots, but a deluge of protesting letters appeared to suggest additions to the list.

To find out where the current in spots are in Los Angeles, New

York, or wherever you're based, ask your industry contacts or your agent. And read the trades and celebrity magazines. Restaurants and chefs are now stars, too.

For maximum effectiveness, focus your power eating. Target places where your colleagues and the people who can hire you go. If you're a grip, grabbing a burger with an industry buddy at a below-the-line joint in the San Fernando Valley is more likely to result in work leads than a fancy dinner at Jimmy's or a breakfast at Hugo's where the D-people (program development executives) and young agents hang out.

Don't forget the studio commissaries: they're great places to shmooze, and not as difficult to get into as many people believe. Even if you don't live in L.A., with some persistent networking you can probably get to know someone who knows someone who works on a studio lot. It could be a student intern, a mail room slave, or a busboy! That person may be able to leave your name at the studio gate with the guards, and voilà—you're on the lot. Your friend can make a reservation at the commissary and you both can enjoy lunch with the working industry insiders at the studio.

The next step is . . .

TABLE HOPPING

Table hopping is a sensitive issue. By all means, if you see an acquaintance, stop by to say hi before you leave the restaurant. You'll be asked about what you're doing, so you need to be ready with an answer and also explain what you're currently hoping to do or looking for. She may have some advice, suggestions, or referrals. Also, be ready with some small talk about the food, a film you saw last night, or the home run you hit at the entertainment industry softball game on Sunday. Shmoozing involves friendly chatting, not just hustling.

If you're thinking of approaching a player you don't know, be cool about it. Be polite and flattering but not fawning. Casual charm is the idea. Add funny and entertaining if you can pull it off without a strain. Whatever you do, don't make a pest of yourself. Autograph hunters and looky-loos are anathema.

You have to have a legitimate reason to approach someone. Perhaps you attended an industry seminar at which he or she spoke. Or the person you're having a meal with may be able to introduce you (agents, managers, and publicists are very useful for this since their jobs involve getting to know everyone in the industry).

But first you have to know who people are and be able to recognize them. Stars are easy, of course, but what about the important behind-the-scenes players? Industry directories can give you the important names and locations. But how will you put faces to the names? You can ask your lunch companions, but what if they don't know? Sometimes even people who've been around the industry for a long time neglect this area of vital career information!

Judy Stangler, a publicist friend, clips pictures from *Variety* and the "Great Life" section of the *Hollywood Reporter* and attaches them to her large Rolodex cards so that she not only knows who Fox topper Barry Diller is but exactly what he looks like, in case she needs to approach him at a restaurant or party.

What to say? *Don't* pitch your latest screenplay until you've built a relationship! *Do* say something complimentary. Most people are pleased to hear that you enjoyed their last show or to receive congratulations on an achievement recently written up in the trades.

Do identify yourself as a serious industry person: "I'm so-and-so's assistant at Columbia, and I just wanted to tell you how much I enjoyed *Super Sequel III*, which we screened at the studio last night." Or, "I'm studying screenwriting with Richard Walter at UCLA and I wanted to tell you I'm a big fan of your scripts."

If you've met the person before, remind him or her of the connection, so there won't be embarrassment if the person doesn't recall you. And, if the table hop goes well, follow up with a call, a note, or a meeting to cement the relationship.

NAME-DROPPING

As these examples demonstrate, name-dropping is de rigueur. Whereas in many other industries this might be considered crass, in the entertainment industry people want to know who you are and what players you're connected with. Otherwise, how will they be able to distinguish you from the thousands of wannabes who approach them everywhere they go? Industry power players get pitched by their dentists, their gardeners, their pool men, and their dog trainers. By letting them know that you are already involved with industry people they know, you separate yourself from this crowd of outsiders.

YOUR NEW BEST FRIEND, THE MAÎTRE D'

Producer Julia Phillips *(Close Encounters of the Third Kind)* shares one of her success secrets in her tell-all tome *You'll Never Eat Lunch in This Town Again:* "Figure out what you like to eat, where they treat you nice, and buy a relationship that you can call on on a daily basis."

Perhaps you won't be ready for this until you land a job that requires you to "meet and eat," plus a hefty expense account, but it's worth thinking about. A little sweet talk and sweet cash in the hands of the maître d' of an appropriate restaurant will do wonders for the impression you make on your lunch and dinner guests. You can use the restaurant as your personal clubhouse to entertain guests. Emmy-winning producer Sascha Schneider ("Hill Street Blues"), for example, has formed such a good relationship with the owners of Mistral, an excellent French bistro near the studios in the San Fernando Valley, that he stores wine at the restaurant and recently cooked for industry friends in Mistral's kitchen!

THE SPORTS CONNECTION

A cynic once joked that it's against the law to be overweight in Beverly Hills. (Don't tell that to Roseanne Barr-Arnold!) Indeed, the entertainment industry does take fitness very seriously, but truly ambitious insiders often combine shmoozing and sweating. There are power gyms just as there are power restaurants. You may also be interested in some of the informal entertainment industry softball leagues, basketball games, and hockey clubs that pop up around town. How to find them? Through shmoozing, of course.

Shmoozing while you sweat can be particularly helpful for less verbal people who are often more comfortable connecting and bonding with others around an activity, rather than just chatting over a glass of wine or Perrier at some event. Team sports are especially effective for these folks.

THE POLITICAL PLAYERS

If combining shmoozing with sweating doesn't appeal to you, perhaps a better way to meet people would be to combine shmoozing and improving the world. Many industry people have strong political and social concerns. If you share those concerns, it makes sense to get involved with some of the industry's charitable organizations.

For example, producer Norman Lear ("All in the Family") and his psychotherapist wife Lyn have created the Environmental Media Association (EMA)—with close buddies Michael and Judy Ovitz (CAA), Michael and Jane Eisner (Disney), Barry Diller (Fox), Bob and Nancy Daly (Warner Bros.), and Ted and Susie Field (Interscope)—to encourage film and TV program makers to include messages about saving the planet in their product. Reportedly, the scene in *Lethal Weapon II* in which Danny Glover's family warns him against eating certain kinds of tuna because of fishing techniques that kill dolphins was the result of EMA lobbying efforts.

EMA is a rather exclusive group that may or may not welcome you as a member (although it's worth finding out if they could use you as a volunteer), but you may be able to join ECO (Earth Communications Office), a $50-per-person membership group founded by entertainment lawyer Bonnie Reiss that is open to people who work in the industry. ECO lobbies entertainment industry people to raise environmental consciousness, change unecological life-style habits (CAA now has low-flush toilets), and create support for saving the planet. Reiss has escorted a number of luminaries like Tom Cruise and John Ritter to the Amazon on fact-finding trips.

Other industry political organizations to be aware of include the Show Coalition, an industry insider club that holds breakfast meetings with political leaders; the Hollywood Women's Political Committee, a group of A- and B-list players that works for abortion rights and other causes; Young Artists United, founded by actress Alexandra Paul to mobilize young Hollywood in support of hands-on neighborhood improvement projects; and Education First!, founded by independent producers Lynda Guber (wife of Peter) and Carole Isenberg (wife of TV producer Jerry Isenberg) to convince Hollywood writers, producers, and directors to include pro-education themes in their programming.

You may want to check out these and other industry political or charitable organizations to find one that fits with your personal values and concerns. Then volunteer or join the group, get active, become visible—and, of course, shmooze.

BECOME AN INSTANT INSIDER: JOIN AN INDUSTRY ASSOCIATION

The most effective networking affiliations you can develop are those that come directly out of your passions and experience.

If you attended a university (especially if you were in the cinema/ TV department), get involved in your alumni association. Some alumni groups are famous in Hollywood for their tendency to hire each other and tip each other off to jobs. For example, the "USC Mafia," graduates of the USC cinema/TV graduate program, have a reputation for taking care of each other. Their alumni association holds events where members can sometimes meet successful graduates who are now powerful industry players.

Even if you don't consider yourself a joiner, make it your business to know about the important entertainment industry associations and join at least one that seems to offer shmoozing opportunities that are appropriate to your targeted career goal.

Perhaps Women in Film would be right for you, or the Independent Feature Project. The American Film Institute is an excellent affiliation. The International Documentary Association is home to many nonfiction film and television producers. The Association of Entertainment Industry Computer Professionals could help you meet computer mavens from many of the studios and production companies around town.

At the Hollywood Radio & TV Society you may be able to attend regular "Newsmaker Luncheons," which are great for networking with a who's who of television luminaries, or their annual holiday party at the Century Plaza Hotel. The American Cinematheque, run by top film people, holds an annual Motion Picture Ball to raise funds for a permanent, Los Angeles-based film showcase. If you're a true film buff, this might be an excellent affiliation where your knowledge of film history would shine.

The Association of Visual Communicators in Pasadena can link you up with others interested in corporate media. Financial & Administrative Management in Entertainment (FAME) is a group of financial and business-side industry executives.

If you're from out of town (or another country), by all means join any groups that help you meet fellow immigrants in the industry. For instance, since I'm Canadian, I try to stay in touch with Telefilm Canada's Beverly Hills offices (they keep resumes of showbiz Canucks on file) and I also like to keep up with the Los Angeles branch of the Academy of Canadian Cinema and Television, which holds screenings and events. A group called Chicagoans in the Industry (CITI) has been created by Jeff Gordon, who runs the Writer's Boot Camp, for all you Windy City refugees in Hollywood. If a group of industryites from your neck of the woods doesn't yet exist, start it!

And of course if you can join a guild in your area of special interest, do so. But don't leave it at that! Get involved, become active on a committee or project, run for office. It's amazing to me how few guild members take advantage of this important affiliation by maximizing their involvement. The board of directors and the staff of your guild are important, respected, well-connected people in this community and getting to know them as working colleagues can be of inestimable value to your career.

As you gain experience and credentials in the industry, you may be eligible to join the Academy of Motion Picture Arts and Sciences and the Academy of Television Arts and Sciences. These are, of course, highly respected and powerful affiliations with many benefits and opportunities. The TV Academy, for instance, has a Writers Repertory Group, in which nonwriter academy members can hear their work read by actor members.

Once you've targeted a couple of organizations that interest you, call and ask for membership information and a current calendar. Then, if you like what you read, attend an event (you can sometimes attend expensive fund-raisers or seminars free if you volunteer to work on the event). Or volunteer to help in the office or on a committee.

SHMOOZY SEMINARS, FESTIVALS, MARKETS, AND CONVENTIONS

As you know, Hollywood offers a wealth of seminars and classes that are open to the public at large. Almost every important industry guild or association holds these seminars, and many local educational institutions (the American Film Institute and UCLA Extension are especially popular) offer them as well. Most are presented in Los Angeles or New York, but sometimes these seminars go on the road. For example, I've been teaching a seminar at the American Film Institute called "Job Search Strategies for the Entertainment Profession," which has been offered about twice a year in Los Angeles and which I have also presented in Dallas and San Francisco.

The benefits of attending an industry seminar aren't limited to the content of the class, however. You may also have an opportunity to shmooze with people who normally might not return your calls: the star panelists. Many of these events feature industry heavyweights whom you can approach at the breaks or after class. In the relaxed classroom atmosphere, you may be able to begin to build a relationship that you can follow up later with calls or letters or even script submissions.

You can also use these classes to create an instant "alumni association." Take an industry seminar in your area of interest—acting, writing, camerawork, or whatever you're most passionate about—and pass around a notepad, collecting names and addresses of fellow students. Pick a bar or restaurant, and send out invitations to a no-host "alumni shmoozer" event so people can keep in touch. Such get-togethers are perfect times to share gossip and information on possible jobs.

Festivals, markets, and conventions are also great places to meet people and shmooze. The ski slopes or après-ski get-togethers at insider festivals like the winter Sundance Festival in Park City, Utah, provide more relaxed, informal settings for industry networking than the usual frenetic Hollywood venues. People who wouldn't take your call in L.A. will be happy to chat over the cappucino in front of a roaring fire.

START YOUR OWN CLUB: THE SUNDAY DIM SUM GANG

A few years ago, my husband and I and a few industry friends started the Dim Sum Club to expand our network and keep up with industry buddies. We picked a popular downtown Chinese restaurant that served great dim sum, and chose a date and time. Then we created a simple flyer and printed it on brightly colored paper (you could also put your message on a postcard, which is cheaper to mail). We delivered invitations to our entertainment industry friends (including people we had lost touch with). We also invited some new folks— people we met at parties, plus a few important players we hoped to get to know better. One of the latter was Tom, an important studio exec that one of our friends had met at a pitch meeting.

Our club get-togethers were informal and lots of fun (and cheap, because they were no-host events where everyone paid their own way). We enjoyed ourselves and got to know people in a new way. After our dim sum breakfast one Sunday morning we went toy shopping in Little Tokyo with Tom, the executive I mentioned above, who collected mechanical toys for his office coffee table. We were able to create a much more personal relationship with him than we ever could have just meeting with him at the studio.

Starting your own organization can help you rise to the next level in your entertainment industry career. At the beginning of this chapter I mentioned the enterprising young development assistant who started the development executives' networking group that Lucas Foster and I belonged to. I was so impressed with her entrepreneurial spirit in getting this group started. As a result of this group, she got to know a number of important people from studios and production companies around town. She was able to network with powerful development execs who accepted her as an equal. Last I heard, she had optioned a literary property and was launching a producing career.

CREATE A MOVIE CLUB

It's also fun to start your own movie club. A few years ago I did this with the story analysts who worked for me at Lorimar. I'd pick a new movie, a day, time, and theater. Then I'd invite the readers and their buddies or spouses to attend. We'd all watch the film and then adjourn to a nearby restaurant or coffee shop where we had some great (and loud!) discussions of what worked or didn't work. We picked apart the premise, the story structure, the acting, the cinematography, the directing. We got a few strange looks from other people in the restaurant, but we had a terrific time.

If starting your own movie club sounds like too much work, you may want to frequent some of the film or video venues in Los Angeles. The Cinema Cafe on Melrose Avenue is a coffee house that features a cinema room with state-of-the-art video/laser equipment and regular evening programs spotlighting the work of independent filmmakers. Vidiots in Santa Monica presents panel discussions with filmmakers like Charles Burnett *(To Sleep with Anger)*. Al's Bar in downtown L.A. holds open screenings by independent film and videomakers and accepts submissions. EZTV in West Hollywood shows video features. These may be interesting places where you could hang out and shmooze.

SUPPORT GROUPS AND ELECTRONIC SHMOOZING

You can also join a weekly entertainment industry career support group—or create one yourself. Get together a group of show business buddies, set a regular time to meet, and, at each session, share the last week's victories and current challenges and assign yourself next week's homework. Group members share contacts and leads (advice is frowned upon) and encourage each other to make those calls!

Another way to meet people is through electronic shmoozing. The Writers Guild has a computer bulletin board through which members can communicate with each other when they're avoiding their screenplays.

SHMOOZING WITH THE STARS

The stars who count in your career are the star players in your chosen niche. How can you meet them?

One good way to get to know people you might otherwise be unable to reach is to use your industry organization affiliations (see above) and put together a seminar on your area of interest or expertise.

For example, if you're a budding set designer you might want to join the Independent Feature Project/West and volunteer to organize and moderate a seminar on production design for independent features. If IFP agrees, you could call up your heroes in production design and ask them to be on the panel. Because you're calling as a representative of the Independent Feature Project, a highly respected industry organization, chances are that not only will your calls get through, but the production designers in question may agree to be part of your program. You'll be working with the panelists to prepare them for the seminar. You may be able to drop by to meet them and fill them in on what will be involved. And on the day of the program you'll have an unparalleled opportunity to demonstrate your knowledge, charm, and competence. And of course you'll want to follow up with a thank-you note or gift and maintain these important relationships for years to come. If you hit it off with any of these stars, you may have found an invaluable career mentor.

Another technique that a friend of mine used to meet people she wanted to know: volunteer to write an article for an industry organization publication (the Independent Feature Project/West, for example, publishes *Montage*) on your area of interest. It could be an overview article on an interesting topic—for which you'll want to interview a number of people—or an in-depth interview with one of your heroes. Either way, you'll have a legitimate reason to call and meet with the folks you need to know. And they'll probably be delighted with the recognition and publicity your article will give them.

GET ON THE HOLLYWOOD PARTY CIRCUIT

A great deal of Hollywood's business is done at parties, events, and screenings. But how to get invited?

If you're a member of a few industry organizations, you'll automatically be invited to a number of gala fund-raisers every year. They're often expensive but can be excellent opportunities to shmooze if you can summon the courage to meet at least two or three new people at the event.

To meet the most people, attend events by yourself or with a friend who is a good shmoozer. Agree to split up at the party as much as possible, but rescue each other if either of you seems to be floundering. Introduce each other to new people you meet.

If shmoozing is tough for you, write a few opening lines for yourself to help you get a conversation started with a new person. Also, you may want to attend sit-down events where you're placed at a table next to others, which makes conversation a little easier.

Party and screening invitations will come into your life as your network of friends expands. Let it be known that you love parties (if you do) and that you're available when things come up. And share your invitations with others. If you're working temp at a studio and get two tickets for a screening from your boss, invite your shmoozing buddy to come with you. Hopefully your offer will be reciprocated.

Give parties yourself if you're comfortable doing so. They don't have to be expensive, but they do need to be creative and entertaining. I used to host an annual "Pick the Hits" party each January when the *Los Angeles Times*'s annual list of upcoming movies came out. Guests would read the sometimes hilarious loglines out loud and then fill out a ballot predicting which would be next year's top-grossing hits. At each party we'd give a silly prize to last year's top hit picker.

HOLLYWOOD PARTIES

Every weekend there are parties all over Los Angeles at which you'll meet industry folks. At a San Fernando Valley baby shower for your cousin's sister-in-law you may find yourself seated next to a hot director or a mail room person from Fox or a writer for "Married with Children." At a casual party in a rambling Craftsman era Silverlake house you may wander from room to room munching cheesies and shmoozing with a young crowd of D-people, agents, and film school graduates.

But sooner or later you'll get invited to an honest-to-goodness high-powered Hollywood party. The most important thing to remember at a Hollywood party (which may be held in Malibu, Bel-Air, Brentwood, or Beverly Hills) is that you're not "less than" anyone else. Even if you're a rank newcomer or a midcareer person who's had a few bad years, hold your head up high. Dress up (or down) with a little style and carry yourself with a positive attitude and you'll be fine.

Don't let yourself be intimidated because the valet parker gives the evil eye to the fake leopard skin seat covers on your beat-up Toyota station wagon after parking the plush Mercedes in front of you. Don't gulp when you see the inside of the house or the power players and celebrities. Just be cool, relax, and have fun. As usual, try to meet at least two or three new people. Remind yourself that you belong in this crowd because you're a creative person and creative people are the lifeblood of Hollywood. Every famous and powerful person in the room was once an outsider or a less-than. Remember that success (and failure) can happen very quickly in Hollywood: next year this could be your house and the person who presently owns it could be drying out at the Betty Ford Clinic.

YOU NEVER KNOW . . .

When you're out shmoozing, don't be snobbish about whom you befriend. The frizzy redhead licking stamps next to you at Women in Film may be writing the decade's next hot script. The quiet little man hovering over the punch bowl at the screening reception may be the producer's father. The secretary you ignore today may be a superstar tomorrow. As a former boss used to warn me, "You meet the same people on the way down you met on the way up." In an industry where job mobility has escalated into a fast game of musical chairs, it pays to be good to people. Even if they are not in a position to be of immediate assistance to your career, you never know. . . . Besides, you'll feel good about yourself if you take a kind and positive attitude toward others. And that good feeling will give you the confidence you need to continue making the right moves.

PHONE SHMOOZING

In Hollywood the phone is a lethal weapon. To win at the game, you need to wield it skillfully.

Although phone shmoozing is less powerful than face-to-face shmoozing, the time pressure and the increasingly global nature of the industry (not to mention the appalling congestion on the freeways) make it indispensable. Agents and studio executives make up to 200 calls a day! While some of these calls are strictly business, most include a certain amount of shmoozing and gossip. Every Monday, film executives all over the world call each other to ask, "Did you read anything interesting over the weekend?" and to chat about writers, scripts, who's about to make it big or be fired.

The first step in effective phone shmoozing is to learn to respect and charm the secretary/assistant. Because "you never know . . . ," it's bad form to treat this person like a nobody. After finding out his or her name, using your two magic words, and stating your business as clearly as possible, interject a little good-humored shmoozing or gossip into the conversation to make a connection. Ask questions if you can, so that your comments are personal rather than general. Even overworked, perennially grumpy assistants have been known to respond to a cheery greeting and a joke. By calling frequently and being a "nice nudge" you can build a relationship with an assistant that can really pay off. A film school student I met at one of my seminars was able to turn a phone relationship with a mogul's assistant who was a Wayne Gretsky fan into a hockey date that eventually led to his meeting the mogul in person.

But what if you actually get through to Marvin Mogul on the phone? Of course you'll use the pitching techniques you learned a few chapters ago, but then what? In Hollywood it's considered bad form to have a cold business conversation without a little shmoozing thrown in to keep the relationship sweet. Perhaps you won't want to try this on a first conversation with Marvin, but on subsequent calls be ready to chat a little. For this it helps to have done some research about Marvin. During one of your "nice nudge" calls, for instance, his assistant might have told you that he is a horse-racing nut. Or you might have read in the trades that he supports the local opera society. If you happen to know something about either of these, you're in luck. Truly ambitious Hollywood newcomers have been known to do special research on their targeted mogul just for the purpose of being able to "give good shmooze" when the opportunity arises.

SHMOOZING ON THE SET

Sets can be exciting places where magic happens. They can also be stressful as crews struggle to cope with the demands of time, budget, art, and ego. But mostly they're boring, because there's a lot of waiting around. That's where shmoozing comes in—how else are you going to pass the time?

A special sort of bonding happens on sets. The team becomes a family—sometimes a squabbling family but still a family. Relationships formed under battle conditions are very potent. Some of the most helpful names in your Rolodex will be folks you met on sets.

Even if you're unemployed or not currently working on a project, you can benefit from on-set shmoozing. Once your Power Rolodex reaches critical mass, you'll probably have at least one or two buddies working on a film or TV shoot at all times. Visit them on the set. Once there, the rest is easy. Between takes, many crew members and creative people have time to sit and shmooze in an informal way that would be impossible if you visited them in their offices. A TV director friend of mine regularly makes the rounds of Hollywood sets, just to shmooze and to remind everyone (without saying so, of course) that he's available.

SPY NETWORKS, GOOD GOSSIP, THE BUZZ ECONOMY, AND TRADING BASEBALL CARDS

The entertainment industry, like Wall Street, thrives on inside information. How do you find out about the jobs that aren't listed in the trades (which is to say, most jobs you'd be interested in)? How do you keep up on who's where doing what to whom? To know what's happening, you need to get into the gossip flow, the "buzz economy." People all over town are sharing information with each other on a quid pro quo basis: if you tip me on a job opening for a production manager, I'll call you when I hear about a good spec script no one's seen yet.

Good gossip is very much a part of Hollywood shmoozing. At the gym, on the cellular phone in a freeway traffic jam, at lunch, on the beach—you can hear the buzz. The industry buzzed with rumors when David Puttnam was floundering. It buzzed over the widely distributed letter written to CAA's top agent Michael Ovitz by a defiantly defecting writer. It buzzed when the Japanese were courting Guber and Peters to head up Columbia Studios and when Peters subsequently left his studio job. It buzzed when the Jeffrey Katzenberg/Disney memo was leaked to the trades. It buzzes each time a project looks like it will be greenlighted (given the go-ahead).

Everyone in your Rolodex can be part of your unofficial spy network and gossip club if you "water" your relationships and nurse them along like seedlings. Try to know someone at every major studio and production company, no matter how lowly their job.

BUT WAIT A MINUTE—WHAT ABOUT NEPOTISM?

This shmoozing is all well and good, you may say. But don't you really have to be related to someone to make it in Hollywood? Some newcomers worry a lot about the unfair advantages enjoyed by players' relatives. Relax. Being related to someone opens doors, and so does shmoozing. But once you walk through those doors, you have to deliver the goods, no matter who you are. There is too much money at stake in today's Hollywood to hire no-talent people to do critical jobs.

My advice: don't waste your time worrying about nepotism. Concentrate on developing your talent—and on your shmoozing.

TALK THAT TALK

Every industry has its jargon, and show business is no exception. As you shmooze your way around town, you're way ahead of the game if you can speak (or at least understand) the language.

Take a few minutes to peruse the glossary at the end of this book. Soon you'll be "taking" relationship meetings at which you chat comfortably about "turnaround projects," "packaging elements," movies that "open," Paramount's new "franchise," your planned trip to Hawaii during this year's "hiatus," Kevin Costner's great "first look housekeeping deal," $3 million "spec scripts," picking up "sides" and checking the "breakdowns," "pay or play" contracts, "story beats," "below-the-line costs," and "wrap parties."

As any good anthropologist will tell you, it helps to talk like the natives.

SHMOOZING BUILDS UP YOUR POWER ROLODEX

It's important to turn all of this shmoozing into serious, ongoing relationships that can help your career year after year. Keep track of the people you meet in your Power Rolodex. Follow up with notes, birthday cards, calls, lunches. Your talent and your relationships are the two best guarantees of long-term career success in the entertainment industry, and cynics would count the latter as far more important than the former.

BUT WHAT IF I HATE SHMOOZING?

If you're a quiet, introverted person, shmoozing may be next to torture on your list of enjoyable things. Under certain circumstances, you can get away without it. For example, if you're a genius writer who lives on a mountaintop in Colorado and you've written a truly astounding script, no one may care if you never wash, have green hair, and communicate in grunts. Your talent will make you popular. You'll be surrounded by admirers and new best friends.

But even this may not be enough to protect you from the necessity to shmooze. You still have to find and communicate with an agent or lawyer, and you'll probably have to attend the dreaded "story meetings" with studio people who will treat you more kindly if you "give good shmooze" than if you clam up in the corner of their office couch and give them surly stares.

So one way or another, everyone in show business has to learn to shmooze at least a little. As you begin to understand the rules of the game, you might even start to relax and enjoy it. Don't take it seriously. As they say in Hollywood, "This isn't brain surgery."

SANITY AND SHMOOZING

It's a good rule not to take either the shmoozing or the rejection personally. One minute you're a nobody having a tough time getting people to take your calls and the next you're the flavor of the week, being shmoozed and romanced by everyone in town. Just stick to your faith in yourself and your projects and keep a level head. This is your best bet for long-term sanity and survival in a notoriously fickle business.

You can't change the industry (at least not until you have more clout) or control the behavior of other people, but you can be fair in your own dealings and honor your commitments. As you build a network of colleagues and contacts, treat them like the valuable people they are. Respect each person you meet as an individual, not just for what he can or can't do for you. Enjoy his company. Be a good, helpful friend.

Stay focused on who you really are as a human being, as well as on where you're going. A good reputation will attract jobs and true friends and colleagues who will be your support system for many years to come.

15

☆

Hollywood Agents

★ ★ ★ ★ ★ ★ ★ ★ ★ ★ ★ ★ ★ ★

THE SUPERSHMOOZERS

Shmoozing is so important in Hollywood that a whole profession has grown up around it: agents. With the demise of the old studio system, agents have become more and more important. They're the glue that holds the industry together. They're information and talent brokers. (The biggest agencies are now providing financing as well.) It's almost impossible to put a project together without them because practically every desirable director, actor, writer—even the producer, cinematographer, special effects genius, and editor—has an agent. Even big corporate deals involve agents: CAA topper Michael Ovitz is credited with arranging Sony's Columbia Pictures purchase and Matsushita's MCA/Universal buyout. (He is also an advisor to Coke.) And former agents hold many of the top positions in Hollywood.

So they're definitely necessary. But are they a necessary evil? If you listen to the Hollywood jokes, it would certainly appear to be so.

HOLLYWOOD AGENT JOKE #1

THE DEVIL

I'll make you the top agent in the business, bigger than Mike Ovitz. But I want the soul of your first-born child and the soul of your first-born grandchild.

AGENT
(suspiciously)

So what's the catch?

HOLLYWOOD AGENT JOKE #2

Q: What do you call six agents at the bottom of a swimming pool?

A: A start.

HOLLYWOOD AGENT JOKE #3

Q: You need a heart transplant. Two hearts are available. One belonged to a twenty-one-year-old, nonsmoking triathlete champion. The other belonged to a fifty-year-old, 250-pound cigar-smoking agent. Which heart should you choose?

A: The agent's, of course. It's never been used.

HOLLYWOOD AGENT JOKE #4

Q: An agent falls overboard in shark-infested waters, yet he isn't attacked. Why?

A: Professional courtesy.

HOLLYWOOD AGENT JOKE #5

NIGHT AT SPAGO RESTAURANT

BEAUTIFUL YOUNG THING slips into an empty chair beside AGENT.

BEAUTIFUL YOUNG THING
(seductively)

Oooh, how nice to meet you.

> AGENT
> (ignoring her)

Mmmmm.

> BEAUTIFUL YOUNG THING
> (moving in closer to him)

Why don't we go back to my place so I can give you a nice back rub? (Hollywood versions of this joke tend to be a little more X-rated.)

> AGENT
> (suspicious)

What's in it for me?

DO AGENTS GET A BUM RAP?

These jokes reflect the ongoing frustration many creative people feel toward agents. And some agents deserve this abuse. They can be cold, calculating salespeople who will do anything—anything!—to make a deal. They live and die for their 10 percent. If you're hot they love you. If you're not, forget it. And the worst crime of all: even if you're their client, they're almost impossible to reach on the phone if you're not a current big money-maker.

It's a great career mistake, however, to hate agents. Agent bashing is a loser's game. Whenever I hear people whining about how their agent hasn't done this or that for them, I know I'm listening to someone who hasn't yet taken responsibility for his or her own career. Blaming your agent just protects your ego: it allows you to avoid facing the possibility that either (1) your work or talent isn't up to Hollywood's standards or (2) you're not putting enough effort into selling yourself and making all the right moves—that is, you're passively waiting for your agent to get you work.

WORKING WELL WITH AN AGENT INVOLVES SEEING THE BUSINESS THROUGH THEIR EYES

Walk a mile in an agent's Gucci slippers and things will come clearer. Let me tell you a story about a prototypical young Hollywood agent, Sammy Slick. No, Sammy is not your agent in disguise, but a fictional character created as a composite of many Hollywood agents I have worked with as a development executive.

Sammy started in the mail room at a major agency. He graduated from a prestige school and has an uncle by marriage whose sister has worked in the industry for many years. She made the call that got him into the mail room.

He had originally hoped to be an actor or writer or director but found that he really didn't have the requisite talent. But he loves movies and TV and he loves creative people. He's fairly extroverted and persuasive. The phone is his medium. He's a good negotiator. He has a fabulous memory for names and faces. He likes excitement and action. Agenting seemed a natural for him. His family and friends told him he'd be great at it.

LIFE AS A MAIL ROOM SLAVE

The mail room was grueling. He found himself working fourteen-hour days, driving all over the city, delivering scripts and doing errands. Because he was eager, he also tried to read scripts for agents and attend plays and films in addition to his mail room duties. Now he understood why the agency preferred to hire very young people. Anyone over thirty would collapse from the ridiculous hours he was putting in.

He kept at it, in spite of an intense desire to retire to Hawaii and dig clams for the rest of his life. Gradually he began to pick up a lot of useful information. When he delivered a screenplay to Sally Star at 10:00 A.M. she was still drunk from the night before. She tried to invite him in for a quickie, but he was already late. He filed that bit of information away for future use. When he delivered flowers to our old friend Marvin Mogul at Fox he saw that the guy's office was filled with model trains. Good tidbit to remember when the time came to romance him. He also made friends (he's good at that) with a pretty mail room assistant at Warners and she promised to copy the latest secret list of the studio's projects for him, which he could pass along to a senior agent at his agency for a few extra Brownie points.

He realized that he was actually learning something useful from this dog work, but he wanted out of the mail room. He found he just couldn't make ends meet on the pittance they were paying him. He decided to really romance Wanda Wonderful, a senior literary agent at his agency, to see if she would take him on as her assistant. Everyone in the mail room was trying to "get a desk," to graduate from the mail room to agent's assistant. He'd be the first to succeed. He'd make sure of that.

SAMMY MAKES HIS MOVE

Being a tactical fellow by nature, Sammy devised a plan. He found out everything he could about Wanda. He chatted up Wanda's current assistant, Joe, and found out that he would be graduating to agent in the next few months. Great! He discovered that Wanda was months behind in her reading and that she had a thing for the theater and that her pet poodle was her life since her boyfriend dumped her.

Sammy set to work romancing Wanda. He made himself as useful as he could. He took her dog to the vet. He read scripts. He passed along the Warners list of projects in development. He hung around backstage at Equity Waiver plays and picked up theater gossip he could entertain Wanda with. He laid on the charm.

It worked. Sammy was elated when he could announce to his fellow mail room slaves that he was moving up. A desk at last! The salary was still pathetic, but he was on his way.

He thought the mail room was tough but was amazed to find that being on a desk was even tougher. Now he was Wanda's slave instead of a mail room slave. His ear developed a callus from taking and placing the hundreds of phone calls Wanda fielded every day. He'd had no idea what being an agent was really like, but now it started to become clear. It was endless, endless phone calls, meetings, screenings, deals. Wanda was on the ragged edge. She really needed him. That cheered him up. He wouldn't let her down.

He started to figure out how the game worked. Wanda got hundreds of calls every day but would only return those that promised a fairly immediate sale and commission. Unless, of course, the caller was an important industry player or her poodle's vet. Wanda resisted taking calls from her clients unless there was specific business to discuss. At first he didn't understand why, but when the clients started pouring out their hearts to him he began to understand. These people needed a psychiatrist, he thought, not an agent. All that whining. They were all terrified they'd never work again.

But he liked the clients who were nice to him, or funny, or interesting to chat with. And he liked the ones who kept it brief and seemed to know how to help Wanda get them work. They were no problem. He found himself reminding Wanda to call them back.

SAMMY'S ON OVERLOAD

Sammy was getting seriously overloaded, though. His hours were getting longer, not shorter. All the phone calls were beginning to rot his memory and erode his attention span. He started getting irritable with people. His girlfriend dumped him when he forgot her birthday and then spent most of a romantic Sunday in a Santa Barbara bed and breakfast reading scripts. His ulcer started acting up and his father told him he was getting worried about Sammy's health. His mother thought that perhaps he had picked the wrong profession.

But Sammy was hooked by this time. How could he give up the excitement and fun of being where the action was? All the top deals went through his agency. He was on the inside. He had buddies and contacts all over town and it was fun to keep up with the gossip. And it was exciting to be part of helping talented people land great assignments. People all over the world would envy his position. Besides, he had found out how much money Wanda was making, and he wasn't going to quit until he too got the big payoff for his hard labor. He had his eye on a red Jaguar and a beach house in Malibu like the one Wanda had bought recently.

The powers that be at the agency had taken note of Sammy's enthusiasm, talent, and drive. His eagerness and hunger reminded them of how they were when they started out in the business. Yes, the kid definitely had it.

And after an all-nighter at the animal emergency room with

Wanda and Pierrot Poodle, she had rewarded him by singing his praises to the top agent. She would help Sammy make agent, she promised.

SAMMY MAKES AGENT

A year and a half later—he thought his servitude would never end!—at last it happened. He was an agent, with his own slave out there answering his phones.

Now he needed clients, of course. The agency had him working for existing clients, but he knew he'd have to bring some new clients in to make the big bucks and to keep moving up. He could develop new talent from scratch or he could try to steal already-established talent from other agents.

Developing new talent appealed to him. He prided himself on his taste and knew he could spot a winner. But selling a new writer to producers and studios could be tough. Wanda had a few of these newcomers she was "developing." Some were actually signed with the agency and some were unofficial, "pocket" clients she did favors for on the understanding that if anything was sold, she'd get the commission. They were usually theater people she'd met who had talent but hadn't yet made any money in film or TV.

HOW TO WOO A CLIENT

Sammy had also watched Wanda romance big-bucks-screenwriter Jeremy Genius, who was a hot client at a rival agency. She wooed him the way Sammy had wooed Wanda. Sammy admired her style. No doubt about it, when she wanted to, Wanda could really turn on the old charm. She told Jeremy that he was being mistreated by his current agent, an industry veteran who was, according to Wanda, losing his grip. On Jeremy's last deal, she said, she could have gotten him much more money than old Chuck squeezed out of Columbia. She flattered him shamelessly, told him that with his talent he should be making more than screenwriter stars like Shane Black, who pulled down over $1.75 million on his last deal. Wanda hinted that $2 million might not be impossible—if he signed with her, of course.

It worked. Jeremy signed with Wanda. The head of the agency

bought Wanda a red Jaguar in recognition of Wanda's talent as a Signer. Other agents might be Holders or Sellers, but a real Signer must be cherished and rewarded by an ambitious agency.

So Sammy developed a plan. He put together a Hit List of talented writers who were making good money. Then he called his spy network (his friends all over town) and tried to find out if any of these writers were unhappy with their current circumstances. He discovered that hot romantic comedy scripter Melanie Mays, who was still loyal to her first agent (a real nobody), might be ready to make the move. He wooed. She signed. Now he was cooking. Melanie was writing a new spec script. When she finished he'd hold an auction. He'd make his mark in this town!

The days sped by, a blur of power meals with possible buyers . . . hurried workouts with his personal fitness trainer . . . freeway carphone gossip with buddies and spies . . . screaming matches with business affairs goons who didn't want to pay his clients' prices . . . political infighting at the agency . . . the brief thrill of getting a wonderful gig for a client he really liked . . . more and more scripts to read piling up on his desk and on his bedside table at home . . . endless agency meetings at which he was always called upon to report the latest news on what was happening at Warner Bros., the studio he was supposed to "cover" for the firm . . . shmoozy evening screenings with stars who wanted to tell him their life stories over drinks at 11:30 P.M. when he was exhausted . . . and of course Melanie's auction—a fifty-two-hour marathon of frenzied phone calls.

In the meantime, he was also getting calls every day from writers who wanted representation. Yeah, yeah. He didn't have time to read their scripts. He was now completely overloaded and his ulcer was getting worse. He was seeing a therapist. She agreed with his parents and his ex-girlfriend that he should get out of the business.

SAMMY FINDS TRUE LOVE

One night he went to the theater, and before he fell asleep in the second act he knew that the guy who wrote this play was incredibly talented. As his eyes were closing, he even started to remember why he had wanted to be a literary agent in the first place.

Sammy stayed after the show to meet Peter Playwright, and invited him out for drinks. He liked the guy. And Peter had no film or TV agent.

But Sammy worried that taking Peter on might not be a smart move. Shouldn't he concentrate on clients like Melanie? Ten percent of Melanie was definitely more lucrative than 10 percent of Peter. And since Peter was a complete newcomer, how could Sammy convince the rest of the agents that they should sign him? He'd really have to put himself on the line for this guy, and if Peter didn't pan out, Sammy's ass would be grass. It was definitely a risky move.

As he was driving home at 1:00 A.M. he called Wanda (the poodle was sick, so he knew she'd be up), and she encouraged him to go for it if he really had a gut feeling this guy was something special. Good old Wanda.

By the time he'd hauled himself out of bed the next day and done five phone calls on the way to the office, he had forgotten all about Peter. But then a call from Sally Star jogged his memory. (He considerately didn't remind her of their previous meeting.) Sally gushed about how thrilled she was that he might be helping her dear friend Peter Playwright, a true genius if ever there was one. Hmmm, thought Sammy. This guy's smarter than I thought. "Get me Peter Playwright," he screamed at Zoe, his new assistant, another trainee. "Who?" she screamed back.

PETER MAKES THE RIGHT MOVES

Peter came in to see him. Even the morning after, the magic was still there. First Sammy carried Peter as a "pocket client," and then, once he'd sold Peter's play to Marvin Mogul, who wanted to turn it into a screenplay starring Peter's dear friend Sally Star (a deal that couldn't have happened without Peter's help, he had to admit), the agency agreed to actually sign the guy.

Peter was the kind of client Sammy liked. Not only was he bright and talented, but the guy hustled. He was out there, meeting people and making friends. It was fun to take his calls. He didn't call Sammy unless he had a good lead that he thought Sammy could close, or a good story to tell him. Sammy even started to think of the guy as a friend. After all, Sammy had few real friends—he was too busy. He and Peter started going to the race track together, which Sammy really enjoyed.

Thanks to both of their efforts, Peter started getting hot. Peter adapted his play for Marvin and he did a damn good job. Sammy was so delighted that he let a few select people see the screenplay (Marvin didn't want him to, but business is business) and soon Peter was getting writing assignments. Sammy and Peter did all they could to help Marvin get the script produced and, miraculously, it was. Even more miraculously, it did well. On Oscar night, Peter thanked Sammy for believing in him when no one else did. Sammy was in heaven. This is why I became an agent, he sighed.

The next day, Superagent Clara Claws called Peter. Would he like to have lunch? She felt she could take his career to a new level, if only he'd leave his agent, Sammy . . .

AN AGENT'S LOT IS NOT A HAPPY ONE

Well, perhaps you're having a little trouble feeling too much sympathy for Sammy's loss of Peter. But hopefully you're beginning to understand the terrible pressure most agents operate under. Frankly, I don't know how they keep it up.

Not every agent is as calculating as Sammy. Some agents, in fact, go out of their way to help newcomers and encourage new talent. But a significant proportion of Hollywood agents get so burned out and ground down by the job that they give up on the idealistic side of agenting and just focus on earning their ten percent. It's understandable, in a way. They have to make a living, and to do that they must focus their efforts on clients who regularly earn serious money.

So what moves should you make to get and use an agent successfully?

HOW TO GET AN AGENT

Now that you understand Sammy's predicament, you're ready to undertake the task of romancing him.

But first, think about who the perfect agent for you would be. Do some homework. Get a copy of a list of agents who specialize in your targeted area (*The Hollywood Agents Directory*, listed in Resources, could be helpful). Also get the list of agents put out by your (prospective) guild—you don't want to be with an agent whom your professional guild doesn't recognize. Talk to your friends and colleagues. Who represents them? Who do they hear is good?

DO YOU WANT AN AGENT WHO'S NICE OR AN AGENT WITH CLOUT?

There are, thank God, a sizable number of agents who both are nice and have clout, but niceness should not be the deciding factor in picking an agent.

Newcomers and veterans who are having a rough time with their careers are often seduced by the hand-holding type of agent who seems so sympathetic and understanding. But if you want a shrink, go to a shrink. If you want a friend, find a real friend. This is not a good criterion for choosing an agent. The wonderful hand-holder may be a complete novice, a perennial loser, or completely unconnected in your area of specialization.

The real criteria for choosing an agent should be: How excited is she about selling your talent? Do you both agree on what your most sellable assets are? Do you share the same vision of where you're headed? Does she have good contacts with people who could buy you and your work? Is she an effective salesperson? Does she have clout? (One of my clients refers to his powerful agent as a "1,000-pound hammer" he uses to hit people over the head.)

Nice is not the issue. Sometimes it's there; sometimes it's not. It's the icing, not the cake.

PUT TOGETHER AN AGENT HIT LIST

No, I'm not talking about bumping off your last two agents or the agent who wouldn't take your calls. I'm talking about an organized way of targeting the best agent for your career.

Think about your exact career goal, your special niche. Perhaps it's directing sitcoms, for example. Watch all of your favorite shows and write down the names of the directors. These lucky people are actually doing the work you want to do. Then call the guild that represents your heroes—in this case, the Directors Guild. When the receptionist answers the phone, say, "Agency, please." The receptionist will connect you with someone who sits in front of a computer. "Who represents Audrey Artsy, please?" you ask. "Sammy Slick at the Hot Agency," he will answer. If you're nice, this computer slave may tell you the agents for three directors in any one phone call, but no more. Anyone can call and get this information because it's considered a service to members who are looking for work. You don't have to be a guild member to call.

Now you can put together a list of agents who specialize in representing directors who do the kind of work you'd like to do. These agents' contacts with the buyers you want to work for—in this case, the producers of TV sitcoms—will probably be better than most other agents', because that's where they're doing business and making money.

But won't agents see a potential conflict in representing more than one director in a particular category? Sometimes agents will tell you, "We already have someone in your area," but you can't let that stop you. Even overworked Sammy Slick took on Peter Playwright. Just be persistent and make all the right moves. Once the agent sees that you're talented, charming, and ambitious, she may decide to place you on jobs that her A-list directors turn down. And soon, hopefully, you too will be on that A-list and she'll be glad to have signed you.

But don't limit yourself to agents who already represent directors. You may also discover an agent who would like to branch out into this area, and although he won't be initially as knowledgeable and well connected as already-established specialists, he may be eager to learn.

Once you've got your Hit List together, work it just the way you'd work a list of potential employers.

NOW, HOW DO I GET SAMMY TO REPRESENT ME?

The easiest way to get an agent to represent you is to be a money-making talent already represented by another agency. Stealing clients is a time-honored career strategy among agents.

The second easiest way to get an agent is by referral. Start asking around; ask everyone in your network if they have any contacts at

Sammy's agency or if they know anyone else who might. Perhaps they know someone in the mail room or an agent trainee or even the janitor. Keep calling until you find someone who can help you. It may take hundreds of calls, but keep doing it; you're building your Rolodex as you go.

An experienced agent will almost never sign a new client unless the client has been referred to her by someone she knows and respects. Remember Sally Star's call to Sammy on Peter's behalf? Perhaps your contacts don't include someone at Sally's level, but you may be able to find another talent represented by Sammy who would be willing to recommend you. You can also do what Peter did—get your work out there in public view and invite agents to attend your play or screening.

The third way to get an agent is to send in unsolicited letters, scripts, resumes, and reels. Give it a shot, but realize that this is seldom an effective way to get the kind of representation you'd like to have. After all, why should an agent take the time to seriously consider you when he's already overloaded? (The good agents are always overloaded. Too often it's only the rank newcomers or the real losers who have time to spend reading unsolicited scripts or considering unknowns.)

Selling to an agent is tough. Being supershmoozers themselves, they know all the angles. Sammy, for instance, is a master salesman and romancer. You just have to be charming, clever, talented, and persistent.

BECOME A POCKET CLIENT: THE "AFRICAN QUEEN" PLOY

Here's a little trick that's worked for Hollywood people for many years. I know a number of writers who've used it successfully. I call it the "African Queen" ploy because it was reportedly used by producer Sam Spiegel to land Humphrey Bogart and Katharine Hepburn for that John Huston-directed classic. Supposedly he told each of them that the other had already agreed to be involved. So of course they both said yes.

In our version, you first find a buyer who agrees to read your script once you are represented by an agent. Many producers are open to reading new material if it comes through an agent, so this isn't as difficult as it sounds. (Producers may also read material submitted by a lawyer, but that wouldn't land you an agent, would it?)

Then call Sammy's office. Of course you'll reach Sammy's assistant, Zoe, the agent trainee, who's having a nervous breakdown. Make her your new best friend. Drop the two magic words—the name of someone she or Sammy knows—so she won't hang up. Even better, perhaps you can have someone she and Sammy know make a Godfather or Godmother Call on your behalf to prepare them for your call.

Explain who you are and that Marvin Mogul is interested in reading your script. If Marvin wants to buy it (or your writing services), would Sammy be willing to represent you on the deal?

Sammy may actually agree to this. After all, what does he have to lose? You're not asking him to do any work to get the sale, just to collect ten percent if there *is* a sale. Besides, he likes dealing with Marvin. Who wouldn't? If Marvin calls, of course Sammy will take his call. Everyone in Hollywood would take Marvin's call. He's a buyer. He's a player. Sammy's impressed that you've gotten through to Marvin. And if Marvin thinks you're good, maybe you *are* someone Sammy should represent.

BETTER YET, HAVE MARVIN'S D-PERSON GET YOU AN AGENT

But how did you get to Marvin? Well, here's a possible scenario. You were at a party at a director's house, and you met Alex, who does free-lance story analysis for Marvin. You romanced him and he agreed to read your new script. He read it and liked it. He passed it along to Sarah, one of Marvin's D-people (development executives). She liked it too. You spoke with Sarah and she asked if you had an agent. You said no, but you'd love her advice on whom you should be with. Flattered, and ever-mindful of her own need to romance agents, she took a minute to think. To whom did she owe a favor? Sammy Slick, she thought. Why not?

She mentioned Sammy's name to you. You were thrilled, because Sammy was on your agent hit list. But you played it cool. You didn't slobber or stammer shamelessly. Would Sarah be so kind as to call Sammy on your behalf? And if not, could you mention Sarah's name and Marvin's interest when you called Sammy?

This tactic can work for actors as well as writers. If you're an actor, for example, you'll need to get to know casting directors (who recommend actors to directors and producers). Perhaps you'll meet them at an industry seminar or a reading (in Hollywood you can pay to read for prominent casting people—a practice the Screen Actors Guild abhors but some actors find useful). If you can, try to talk privately with the casting person and ask for his suggestions about who would be a good talent agent for you. Then call that agent, saying the casting person spoke highly of the agency and referred you to her. Your two magic words are the casting agent's name.

An even more common way for actors to get agents is to take a good class and get referrals from the class teacher and the other students. And tell everyone you know that you're looking for an agent. You'll get referrals, and maybe even some Godfather Calls.

DO FILM EDITORS, PRODUCTION DESIGNERS, AND CINEMATOGRAPHERS NEED AGENTS TOO?

These days, every important creative category in Hollywood seems to have its agents. Even cinematographers, assistant directors, production designers, costume designers, and film editors now have representatives like all the other serious talents in the business. And many producers (especially line producers and unit production managers) have agents too. Even creative producers often make special deals with agencies that help them put their projects together and sell them.

In putting together your agent hit list for the below-the-line crafts, you may want to consult an industry Who's Who, like the *Cinematographers, Production Designers, Costume Designers and Film Editors Guide,* to see what agencies are listed as contact addresses for your heroes. Call each agency and ask for the name of the agent who represents the talent in question. If there is no agency listed in the publication, call the appropriate guild and ask who the talent's agent is.

IS ANY AGENT BETTER THAN NO AGENT?

My opinion: yes (especially at the beginning of your career). A lawyer can be an effective substitute later on, when you're well known and work comes to you effortlessly, but for most people, an agent is a credential that proves your legitimacy. Having an agent says you're in the game.

If, in spite of all your best efforts, the only agent you can get to sign you is Louie Loser, who operates out of a hole in the wall on Hollywood Boulevard, you may decide to go for it—if he's on the SAG, WGA, or DGA list. Just don't expect him to be effective. You'll have to do all the work and, if you can prop him up, use him to make the closing call and collect the money. (Have your lawyer look over any contracts, of course.)

Why is he worth his ten percent to you? Because people without agents are looked down on in Hollywood, and Lou is your starter agent. When people ask you, "Do you have an agent?" you can answer yes. They may groan when you mention Lou's name, but that's OK. If they take pity on you, ask them to call an agent they know and see if that person will take you on. (Even if you signed with Lou, if he hasn't gotten you any work within a certain time period, guild rules may entitle you to break that contract.)

Just as it's easier to get a job when you're already employed, it's easier to get an agent if you've already got one. Most agents, like Sammy, would rather steal someone from another agent than take on an unrepresented novice. After all, if an agent has seen your work and thinks enough of it to represent you, it's a vote of confidence—even from a loser like Lou. It's better than nothing.

If an agent like Lou sounds just too awful, think about romancing an agent trainee who will hopefully take you on when she makes agent. In the meantime, she may be able to help you with information and advice and if a deal looks imminent, she might be able to talk her boss into closing it for you, making you a sort of de facto "pocket client."

New agents are a mixed blessing, however. Although they haven't yet lost their idealism, are open to new talent, and are still excited about the whole process, they don't yet know the game the way the experienced players do, and can make serious boo-boos.

HOW TO USE YOUR AGENT TO CREATE WORK

Notice that I didn't say, "How to get your agent to get you work." That's your job. You're just going to use your agent to help you make contacts and close the deal.

At a Directors Guild seminar I taught last year, director Michael Schroeder recommended that a client approach his agent the way he approaches God: "Pray like it depends on God; work like it depends on you."

I always advise my clients—especially clients who aren't yet successful enough to be with powerful agents—to expect nothing from their agent and be pleasantly surprised when he picks up the phone on your behalf. Let go of your fantasies that Sammy will actually get you work. Assume you'll have to do it all yourself and you won't be disappointed or join the legions of losers who hang out in bars beefing about their agents.

So why do you need an agent if he's not going to get you work? You need him not only as a credential but also for his information and network of contacts. All the years that Sammy's been out there shmoozing and spying are incredibly valuable to you. Sammy knows who's who, who's doing what to whom, and who's buying. He knows where the bodies are buried. When you give him ten percent you're paying him for that knowledge and those contacts.

USE YOUR AGENT'S CONTACTS

The first step is to make it easy and convenient for Sammy to advise you and make phone calls for you. Above all, don't whine and don't waste his time.

Make it your job to learn everything about your agent that you can. Make sure you know who else he represents. (Hopefully you did this research before you chose him. If not, your network, the trades, the guilds, and the entertainment industry libraries are your best sources of this information.)

Romance Zoe. You'll probably be talking with her five times more frequently than you talk with Sammy, so make her your new best friend. She, like many agents' assistants, may one day be an agent herself. Draw her out. Listen to her tales of woe and pay close attention when she tells you about Sammy's idiosyncracies, hobbies, other clients, contacts, habits, and schedule.

When is the best time to talk to Sammy? One agent I worked with sometimes liked to stay in her office during lunch and eat her sandwich at the desk (very unusual behavior for an agent!). I found it very effective to call her assistant in the late morning and see if she would mind if I dropped by for five minutes just after noon. She often said yes and we had some very productive impromptu lunch meetings.

Observe your agent's style. Some agents are all business and others like to shmooze. Some enjoy a good joke, and others want to talk about the Lakers game. Know your agent. Talk to him in a way he can understand and relate to.

MAKE IT EASY FOR YOUR AGENT TO TAKE ACTION ON YOUR BEHALF

Before you meet with Sammy, prepare a list of items you want to discuss and specific things you'd like him to do for you. The operative word here is "specific." Don't just say you need work. Express enthusiasm for getting involved with a particular person or project or company. For example, you may want to tell Sammy the title, logline, and movie cross on your new spec screenplay and ask him who he thinks might spark to something like this.

And don't just wait for Sammy to come up with ideas. Tell him that you heard that Helen Hustler is looking for action comedies and does he think that your project might be right for Helen? If his contact with Helen is good, he may bite. If he sounds reticent, it may be that he had a screaming fight with Helen at Morton's last Monday night. Let it pass. Find another way to get to Helen.

Once he agrees to call someone, reinforce this by telling him you're thrilled that he'll be calling Marvin Mogul (or whomever he's agreed to contact) on your behalf.

And to further reinforce this promised action, talk to Zoe on your way out of the office. Tell her that you're delighted Sammy will be calling Marvin about your new screenplay, because by the time you're out of the door Sammy may well have forgotten he was going to do so. Also, when you call in a few days to find out if Marvin has any interest, Zoe will know what the hell you're talking about.

Working with your agent can be an enjoyable process—like brainstorming with a very well-connected friend. Hopefully together you'll come up with two or three people Sammy agrees to call on your behalf. You'll have to stay on him, of course, to get him to actually follow through. He's got a million other things to do, and lots of other clients. How can you keep your needs fresh in his mind?

Well, we're back to being a nice nudge. Go to the office frequently to say hi, but don't be a pest. Always have a reason, and don't overstay your welcome. Continue to romance your agent and your agent's assistant. Treat them like the valuable resource they are. Demonstrate your enthusiasm. Be as good a client as Peter Playwright is, and Sammy will remember to call Marvin to tell him about your new project.

BE A GOOD CLIENT

Agents really appreciate clients who do their homework and who don't waste their time. They respect someone who's enough of an industry pro to know how to use agents effectively and who charmingly makes it easy for agents to do their job: to make the calls that count and to close deals.

A good client also has to regularly provide the agent with something new to sell. If you're a writer, keep writing more and more material. If you're a director, direct theater, commercials, music videos, magazine segments, industrials, a showcase project. If you're an actor, work hard in class, get to know casting people, get a role in a play, do whatever it takes to get some tape on yourself.

SELL TO YOUR AGENT

Some misguided clients think that once the marriage with their agent has been consummated, they can get away with not brushing their teeth in the morning and with putting on ten pounds. No way.

When you talk to your agent, be on your best behavior. Sharing too much discouragement or negativity can cloud your relationship. It's your job to pump up your agent on your talent and projects, to express enthusiasm, excitement and passion for your work, to tell good stories, and to feed your agent good material and good lines to sell you with.

Always act as though you're still dating and the relationship will stay sweet.

HOW OFTEN SHOULD YOU CONTACT YOUR AGENT?

Contact your agent as often as he'll tolerate. Find reasons, pretexts, or occasions to get face-to-face with your agent as often as possible. "Out of sight, out of mind" was never more true. Some clients make a regular practice of dropping by the agent's office to deliver a script, an invitation, a present, good news . . . or just to say hello because they were "in the neighborhood."

Also, talk with your agent about how frequently it's appropriate to call, and make sure you do. Most clients undercontact their agents. They're afraid of being too aggressive (to an agent there's no such thing!) or a pest. You don't want to go overboard, but it's important to be a squeaky wheel. Otherwise you're liable to be forgotten or eclipsed in the agent's mind by more assertive clients (or clients with assertive managers).

SHOULDN'T AGENTS BE MORE SERVICE-ORIENTED?

Yes, agents should be service-oriented. But most haven't yet caught up with the nineties' trend of selling service. A few agents are ahead of the pack, focusing on building lasting relationships with both buyers and clients whom they treat like gold. May their kind multiply.

WHEN SHOULD I LEAVE MY AGENT?

Some industry people believe that you should change agents every two years if you've exhausted their contacts. I think that's a bit drastic. Stay with an agent as long as it's working and you're working. If the periods of unemployment seem to be growing rather than shrinking, then it's time to discreetly begin the search for a new agent.

When you leave, try not to burn bridges. Don't beat up on your agent for all the things she didn't do for you. Just keep it impersonal and friendly—"The time seems right for a change." Thank her for all she's done for you (even if it's been precious little) and say good-bye. Even after you've moved on, touch base every once in a while. Be friendly. Call on a birthday. Send a note if you see something in the trades about an accomplishment. You never know when you might need your former agent again.

SHOULD I BECOME AN AGENT?

After reading my description of the daily life of Sammy Slick, you may be surprised that I believe agenting can be an excellent career for people who have natural sales talent. It's exciting work in an exciting business.

There are different kinds of agents: talent agents (who represent performers), music agents, voice-over agents, literary agents (film or TV), so-called packaging agents who put together the elements for a TV show or feature (sometimes including the financing), and, as we've seen, there are agents who specialize in representing directors, cinematographers, film editors—you name it.

Even if you don't see agenting as the right life-long job for you, a few years as an agent is terrific training ground for a career as a creative producer or studio executive. You'll get a behind-the-scenes, hands-on education in how to get a project made. You'll learn the business from the inside out and get to know the most important players.

An over-40 agent told me about another benefit of agenting: it's one of the few careers in the entertainment industry where one can enjoy a fairly stable, lucrative job and grow old somewhat gracefully. Heads of studios come and go; directors seldom sustain a hot career for over a decade; but agents can wield power for half a century. Senior partners in agencies are often wealthy, respected industry figures. Many of them have been with their agencies since they started in the business many years ago—an amazing record of stable employment in this business. Some of these senior agents, like the famous Swifty Lazar of Oscar-party fame, keep going well into their eighties.

16
☆

Managers, Lawyers, Publicists, and Headhunters

★ ★ ★ ★ ★ ★ ★ ★ ★ ★ ★ ★ ★ ★ ★

WHO NEEDS 'EM?

THE PERSONAL MANAGER

If you have an agent (who usually takes 10 percent of your paycheck) why do you need a manager (who, being unregulated by the state, can often take 15 percent or more of your income)? If your agent is really good and you have a trustworthy lawyer, you may not need a manager at all. After all, 25 percent of your income is a lot to shell out.

But managers do have their uses. A good manager is like a well-connected career coach. Although you may change agents every few years, you'll hopefully be with your manager for a long time, and she will give you advice about good, long-range career moves and strategies—and then help you implement those strategies. She will introduce you to the people you need to meet and will help you get the right support folks (agent, lawyer, publicist, business manager) around you as you become more successful. In fact, a good manager may get you set up at a better agency and will stay on your agent to make sure your agent takes action on your behalf.

For this and many other reasons, some agents don't like managers. They may worry that managers sometimes use their hot clients to further their own producing careers (and, indeed, a number of managers do become producers by helping star talent put together projects, which state-regulated agents cannot do). Managers counter these arguments by saying that agents are short-sighted and think only of the immediate 10 percent commission they can earn, not the long-range career benefits of any particular job or project. Managers also point out that agents represent many talents (some in competition with each other), while a manager represents just a few and can thus give more personal care and attention to each client.

Personal manager Ron Kramer, whose clients include Charlene Tilton ("Dallas"), Christina Pickles ("St. Elsewhere"), Nicholas Walker ("One Life to Live"), and actress C.C.H. Pounder *(Bagdad Cafe, Robocop III)*, explains the function of the manager this way: "Many agencies have far more clients than they really have the right to represent. An agency may have a couple of hundred clients, and there's just no way they can be on top of it all the time." (In contrast, a typical manager may have eight to ten clients.) "The agency ends up gravitating to those whom the producers and casting directors already want and those who earn the lion's share of the income for the agencies. Many other clients who aren't as prominent or who are in the beginning stages of their careers don't get the opportunities because agents are too busy working for those who are going to generate immediate dollars.

"There are certainly agents who are creative and will work with young talent or midcareer talent looking to move to a higher level, but that is, unfortunately, not the norm. The manager can create the squeaky wheel syndrome. In many instances I must call the agent and insist they get a client in on a project. They may have been aware of the project but, because of the enormous amount of talent they represent, they may not have pushed as hard for my client.

"I also make them aware that there are Caucasian roles that may be appropriate for a client who is Hispanic, Asian, or Black, or opportunities to cast a female in a male role, or vice versa. If you give creative input, it can help a client be seen for a role they might not otherwise have been considered for.

"In many instances I as the manager, in tandem with the agent, may speak to casting directors. I will often take it upon myself to call the director or producer. It just adds a little more substance. If a manager calls, it's a special call and the client seems to get a little more consideration."

WHY MANAGERS' CLIENTS SOMETIMES GET MORE ATTENTION FROM THEIR AGENTS THAN UNMANAGED CLIENTS

To understand the possible importance of a manager to a client's career, consider the following hypothetical example: actress Brenda Beautiful is a client of talent agent Monica Maven at one of the big agencies. Brenda and two of Monica's other clients have powerful Sidney Shmoozer as their personal manager. Sidney also manages two writer-directors who are with other agents at the same agency.

Monica represents fifty actors. Sidney has a stable of eight performers and four writer-directors. Monica doesn't particularly like Sidney, but she is aware of his power at her agency and around town. She knows that he's a serious, long-time player and that he'll probably continue to be a player for many years to come. She knows who his clients are and what agencies he has placed them with. It would be a major feather in Monica's cap if she could steal Sidney's biggest client, hot young thing Tommy Talent, from CAA. To that end she likes to keep her relationship with Sidney sweet. When a role comes up that Brenda might be right for, Sidney is on the phone to Monica.

Monica has a choice: she can push Brenda for the role or she can push five of her other clients who aren't managed by Sidney.

Guess who gets Monica's best efforts?

THE JULIA ROBERTS STORY: MANAGERS SOMETIMES SHAPE CAREERS

Julia Roberts's first show business representative was manager Bob McGowan. He suggested that she get rid of her thick Southern accent and take acting lessons. According to the *Los Angeles Times*, McGowan then used chutzpah tactics to bring her to the attention of agents. To land her a role in a movie about an all-girl rock band he told the casting director that she was a musician and then enrolled her in a crash course in the drums, "the easiest instrument to learn." She got the part and met producer Alan Greisman, the husband of Sally Field, who was influential in getting Roberts into *Steel Magnolias*. And McGowan got her an agent by offering the William Morris Agency 10 percent of the deal if they signed her.

The rest, as they say, is history.

CHOOSING A MANAGER

When looking for a manager, try to find someone who is savvy about the business and fairly well-connected, although he or she doesn't have to be a superstar manager like Sidney—especially if you're not yet a superstar talent. A creative, strategic mind is even more important in a manager than an agent. And look for a responsible, honest, and reliable person who is extroverted enough to be able to shmooze and do business with players. Emotional supportiveness is a plus (much more so than for an agent), because the two of you will probably spend a lot of time together. A good manager may well become a business friend, if not a personal friend. He will be a combination of coach, priest, cheerleader, parent, shrink, military strategist, executive producer, matchmaker, and nanny.

As you begin to become successful, the question of whether to get a manager will probably become more urgent. Talk it over with friends, advisers, and mentors. Learn about other peoples' experiences with managers. Carefully weigh the pros and cons of having a manager at this stage of your career, and research the background of any particular person you are considering. Be cautious—because they are unlicensed, personal managers range from honestly superb all the way to totally unscrupulous.

If you decide to work with a manager, consult with your lawyer before signing any contract. Your lawyer will probably advise you to sign with a manager for the shortest possible period (perhaps a year) so that you will have the opportunity to assess your progress with the manager without obligation. The rule of thumb: your manager (or your agent, for that matter) should be able to raise your income by at least the percentage that you're paying her. For example, if she takes 15 percent of your income, she should be able to raise your income by at least that amount for the arrangement to be worthwhile to all concerned.

THE BUSINESS MANAGER

Unlike the personal manager, the business manager handles your money for you (once you begin to make some!). But be extremely careful about letting someone control your funds and assets. A number of Hollywood people have been badly burned by dishonest business managers. Before turning your money over to a business manager, consult with a certified public accountant for further advice. You may also want to speak with your lawyer.

THE LAWYER

I believe that everyone in the entertainment industry should have a good show business lawyer whom they can hire for advice and deal-making expertise when needed.

Neither an agent nor a manager is a substitute for a lawyer. Agents negotiate deals, but not always well. It's nice to be able to run contracts by your lawyer, although agents often believe that lawyers can be nit-picking deal-killers if you don't watch them carefully.

The nice thing about many lawyers is that you can usually rent them by the hour (except for the star lawyers who won't take you on even if you do pay their outrageous fees). And some lawyers will work "on spec," taking a percentage of your earnings—but only if you work regularly. When you first come to Hollywood and don't yet have an agent, get a lawyer. Producers may agree to read your agentless script, for example, if you have an entertainment industry lawyer submit it on your behalf.

Don't begrudge the money for a brief initial meeting with your lawyer. It's important to build a positive relationship with this important career support person, and the advice she gives you may save you a lot of grief. Sometimes lawyers will even refer you to buyers or other career support professionals.

To find the right lawyer for your specific needs, nudge your network. Find out if any of your contacts have entertainment industry lawyers and what their experience with them has been. If you're referred to a lawyer you hear good things about, ask your friend to make a Godfather or Godmother Call to sweeten the introduction.

If you strike out with your network, you may want to contact the following referral services: the Beverly Hills Bar Association, the West Hollywood Bar Association, and the Los Angeles County Bar Association. Don't forget to specify that you're looking for an attorney who specializes in entertainment law.

PUBLICISTS: TOOT YOUR OWN HORN—OR HIRE SOMEONE TO TOOT IT FOR YOU

Veteran Hollywood public relations consultant Bill Barron believes that a good PR campaign is an integral part of creating a positive "job climate" for yourself. "This town is pretty unique," he says. "Unless you have recognition and mention in certain publications and columns, Hollywood people don't know you're alive. They figure you're either dead or in Europe."

But, he warns, a "good sound PR campaign has to be based on truth and reality. There's got to be a lot of integrity involved with it or you're doing yourself a terrible disservice. The days of pure flackery are gone. You can't get out there with a lot of baloney. You have to deal with hard news, facts. You have to be aware of where you fit into the total Hollywood news picture. Are you worth a word, a sentence, a picture? Just because somebody else has it doesn't mean you qualify."

Professional publicists will be well enough connected at the trades to give you the best possible shot at coverage, but you have to have something for them to toot the horn about—something truly newsworthy about you or your project.

Barron points out that the marketplace is very, very small. The trades, which are read religiously by everyone in Hollywood every day, each have a circulation of approximately 20,000 people, of which Barron estimates that half are out-of-work actors or others seeking work. "Our industry is pretty much a cottage industry, with very few [key] people. You have to target the specific opinion makers you want to be aware of you: the networks? studio heads? casting directors?"

Professional Hollywood PR guidance isn't cheap. The lowest fees in town are approximately $2,500 a month, plus expenses. A typical producer, director, or actor might pay a $5,000-a-month fee to his or her publicist. New publicists might be able to cut a special deal with you or consult with you on an hourly rate.

Barron has a few tips for people who can't yet afford to put a public relations consultant on retainer:

★ Write a good biography on yourself, "short and to the point," which includes your major achievements plus interesting material on your background. (Some Hollywood job seekers use this bio in lieu of a resume in certain circumstances.)

★ Even if you aren't an actor, have some good 8″ × 10″ black-and-white stills of yourself available for the media.

★ If you're working on a TV show or feature, meet the still photographer attached to the project and, if possible, get some stills of you working.

★ While you're working, take the time to meet with the publicist connected with your show, company, or network. Be prepared to provide newsworthy tidbits about yourself that might be used when promoting the project or film. Offer to be cooperative and available. Provide your bio and stills if your publicist needs them.

★ If you're arranging a screening for your showcase film or a performance of your theater production, in addition to the usual industry presentations, consider special nights when you invite a group of people related to the topic of your project. For example, if your project is about fire fighting, hold a special event for fire fighters and alert the nonindustrial press. Sometimes you can bring yourself to the attention of the industry through good coverage in the general media.

★ Don't wait until you've completed your film to think about bringing a publicist on board. Consult a PR person early in the process of putting together your project, so she can make sure that you'll have everything you need for maximum media coverage— good stories, clever press angles, useful still photographs, newsworthy interviews.

★ Learn how to give a good interview. Remember that your purpose is to create a "want to see" attitude in your audience. If you don't have a professional publicist to set up the interview for you and to lay the groundwork with the media about what will and will not be covered, it's especially important to stay on track and not ramble on about irrelevant subjects.

Some additional do-it-yourself advice I would add to Barron's: gain visibility in the Hollywood community by becoming active in one or two entertainment industry organizations; run for office; moderate panel discussions; produce seminars and events; write articles for newsletters. The chapter on shmoozing gives you some ideas on how to get involved.

THE KEYS TO HOLLYWOOD PR: AWARENESS, INTEREST, ANTICIPATION

Barron emphasizes the three goals of entertainment industry publicity: awareness, interest, and anticipation.

The classic show business campaign was, of course, *Gone with the Wind*. It started with the purchase of the novel, for what was then considered an astronomical price. Then came the two-year talent search for Scarlett O'Hara, followed by the much-publicized screen tests of Hollywood's biggest stars. By the time the picture came out, the public was so involved in the production they almost felt that it was their own film.

This campaign admirably met the three criteria: awareness (was there anyone in America who hadn't heard of the novel or the search for Scarlett?), interest, and anticipation. The payoff at the box office was extraordinary.

When you think of your own personal PR, apply the same criteria. Build awareness of your name and your special talents, interest in your activities, and positive anticipation—the desire to work with you.

EXECUTIVE RECRUITERS

Agents, managers, lawyers, and publicists are people you hire. They work for you. Executive recruiters, on the other hand, don't work for you—they work for companies who may need you. In this sense, they are very different from the entertainment industry employment agencies that place temps and assistants.

The emergence of executive recruiting firms that specialize in finding high-level employees for entertainment industry corporations is a relatively new phenomenon in show business. Until recently the "old boys network" was the predominant method of finding executive talent in Hollywood. After all, it's a small industry, and people felt that they knew everybody who was anybody, so why pay a recruiter when you could call up old Joe or Manny and ask him who was available? But as Hollywood becomes more corporate and more global, with giant firms taking over most of the studios, the customs of international business life are finally catching up with Tinseltown.

The executive recruiter firms are hired on a retainer or contingency basis by an employer to find the perfect employee for a particular job. Retainer firms are paid a fee for doing an exhaustive search, whether or not they find an applicant who is hired. Contingency firms work on a speculative basis, being paid only if the company hires one of their applicants. Retainer firms feel that they're a notch or two above the contingency firms.

What does all this mean for you? If you're already employed in an over-$60,000-a-year job and have a fair amount of visibility in your field, you may be one of the lucky people who are contacted every year by executive search firms. Search firms are looking for proven winners with an impressive track record in exactly the area needed by the employer. It's ironic that executive recruiters are usually looking for people who have the least, not the most, need of their matchmaking services!

Search firms usually have a "Don't call us, we'll call you" attitude, but many will accept resumes from people with impressive credentials in an area they do searches in. Your resume will be kept on file in case the firm lands an assignment to find someone with your background, skills, and experience. Traditionally, they have focused on business, financial, legal, and technical positions, but now they deal with creative executives and even on-camera talent (primarily in TV news) as well.

They're professional connecters and networkers, just like agents. They're gold mines of information.

You may be ready for an executive recruiter sooner than you think. And once you have a few years of solid achievement and visibility under your belt, it will be time to contact them if they haven't contacted you.

Using your networking and shmoozing talents, find a way to meet a few recruiters—at a seminar where they're speaking, at a luncheon arranged by a friend, whatever. Let them get to know you. Ask their advice. Update them on your activities. They like to keep up on the up-and-comers around town. A note of caution: if a so-called head-hunter tries to charge you a fee for doing your resume or placing you, this person is not the genuine article. True executive recruiters are paid by the employer, not the employee.

17

☆

Crossover Moves and Midcareer Crises

★ ★ ★ ★ ★ ★ ★ ★ ★ ★ ★ ★ ★ ★

BETH BOHN: A WEALTH OF TRANSFERRABLE SKILLS

I met Beth Bohn at a "Career Crossover" seminar I taught at the Academy of Television Arts and Sciences in 1989. Beth was a successful district sales manager for Avon cosmetics with an impressive record of achievement. She had increased sales in her district by 31 percent and had raised the number of distributors from 135 to 210 in less than a year on the job. She had also worked as a corporate sales trainer for Avon and as telephone sales manager and territory sales manager for the Sweetheart Cup Corporation, where she was responsible for $100,000 in sales from new accounts.

Beth was hoping to transfer into the entertainment industry. She is wonderfully extroverted and enthusiastic, and an incredibly diligent worker. She has energy to spare and a "big personality." But that was the problem. In "straight" industries, people with dramatic, entertaining, larger-than-life personalities can sometimes have problems. They're seen as a little "too too"; they somehow don't fit the corporate mold. They're a little too free-spirited, too entertaining, and too spontaneous for the comfort of their colleagues.

But Beth's customers loved her. They got a kick out of her—she made them laugh. And she made them buy! Her sales track record was extraordinary.

Beth wanted to meet privately with me. She had a question: did I think she'd fit into the entertainment industry? I knew that people in Hollywood would absolutely adore her.

We went over her strengths. Beth is terrific both on the phone and in person. She has an uncanny ability to make you her best friend in thirty seconds. And it's totally sincere. Her energy is inexhaustible. She can meet with and talk to hundreds of people a day and still be her normal, bouncy self. She also loves television. And reading.

I didn't have to think too hard to come up with my suggestion: what about becoming a TV literary agent and packager? We mapped out a plan. Beth knew she'd have to "pay some dues" as an agent trainee before becoming a full-fledged agent. Because she is in her thirties, she decided not to go the mail room route at a major agency but to join a small, boutique agency where she could be an experienced agent's right arm.

And that's just what happened. After brief stints as an assistant at The Agency and The Irv Schechter Agency, Beth became an agent trainee. She's now an agent with Cindy Turtle of the The Turtle Agency. Every day she works with Cindy, meeting with writers, reading scripts, doing lunch, attending readings, pitching at CBS and NBC, and shmoozing on the phone with industry buyers.

She loves Hollywood. And Hollywood loves her.

CROSSOVER MOVES

How possible is it to transfer into the entertainment industry from another field? You can do it *if*—like Beth Bohn—you can answer yes to most of the following questions:

★ **Do you have talents, skills, and experience that the industry needs?** If you've done the exercises at the beginning of this book, you're probably ready to answer this question.

★ **Will your personality fit well into the Hollywood culture?** If you're intelligent, creative, entertaining, fun-loving, talented, and imaginative, you'll fit right in. If you have a little dramatic flair to your personality, all the better.

★ **Have you done your homework, attending industry seminars, reading books, getting advice so you really understand the business and know where**

you might fit in? You're reading this book, so you've already got a head start on this question.

★ **Are you OK with the fact that your crossover move may mean a temporary cut in status and pay. Could you handle that?** When you put together your Hollywood Pitch and your resume, be prepared to show how your current skills and background will benefit an entertainment industry employer. If you're lucky and smart and a good self-marketer, you may be able to cross over at your current level or even higher. But it's also possible that you'll have to take a short step backward until you learn all you need to know about the business.

★ **Are you ready to "pay some dues" in your new field?** Just because you're a hot shot in another field doesn't always mean that Hollywood will welcome you with open arms. You may still have to earn your way in, working long hours under tough conditions. If you relax and don't develop an attitude about it, paying your dues will be the best education you've ever had.

★ **Are you willing to move to where the action is?** This is often a conversation stopper. Many people take a big gulp at the thought of uprooting their whole life and their families to move to Hollywood.

DO I *HAVE* TO MOVE TO L.A.?

This is a tough question for anyone seriously interested in a successful career in the entertainment industry. Here's my advice:

1. *Don't move to L.A. until you've exhausted local opportunities and resources.* This may never happen, especially if you're interested in areas other than network TV and studio feature films. You may find success in independent features, local television, news, commercials, and documentaries right in your own back yard. Perhaps that success will bring you to the attention of Hollywood powers that be. Then you'll have a decision to make.

In the meantime, join all the local film organizations and meet everyone you can. Check your state film commission for information on what out-of-town films are shooting in your area. Meet those folks too. Many of your local and on-location Hollywood contacts will stand you in good stead if and when you go to L.A.

2. *Don't move to L.A. until you're good enough to compete with talent from around the world.* It's often better to be a big fish in a smaller pond than an unemployed fish in the big-time shark tank.

3. *Try being the "star from afar."* It's amazing how many Hollywood people will agree to meet with you if you call long-distance and say, "I'm flying into town next week for a few days and would like to meet with you." If you lived in Burbank, no one would even take your call!

You can swan into town and do the rounds, taking meetings and dropping off projects or pictures. The problem is that very few people sell a script or get work from just one meeting. You have to be able to stick around for second and third meetings for a "Hollywood Sniffing" until folks trust you enough to say yes to you. Sooner or later, you'll need to make the move.

4. *Don't move to L.A. without weighing the personal, financial, and family costs.* If your loved ones threaten to leave you if you decamp to the Big Orange . . . if you don't have a financial nest egg to cushion you during the months and months of meetings and unemployment before you get work or sell a project . . . if you haven't yet written at least three spec scripts . . . if the thought of living in the Urban Jungle or the Smoggy City makes your creative juices dry up . . . WAIT AND THINK TWICE!

5. *Be bi-urban.* It's tough, but I know a few people who have made it work. Producer Sam Grogg, for instance, started out in Texas as the head of FilmDallas, which was involved in producing specialty films like *Kiss of the Spider Woman*, *Choose Me*, and *The Trip to Bountiful*. Now he's teamed up with John Dykstra, the Oscar-winning special effects wizard best known for his work on *Star Wars*, at Magic Pictures. Magic has offices in both L.A. and Dallas, where Grogg lives. Texas is a "right-to-work" (no obligatory unions) state and Grogg believes that his company has the best of both worlds—the L.A. contact with industry power players and creative talent; and the "top-drawer creative and below-the-line" people in Texas.

To function effectively in two locations, you'll need a number of indispensable items: enough cash flow to cover frequent plane trips back and forth and L.A. friends who'll let you crash on their sofa and use their phone and mailing address. Hometown friends who have moved to the city are great for this. *Really* good friends might also allow you to set up an additional phone in their house with an answering machine or automatic call forwarding to your out-of-town number. If your friends don't want to forward your mail, rent an inexpensive post office box with a nice address and pay the post office to forward the mail. Some job hunters have told me that putting an L.A. address or phone number on resumes and cards is much more effective than using a hometown address.

WHEN YOU MOVE TO L.A., BRING FRIENDS!

Busy actor Noble Willingham (*The Last Boy Scout, City Slickers, Good Morning, Vietnam*) has some advice for people thinking of moving to Hollywood: "Don't come out here unless you really have to. It's hard to get work. But if you come, bring some money—and a friend or two. Hollywood doesn't lend itself to making friends. And know who you are and how to find work before you come. You won't find your real identity in Hollywood."

Set dresser Jim Marchwick came to Hollywood with a dozen friends. Jim and his buddies all went to film school at Montana State in Bozeman. They knew it would be tough to make it in Hollywood, so they made a pact—they'd all move to L.A. and help each other make it. "We knew we didn't have the nepotism factor going for us, so we had to collude," says Jim. And that's what the friends did. When one would land a gig, he or she would help the others get hired on the project if possible. Jim started out as a production assistant, moved up to carpenter, and then set dresser. Now he's a lead man (head set dresser).

HOW JOHN JORDAN CROSSED OVER FROM PR TO DEVELOPMENT

Twenty-seven-year-old John Jordan grew up in a small town in upstate New York. His mom is a secretary at the local junior high school and his dad works in marketing at a Fortune 500 company.

"When you announce at fifteen that you're going to make films in Hollywood," John says, "people look at you funny."

He heard that writing a screenplay was the best way in, so he got a degree in screenwriting at Syracuse University and completed a few scripts. But at twenty-one he realized that he "didn't have a lot to say" as a screenwriter and that he wouldn't be able to compete in this arena. He'd always liked writing on the school paper, however, so he thought about public relations.

John heard a lot of horror stories about Hollywood from film school grads, so he decided to go to New York instead. He did PR for Tri-Star, for famed show business publicity firm PMK, and for *Rolling Stone* magazine. But he still hadn't given up his dream of making movies in Hollywood. He thought that perhaps he could parlay his *Rolling Stone* experience into a development job. "This is a creative business and it takes a creative person to figure out how to get into it," he says.

John made a few exploratory trips to L.A. and found that, as he had predicted, TV producers were indeed eager to meet with him because he had advance knowledge of upcoming *Rolling Stone* stories, which are often seen as excellent raw material for movies. Encouraged, he loaded his belongings into a U-haul and moved to town. But when he hit L.A., reality set in. He had no job interviews for a whole month.

Finally he signed up at a temp agency. He told the agency he wanted to work for a top producer in a busy, action-oriented office. As luck would have it, a high-powered executive producer at Spectacor Films (which made "The Highjack of the Achille Lauro" for NBC and "The Preppy Murder" for ABC) needed a new assistant. The agency helped John rewrite his resume to tone down his managerial background and highlight his typing skills. He got the job.

Today John is manager of development for TV movies at Spectacor. He works at turning true stories, books, and spec screenplays into highly rated programs. He's currently working on the true-life "fatal attraction" tale of a schoolteacher who murdered her lover. He adores his job and is glad he crossed over from PR.

THE SECRETS OF A SUCCESSFUL CROSSOVER

★ **Establish a track record of success in your present field.** Hollywood respects winners in any area.

★ **Try not to cross over geographically and occupationally at the same time.** When you're totally frustrated with your present job, it's very tempting to chuck it and move to L.A. to start a new life. There are things to be said for this drastic approach. No one knows you in your previous incarnation, so you don't have to buck the typecasting and pigeonholing. The downside is that, like John Jordan, you may hit town and find no immediate offers except temp work. It might be easier to make your move to L.A. in your present non-show-business occupation and *then* scout around for industry jobs. That way you'll have a steady income, which will save you from committing one of the two Hollywood sins: being desperate.

★ **Don't be too quick to throw out the baby with the bathwater.** If at all possible, use your current occupation to leverage yourself step by step into your dream job. Even if you hate law or accounting or sales or insurance or whatever else you've been doing, it may make sense to break into the industry by parlaying that skill into steady industry employment at a nonclerical pay rate before crossing over into your target occupation. You can learn a lot doing entertainment law, business affairs, production accounting, distribution sales, or production insurance that will come in handy once you're ready to make the next move. Yes, you may get pigeonholed, but as you'll see in the next section, clever marketing can help you overcome that problem. And in the meantime, you'll avoid the necessity of competing with the thousands of entry-level people who want to do industry temp work, production assisting, or gophering.

WHAT IF YOU'RE STUCK IN THE WRONG ENTERTAINMENT INDUSTRY JOB?

Sometimes your dreams can get lost somewhere along the road to Hollywood success.

One of my clients who wanted to be a director found himself trapped at midcareer in a lucrative position as a gonzo unit production manager. He worked on the big Hollywood features. Everyone loved him. But he hadn't even taken the time to make a showcase film, and his creative needs were not being met by his present job.

Another client was dissuaded from pursuing her dream by pressure from family and friends. They convinced her that it would be more "practical" to pursue film editing than on-location production work. And this is a woman who feels "cooped up" when she's confined to one place for a long time!

For both of them, it was time to take their dreams out of mothballs and to launch a crossover campaign.

PREPARING YOURSELF FOR THE CROSSOVER CAMPAIGN

It's important to make peace with yourself over how your career has gone up until now. Forgive yourself and other people for any "mistakes" you feel have been made. And give yourself credit for all you've learned and achieved in the entertainment industry so far. Add up your *transferrable assets*:

★ your knowledge of the industry

★ what you've learned about audiences

★ what you've learned about film and television making

★ any special knowledge and know-how you've acquired

★ what you've learned about storytelling

★ contacts you've made

★ your current reputation—the number of people who know who you are and what you can accomplish in your present field

★ personal and professional development and achievements

"BEFORE" AND "AFTER" SHOTS: HOW THEY SEE YOU VS. HOW YOU WANT THEM TO SEE YOU

How would most people in the industry currently describe you? This is your "before" shot. Your "after" shot is how you'd *like* them to perceive you. To bridge the gap, redo your Hollywood Pitch to convince people that what you have been doing (your "before" shot) is the perfect background for what you want to do next (your "after" shot).

Now you're ready to make some crossover moves. Does Hollywood see you as a lover-boy soap actor rather than a director who specializes in powerful, emotional drama? Start directing gut-wrenching small-theater productions and send out thousands of eye-catching invitations and hundreds of punchy press releases. Invite all your industry contacts to see your show. Lobby important decision makers, agents, studio and network types. Teach a directing class for underprivileged high school students and make sure the powers that be hear about it.

Hollywood knows you as "good old dependable Jessica, the production manager to call on a really tough show." If you'd like them to see you as "that hysterically funny sitcom writer, wacky Jessica," start by writing yourself some routines and practice them on the set. Pretty soon it's "good old dependable Jessica who's also a very funny lady." And there's no substitute for going home and applying your rear to the chair and writing a script, or two, or ten. Then look for opportunities on the set or through your contacts to show your stuff. Every chance you get, let people know who you really are, what you're doing, and what you're aiming for. If *you* believe it, pretty soon *they'll* believe it and the word will get around.

IRENE NACHREINER'S "BEFORE" AND "AFTER" SHOTS: CROSSING OVER FROM VIDEOTAPE EDITING TO SCREENWRITING

Here is budding screenwriter Irene Nachreiner's story about some of the moves she's been making to cross over from videotape editing to television scriptwriting:

"After spending eight years locked up in the video tape dungeon at CBS, I realized that if I was ever going to change careers from technical to writing, I needed a broader base of contacts. The problem was: how? I didn't know any writers. I didn't know any producers. All I knew were guys with plastic pocket protectors who loved looking at oscilloscopes all day.

"Since I was already a member of the Academy of Television Arts and Sciences through my credits as a videotape editor, I thought I would start there. I volunteered my services to the Activities Committee. They had never heard of me and didn't know anyone who had. I was shooed off like an annoying gnat.

"I expressed my disappointment at this brush-off to a friend who, coincidentally, was running for the ATAS board of governors. A month later, after learning he was elected, I congratulated him for his good fortune and casually mentioned that if he needed any help as governor, I was available. Two weeks later, much to my surprise, he appointed me to the National [Emmy] Awards Committee. His reason? I was the *only* person who had expressed any interest in helping out.

"From that point on, things began to happen. I was accepted into the Academy Writers Group [a special group for nonwriter members of the academy who want to develop their writing skills]. I was asked to contribute a skit for a program being presented at an annual charity party given by the academy. The next year I was asked to be the story editor for the show. Then I was asked to be the executive producer of the Writers Group. Most recently, I was asked to write the entire program for a tribute the Academy was giving for Leonard Goldenson, the founder of ABC.

"Basically, by volunteering my services, I went from knowing nobody to being acquainted with quite a few people in many areas.

"All of this was possible because I have been willing to sacrifice a little of my time. I was able to help others and at the same time really enjoy myself. The one thing to remember when performing community service is that whatever you do must be your magnanimous gift to others. If you have the attitude that everything you do is a favor that must be returned, you will end up very disappointed and bitter. Get involved with the community, and not only will you have a good time, but it will give you an opportunity to let your light shine so your talents can be recognized."

COLLECT INSPIRATION

Start collecting crossover success stories to inspire you. Producer Renee Valente started as a secretary . . . Leonard Nimoy used to be the actor who was cursed with pointy ears . . . Lew Wasserman was a PR guy from the Midwest . . . Billy Friedkin was a documentary filmmaker from Chicago . . . Kevin Costner was just another pretty face . . . Ron Howard was forever Opie, and Rob Reiner was the beloved Meathead.

The beauty of the entertainment business is that change is a way of life in Hollywood. If you show people a great script or a beautifully directed play or a reel in which you do something you've never done before—sooner or later the industry will come around to seeing you just the way you'd like them to—as the person you really are.

ONCE YOU CROSS OVER, SHOULD YOU TURN DOWN WORK IN YOUR OLD CATEGORY?

This is a very sensitive question that many Hollywood people agonize over. At a seminar I taught at the Directors Guild, a member of the audience asked one of my panelists who had crossed over from assistant director to director if he had turned down work in the A.D. category once he got his first directing job.

The director deadpanned: "I like to eat." The industry audience laughed appreciatively. He went on to say that after the release of his first feature film he turned down all nondirecting offers for six months. Finally he realized that directing offers were few and far between and he was going to kill off his lucrative B-career if he no longer took any work as an A.D. So he took a job and continued to look for directing work and market himself as a director. Soon he lined up another directing gig, which was followed by another A.D. job. It took him three or four years of doing both before the transition was complete.

Many Hollywood career changers are given the advice that once they change categories, they must turn down all work in the old category or no one will take them seriously in their new role. And in many ways this makes sense, because industry people do tend to pigeonhole each other. The only problem with this is that transitions aren't always smooth and success isn't guaranteed. It may be a juggling act to keep your old and new careers in the air simultaneously, but it can be done. You'll need to be a real diplomat to reassure those who want to hire you as, say, an assistant director that your heart is still in it and you'll do a great job for them, and also convince those who might hire you as a director that you really *are* a director now.

ANOTHER MIDCAREER CHALLENGE: THE STALLED CAREER

Marlene is an experienced unit production manager. She's worked in series television for over twenty years, and her credits include some top shows. Recently, however, she found herself working less and less. She came to me for help.

She didn't want to change careers or make any crossover moves; she just wanted more work in her chosen field. And she wanted to move up to line producing.

One of the first things we discussed was what Marlene's reputation in the business was like. When her name came up on the inevitable lists, what were people saying?

This wasn't an easy question to find answers for. Marlene thought people liked her, but she wasn't really sure what previous employers would say. She had gone over budget on the last two shows she had worked on. And she had some personal problems recently that might have affected her work.

An industry friend of hers, Bruce, posing as an independent producer who wanted to hire her, called around town asking about Marlene. He heard some good things—people saw her as reliable, knowledgeable, conscientious, hardworking, and fun to be with—but there were reservations. One person mentioned that she seemed to be perpetually grumpy on the last show she did, and that she'd had a few run-ins with the producer. Another was concerned about her shows coming in over budget. Yet another thought that she'd been around for a long time and perhaps was burned out.

When Bruce shared the results of his informal survey with Marlene, she was very upset. At first, she was angry that people had said negative things about her. Then she feared she'd never work again.

One by one, we tackled the issues raised by Marlene's former colleagues. Marlene admitted that she'd been experiencing burnout. Two years ago she had worked horrendous hours on a very tough show with a notoriously difficult producer and star and had never really recovered from that experience. During that time her marriage had broken up, and she'd started therapy. It had taken her a while to recover from the double blow, but she was now feeling better than she had in a long time.

On that ill-fated show and the one that followed, she had budget difficulties, but she felt that these were the result of her burnout and would no longer be a problem on future jobs.

I asked her what job search methods she was using. Over the years she had built up a list of industry contacts she'd worked with, and she called them whenever she wasn't working. Up until recently, that tactic had resulted in new jobs. Now she was calling the same old contacts over and over with no success.

We came up with a new strategy for Marlene. She had to break out of her small circle of previous contacts and demonstrate to the industry that she was an energetic, organized, and efficient unit production manager and line producer.

She joined an entertainment industry charity and volunteered to produce a fund-raising event featuring some of the top people in television. The industry insiders on her committee and in the organization at large were impressed with her "can do" attitude and smooth organizational abilities. She got along with everyone beautifully, and they sang her praises. Through one of her new contacts, she was recommended for a job line producing a network special. She took the job and brought the project in on time and under budget.

Marlene's career was back on track.

EVEN VETERANS MAY HAVE TROUBLE UNDERSTANDING THE SYSTEM

I've seen a number of people in my practice who, in spite of years spent working in the entertainment industry, still don't understand how it really works. Their frustration and bitterness over their failure to achieve substantial career success were heartbreaking.

Jay, for example, is a film composer who had some early success scoring TV shows. In the 1960s he had taken a bus to Hollywood, sent his tape around, and the work had come. In retrospect he thought that perhaps it had come too easily, because he was lulled into believing that it would continue forever, without his having to make any particular effort.

Styles changed. He found himself not quite as sought-after. His agent let him go and he signed with someone less desirable. His anger at the industry mounted. What was wrong with them?

He looked around at the people getting hired now. They all seemed to him to be poorly schooled rock musicians without his impressive classical background, training, and experience. And they all seemed to be getting their jobs by brownnosing.

What Jay didn't realize was that the brownnosing was really shmoozing and networking, now an essential part of the film composing world. In the past, composers seemed to be exempt from this particular industry ritual, but no more. Over the years, as more and more people flooded into the business, things became much more competitive than when Jay started out. Savvy marketing and networking were now critical, and Jay hadn't realized that he wasn't doing what it takes to get ahead in today's entertainment industry.

We came up with a plan. First, he agreed to open-mindedly explore new musical areas. This was exciting to him, and he bought some new, state-of-the-art electronic equipment and started creating some wonderful sounds.

Second, he made a tape that combined his new work with his older work and got it out to agents, who were impressed with his new direction, although they weren't yet ready to sign him.

Third, he scored a student film for free. Once he got over his anger at having to "work for free" he threw himself into this project, which he found more stimulating than anything he'd done in years. Working with the eager young filmmaker seemed to reinvigorate him. He invited everyone he knew to the premiere. The response was excellent. His friends were amazed at "the new Jay."

Last but most important, Jay began to get out more. He met new people through his involvement with a number of entertainment industry associations, and he took the time to have lunch and shmooze, even though this was difficult for him as a dyed-in-the-wool introvert. But slowly he began to enjoy it.

The result? His career was revitalized and he began having more fun than he had in years. And, slowly but surely, work began to come his way.

18

☆

Don't Be Desperate

★ ★ ★ ★ ★ ★ ★ ★ ★ ★ ★ ★ ★ ★ ★ ★

PERSONAL SURVIVAL ISSUES

All careers in the arts resemble life on a roller coaster. First, the painstakingly slow and steady climb; next, reaching a peak; now a sickening plummet from grace. Up again, up, up—and down! Again and again.

—GARSON KANIN

FINANCIAL SURVIVAL AND "F-YOU" MONEY

To survive the up-and-down cycles that are inevitable in any Hollywood career, it's important that you NOT live on what you make—live on two-thirds of your income, at the most. This sounds drastic, but a little arithmetic will explain my suggestion. In an insecure, heavily free-lance field, you should be conservative in your estimates of how much you'll really work. If you work two-thirds of every year and work steadily two out of three years, you're doing great! But you must plan to put money aside to tide you over the rough months.

Fortunately, when you do find work in show business it often pays well (once you're beyond the novice phase). But don't be seduced by the numbers on your paycheck. If you're taking home $1,000 a week, for example, plan on stretching that so it can support you for one and one-third weeks. In your mind, think of it as $660 a week, and you'll be closer to the mark. $330 should go into the bank to cover you in tough times.

The mistake many people make is to assume that when the good times roll they'll never stop rolling. They forget that after the roller coaster goes up, it comes down again before it rises once more. So when they hit a nice gig, they run out and buy the BMW convertible and the condo in Malibu. They can well afford the payments when they're working, but if there's a strike or the job ends—it's desperation time. And we all know what desperation does to your chances of getting another job.

During the last industry strike the screams and groans could be heard from Toluca Lake to Venice Beach. Industry people who were grossly overextended were auctioning off their real estate, paintings, and Jaguars at fire sale prices. Marriages were cracking under the strain. Spouses were whining, "Why don't you get a *real* job!" It wasn't a pretty picture.

Don't let yourself get into this predicament. Resist playing the status game any more than you have to. Talk to your bank about automatic withdrawal arrangements so you don't even SEE one-third of your check. You'll be glad you did.

What's this about "F-You" money? No kidding, this is a real industry term. Having F-You money means having enough of a financial cushion that you don't have to take any lousy or demeaning jobs because you're desperate for cash. It also means that if you're on a job that's unbearable, you can afford to say "F-You!" Although I don't usually recommend that people quit jobs, there are times in a person's life when you have to draw the line. So start that F-You savings account now.

A-SKILLS AND B-SKILLS

Another way to avoid the sin of desperation is to have a viable B-skill in addition to your A-skill. Your A-skill is your best gift, your true career goal. It's your heart's delight, your "bliss," as mythologist Joseph Campbell says. Your best efforts should go into finding a way to express this precious talent. Your B-skill has a much more mundane function: it's a practical skill you can rely on to make cash when your A-skill isn't paying the bills. During a down cycle, when there's a strike, if you're between jobs or on hiatus—you may need your B-skill to make ends meet.

What's a good B-skill for an entertainment industry person? Usually it's something that won't interfere with your primary occupation but will pay a decent amount of money. Hopefully it's work you truly enjoy doing, although of course you don't enjoy it as much as your A-skill or it would *be* your A-skill. Ideally it's an occupation where there are fewer applicants for every available slot than there are in show business.

Entertainment industry people argue about whether it's better to have your B-job in the industry (so you can develop contacts and learn more about the business while you're earning your income) or outside of the industry. The outside-the-industry contingent believes that you should keep things simple and uncontaminated in a business that is notoriously quick to typecast people. If you're a writer, present yourself as a writer. Don't confuse everyone by working as a production assistant too. And, they say, no one will take you seriously as a director if your B-job is a below-the-line craft like script supervisor. Folks of this persuasion can be very creative about coming up with B-skills that don't cramp their style in pursuing their heart's desire within the industry. Tammy, for example, is a screenwriter. That's her A-skill. She's also a registered nurse, and whenever the writing work isn't happening, she calls the nursing registry and takes temporary jobs a few nights a week and weekends. She continues to write spec screenplays and teleplays during the day. For Tammy, it's a nice balance. And it's good for her ego to take a break from the supercompetitive writing game and be in a situation where people are eager to hire her!

Sometimes B-skills that are seemingly outside of the industry can pay off inside the business. Hollywood is catered to by thousands of service people who regularly meet important players. For example, Cary is an aspiring actor who works for an aquarium service that takes care of the office aquariums (indispensable stress-reducers for harried players) at some of the studios and production companies. A watery emergency recently enabled Cary to shine heroically, saving some very expensive fishies for Craig, a harassed TV executive. After the emergency was over, the aquarium's grateful owner chatted briefly with Cary, who told him of his acting ambitions. Craig arranged for Cary to meet the company's casting director.

B-SKILLS IN THE INDUSTRY

The keep-it-in-the-industry folks feel that the benefits of working in the business outweigh the disadvantages. They argue that even though you run the risk of being typecast in a career that's not your true love, you can use your B-job to make contacts and advance your A-career. The script supervisor who wants to be a director, for example, can acquire valuable transferrable skills on the job, while getting paid to watch directors direct. If he's lucky, he may even find a senior director willing to mentor him into entry-level directing jobs.

BARB'S B-JOB PAYS OFF

Barb Mackintosh has two loves: screenwriting and computers. Screenwriting is her favorite by far. But her computer skills have come in handy in Hollywood.

Barb fell in love with computers while she was in graduate school at San Diego State. She stumbled onto an old DEC-Mate 1 digital processor and became fascinated with her new toy. When she graduated and went to L.A. to break into show business as an aspiring screenwriter, Barb needed a B-job to pay the rent until she sold a script. All that fooling around on the DEC-Mate 1 paid off: she landed a night job at a company called Data-Scan, doing text conversions from 5:00 P.M. to 2:00 A.M. Barb never dreamed that this B-job would turn out to be her ticket into screenwriting's inner circle.

One day Barb read an announcement in the *Hollywood Reporter* about a meeting to be held by an organization called the Association of Entertainment Industry Computer Professionals. Barb showed up and was thrilled to meet other show business people who shared her passion for computers. She got involved with AEICP, volunteering her services to help plan and implement future events.

The organization's founder, Larry Saltzman, was a systems analyst at Orion Pictures. He was so impressed with Barb's enthusiasm and talent that he hired her to do some script word processing at Orion, where she meet writer-producer John Whelpley ("Trapper John"), who was working on a short-lived doctor series to be shot in Toronto called "Kay O'Brien." Barb and John hit it off well, and John hired Barb to go to Toronto to do computer training and additional script processing. When John moved on to the TV series "MacGyver," Barb went with him as his assistant.

Through her script processing and her work as a writer's assistant, Barb picked up the tricks and lingo of television scriptwriting. She told me that she learned "how to maintain the integrity of a screenplay" when other people's creative notes threatened to muddy the waters. She was getting a wonderful, hands-on, paid education.

But that wasn't all. By this time she had completed two spec scripts of her own: a "MacGyver" and a "Murphy Brown." The executive producer of "MacGyver," Steve Downing, read her material and was impressed. He gave her an assignment to write a "MacGyver." She got paid, she got an agent, and she got in the Writers Guild! All thanks to a terrific B-job.

Barb is currently writing more spec scripts. In her new B-job, she works as the Los Angeles production coordinator on "MacGyver."

WHEN ALL ELSE FAILS, DRAG OUT YOUR C-SKILLS

Sometimes in Hollywood you've gotta do what you've gotta do to get where you want to go. Let's not knock waiting on tables, answering phones, driving limos, or any other skills that just might come in handy when the rent is due.

TAKE GUILT-FREE VACATIONS!

Now that you've solved your financial problems by putting aside F-You money and working at your B-skill, a word of advice: schedule regular, guilt-free vacations. When a project or job finishes, take a week or two to recuperate from overemployment so you're fresh when you start your job search campaign (if you haven't already lined up a job through great networking on your present job). But don't take six months off—it can be hard to get back on the merry-go-round once you've been off too long. It's also a good idea to take a vacation before you start a new job, if possible. That way you're in good shape to start a new project and ready to hit the ground running.

Many people take vacations during the TV hiatus in the spring, when the series take a break. Christmas vacation is also a good time to be away—the town is dead. In fact, you'll probably meet more Hollywood people on the beaches of Hawaii or the ski slopes of Utah or Colorado during that time than at the Warners commissary. August, on the other hand, can be a good time to stay in town and job hunt. People don't tend to leave until just before the Labor Day weekend.

WHO *REALLY* LOVES YA, BABE?

With all the shmoozing and the new best friends in your life, it's easy to lose perspective on who your *real* loved ones are. Your life expands along with your Power Rolodex and you can fall into the trap of mistaking mere work contacts for true, personal friends who really care about you.

A friend of mine found out about the dark side of Hollywood friendships the hard way. She was married to a top television producer. She entertained "*tout* Hollywood" at their palatial estate in Beverly Hills. She hobnobbed with network executives and their spouses. Her children played with the children of stars, studio heads, top writers, and producers. Everyone *loved* her!

Then she and her husband divorced. She was shocked when almost all of her entertainment industry friends evaporated into thin air.

You can also be dropped if you suddenly become successful. An actor who works steadily told me that when he began getting regular gigs, his acting school buddies were so jealous that they stopped seeing him because it was too painful. His happiness only reminded them of their failure.

It's important to keep healthy boundaries between work and personal life. Trying to get love needs met in the workplace leaves you open to terrible exploitation and disappointment.

CHERISH YOUR *REAL* BEST FRIENDS: BUILDING A SUPPORT SYSTEM

Make a commitment to yourself and your family to remember every day who your real loved ones are and to put precious time aside to nurture those relationships. Your spouse, your children, your relatives, your old friends—they must come first. If you ever get too busy to take their phone calls, may a big, noisy, red-light alarm go off in your head! Hollywood is warping your values. Try to keep your life in balance. It's easy to have your whole existence revolve around the industry, working and socializing with Hollywood folk. Always have a few friends who have nothing to do with the business. You'll need their refreshing sense of perspective to keep you grounded.

IS THERE SUCH A THING AS A HAPPY HOLLYWOOD MARRIAGE?

A cynical friend of mine claims there are three possible "states of being" in a marriage where both people work in show business. (1) They're both equally successful. This sounds great, but it can't last. Sooner or later the roller coaster will turn downward for at least one of the partners. (2) They're both equally unsuccessful. Depressing, but sometimes good for the marriage because misery loves company. They both have someone to commiserate with. (3) One is up, one is down. The worst of all. The successful one feels guilty watching the partner who's having a tough time. The partner who's down can come to envy and resent the other's success.

It doesn't have to be this way. True life partners know that "for richer or poorer" means being emotionally supportive of your loved one whatever his or her current status on the roller coaster ride. Genuine support for the aspirations of both partners is the key to a successful entertainment industry marriage. Creative people *have* to find an outlet for their gifts or their souls wither and die. If you love a creative person, stick with her through thick and thin as she struggles to get her talents out into the world. And, even more importantly, stick with her when she becomes successful and is being seduced by insincere hangers-on and her own publicity. Ironically, the time when a person most needs an honest, true, loving friend is when she makes it (although it's nice to have real friends when you fail too).

WHAT ABOUT SEX ON THE SET?

There's no denying that the intense camaraderie, long hours, and on-location travel on any film or TV project can create sexual temptation of the most interesting kind. Show business people are, by profession, attractive and emotional. On-set romances aren't unusual. Many people find a "location" boyfriend or girlfriend for the duration of the shoot. That's why some spouses prefer to go on-location with their mates if at all possible.

Surprisingly, however, these flings (which often evaporate once the crew breaks up) aren't the worst enemy facing a show business marriage. A pioneering study of entertainment industry marriages by family therapist Annie Coe of the California Family Study Center in North Hollywood revealed the principal stress factor to be the unpredictability inherent in entertainment industry careers. All the people in Coe's study experienced high levels of stress when working, plus varying degrees of anxiety and depression when unemployed. Coe found that marital discord caused by one partner's career in filmmaking was worst in the early years of marriage, and that couples learned to cope with the unpredictable life-style better as the years went by.

STAYING SANE AND HUMANE IN A CRAZY BUSINESS

You will have to develop your own methods for emotional survival in Hollywood. Insecurity and lack of control over your life (and your films or TV shows) will be your toughest adversaries.

Here are some tried-and-true tactics used by the pros:

★ **Don't lose your sense of humor and your sense of perspective.** Remind yourself that "it's only a movie." Enjoy the absurdity of it all. Have a good laugh with friends over the crazy experiences and adventures an entertainment industry career brings into your life. Producer David Permut (*Dragnet, Blind Date*) knows how to do this. Wearing a T-shirt emblazoned with "I survived the reshoot of *The Marrying Man*" (the much-troubled Alec Baldwin/Kim Basinger starrer), he advised: "You have to keep your sense of humor about all this. We're only making movies. We're not solving world hunger or building world peace."

★ **Don't let the bastards get you down.** Use that sense of humor to keep you sane when you deal with the inevitable animals in the Hollywood zoo. Don't take things personally. And learn to deal with the normal conflict between art and business that has always been part of the industry. Every project unfortunately involves some compromise to the demands of producers, stars, lawyers, time, and budgets. Do the best you can within the limitations and then let it go. Don't make yourself sick over it.

★ **Don't let your irrational fears take over.** Almost everyone in the industry knows what it's like to be absolutely convinced that you'll never work again. Remind yourself that this is your fear talking, not your rational mind. Counter fear statements with rational reassurances. Right now you may be unemployed, but stick with your job search campaign and you *will* find work.

★ **Stay in good physical shape.** A regular health and fitness program can save your sanity and also give you the extra energy you need for the inevitable spurts of overwork. Take time to eat properly, even on the set. Avoid drugs and alcohol—very "out" in today's Hollywood.

★ **Don't forget to feed the artist in you.** Sometimes people get so caught up with "making it" in the industry that they forget why they got into it in the first place. Cherish your innermost creative self. Make time for this part of you in the same way you make time for your other loved ones. Otherwise you may find yourself creatively blocked, becoming a hack, depressed or embittered by the business. Some people even believe that if artists don't find an outlet for their natural creative energies they may become physically ill.

Try to stay fresh by regularly practising your art and honing your craft. If you're an actor, do whatever it takes to act, even if you're not being paid what you'd like to be paid. Work out in class, get into Equity Waiver theater, whatever. If you're a director, direct. Theater, super-8, anything that strikes your fancy. Just keep directing, experimenting, stretching. If you're a writer, keep writing. Poetry, novels, screenplays—anything that gets your creative juices going. Sometimes industry pros resist this advice because they feel that, for professionals, unpaid or low-paid work is somehow demeaning. Don't let a sense of false pride inhibit you. A pianist who doesn't touch a piano for months on end loses her touch. Use it or lose it!

Practising your art can be especially important for industry folks who are employed but are not getting to do interesting or creative work. On a long-running TV series, for instance, you can easily get burned out or find yourself becoming a highly paid hack. A successful TV series producer-director I know is writing experimental screenplays and doing conceptual paintings to feed the artist in himself.

★ **Don't neglect the spiritual side of your life.** Hollywood can be a tough place not only for the creative artist in you but also for the deep, sensitive part of you that cares about values and spiritual connections. Is it possible to hang onto your soul in the land of the endless hustle, the new best friend, and the instant deal? Yes, but it takes a commitment, just as holding your family together in Hollywood takes a commitment. It won't happen naturally. You have to work at it.

★ **Don't forget your life's purpose and mission.** Keep your eye on the ball. Remind yourself regularly why you're in this particular industry. What are your gifts and who needs them? Write your mission on a big sheet of paper and put it on your wall where you see it every day. It will keep you focused.

19

☆

Don't Shoot Yourself in the Foot!

★ ★ ★ ★ ★ ★ ★ ★ ★ ★ ★ ★ ★ ★ ★

SUCCESS CAN BE SCARY: THE SHANE BLACK STORY

When I was working in feature film development, I met twenty-four-year-old wunderkind screenwriter Shane Black at a lunch at the Panda Inn in Westwood.

Shane had just landed a small acting role in producer Joel Silver's *Predator* (which starred Arnold Schwarzenegger and Carl Weathers). He had also just sold a clever cop script, *Lethal Weapon,* to Joel and Warner Bros. for $250,000. Shane was the current flavor of the month.

He had gone from being a UCLA theater major, sometime stand-up comic, would-be actor, temp typist, Westwood movie usher, card-carrying member of the Pad O'Guys (a West L.A. apartment that served as a hang-out for Shane and a dozen of his UCLA buddies), and aspiring screenwriter to one of the hottest writers in Hollywood in just a few short months.

Shane Black had hit the pot of gold at the end of the Hollywood rainbow. What shocked me was that he appeared to be miserable about it.

We talked briefly, and I could see that he was really hurting. For Shane, as for many people, winning seemed to be much more uncomfortable than not winning. Most of us are familiar with the latter. It may not be pleasant, but we've gotten used to it. And as nonwinners we have lots of company. Sudden success, on the other hand, can be a frightening and isolating new experience. Everyone with Hollywood dreams and aspirations envied him.

A few years later, he was able to reminisce about that painful time: "I guess I didn't really deal with success very well for a while. I didn't feel I deserved it."

His friends feared he was sabotaging his newfound success when he wrote the sequel to the wildly successful *Lethal Weapon* and killed off the Mel Gibson character. Warner Bros. was not amused, and Shane left the project.

He didn't write for two years. "I was afraid to do the next project, afraid of failing, afraid of being a fluke," he told the *Los Angeles Times*.

Luckily there is a happy ending to this story. At last Shane worked his way through his dilemma and was able to start writing a new screenplay, *The Last Boy Scout*. In 1990 the David Geffen Company bought it for $1.75 million, and in 1991 it became a successful Christmas release starring Bruce Willis.

THE ART OF SELF-SABOTAGE

Sometimes, in spite of your best intentions, you end up sabotaging yourself and your career. You *want* to write that sitcom script . . . you *intend* to make those calls . . . you're *sure* you filled the gas tank before leaving for the big pitch . . . you have *no idea* why you lost your voice the night of the shoot . . . you *meant* to follow up on that wonderful opportunity . . . you're *making an effort* to get along with your boss and the crew. . . . But somehow things just don't seem to work out.

Sound familiar? Perhaps it's time to take a closer look at your life and your career. You may be shooting yourself in the foot! If you're wondering whether or not you're sabotaging your best efforts, ask yourself if you're really and truly ready, willing, and able to let yourself be successful.

ARE YOU READY TO WIN?

One of the most important precursors of lasting entertainment industry success is a difficult-to-define factor, which I call ready-to-win. Not just ready-to-win in show business, but ready-to-win at life.

Some lucky people learn it from parents who are letting themselves succeed in life. But many of us who come from dysfunctional families of one sort or another (families with addictive or compulsive behaviors, failure and loser patterns, chronic illness, abuse) have to be taught as adults how to love and value ourselves and our talents and to allow ourselves to be successful.

Do any of the following problems sound familiar? Check off the areas where you feel you need work.

___ PERFECTIONISM: THE FEAR OF FAILURE

Because of unhappy things that happened to you when you were little, you may have a deep, shameful feeling of not deserving the love, success, and good things that other people seem to have. (This is what author John Bradshaw calls "toxic shame.") To "earn" the right to exist as a normal human being and to cover up for your (or your family's) shame, you go into "superachiever" mode, pushing for total perfection in everything you do. If you're not the best, you're nothing. If you're not 100 percent, you're zero.

On an internal level, the inner critic tries to "help" by beating you up for every supposed imperfection or infraction (which, of course, further lowers your self-confidence). The inner child has two choices: (1) Try to go along with the program. This often creates some success in the short run. But as you push to live up to impossible standards, you become increasingly exhausted, stressed, and burned out. The end result is often physical illness or a refusal to go on with the torture. (2) Rebel from the start, refusing to even try because you know that whatever you do won't be good enough to satisfy the mercilessly perfectionistic inner critic. Give up.

In either case, you can see that the end result of perfectionism is failure.

The way out of this bind is to work on your basic self-esteem issues. You aren't a piece of scum—you're a human being like everyone else, with strengths and weaknesses. Give yourself permission to be human. You don't have to be perfect to succeed. In baseball, batters don't have to hit a home run every time they come up to the plate; they just have to keep swinging, hitting some and missing some, until their averages get better and better.

— PROCRASTINATION

Which of the following sounds like you?

1. **Nonprocrastinator.** You make a plan and work to the plan. You start early and are done in plenty of time.

2. **Procrastinator #1:** You put off your work until the last possible minute. Then you go into high gear, pull an all-nighter, and achieve great results. You turn your work in on deadline, but you feel exhausted and vaguely guilty about your wacky work habits. Why couldn't you have started earlier and avoided the last-minute crunch?

3. **Procrastinator #2.** You wait until the last minute before doing the work. The added pressure gives you an excuse for not doing your best work. ("It would have been better if I'd had more time.") You're not thrilled with the results, but you hand in the work on time.

4. **Procrastinator #3.** You put off doing what has to be done, ignoring your own inner commands to get to work. You alternate between goofing off and beating yourself up for not working. You don't get the work done and are disappointed in yourself. You feel guilty and ashamed that you can't discipline yourself effectively.

I have different advice for each of the types:

1. **Advice for the Nonprocrastinator.** This is a productive and effective approach to getting work done, especially if you're in a noncreative field. If you'd like to stretch your creativity a bit, experiment with fewer "to do" lists and a less-rigid work schedule, allowing your inner creative child a little more leeway to work at a sane pace and timetable. Your best ideas may come to you when you're just kicking back at the park or driving along the freeway. Keep a tape recorder and notebook handy to jot down unscheduled inspirations. If you're a compulsive workaholic, a driven overachiever, or overcontrolled/overcontrolling, you may want to work on overcoming these fearful approaches to life.

288 ★ All the Right Moves

2. **Advice for Procrastinator #1.** My students and clients are often surprised when I tell them to relax and enjoy this pattern. This is normal behavior for a "perceiving" personality (see chapter 4). It's fairly typical of many successful entertainment industry people, who alternate between periods of intense creativity and periods of recuperative vegging out. It only becomes a problem if you don't leave yourself enough time to do your best work, don't allow yourself to recuperate after a superstressful project, or don't set deadlines for completion of your work.

You tend to work best with deadlines, so you'll need to create them for yourself if they're not inherent in a project. Tell a friend you'll show him the script on Thursday, which will put the heat under you to get it done even if it takes a round-the-clock orgy to deliver it. Or join a support group where you'll be reporting on the phone calls you made that week.

3. **Advice for Procrastinator #2.** You're preventing yourself from doing your best work. You may be trying to protect yourself either from failure or from success by giving yourself an excuse for underachieving. Do some soul-searching.

4. **Advice for Procrastinator #3.** This is a serious problem. If it isn't conquered, you have almost no chance of success in the entertainment industry or anywhere else.

PROCRASTINATORS OF THE THIRD KIND

Toxic procrastination, like perfectionism, is caused by a nasty combination of low self-esteem and impossibly high standards. You pound away at yourself to make those phone calls or write that script, but somehow your inner kid drags his feet, never getting around to it.

Author John Bradshaw (*Homecoming*) believes that undisciplined behaviors are the result of the inner "wounded child" contaminating the rest of the self. "The undisciplined inner child dawdles, procrastinates, refuses to delay gratification, rebels, is self-willed and stubborn, and acts impulsively without thinking. The overdisciplined child is rigid, obsessive, overly controlled and obedient, people pleasing, and ravished with shame and guilt. . . . Most of us who have a wounded inner child fluctuate between undisciplined and overdisciplined behavior."

HEALTHY SELF-DISCIPLINE COMES FROM GOOD SELF-PARENTING

To get off the seesaw of over- and underdiscipline, you need to improve your self-parenting technique. As you go about your life, try to become increasingly aware of how you are presently attempting to discipline yourself. Do you alternate between letting yourself flake off and beating yourself up? Or do you pound away at yourself mercilessly all the time, which you've learned to ignore? What tone of voice do you use when talking to yourself? Is it kind but firm, weak and depressed ("Oh, well, what's the use?"), or cruel and sadistic ("You're a total loser"). If you don't like what you discover, you can create an alternative to the poor self-parenting you've been doing until now. Self reparenting is the "big thing" in therapy these days, and many books, workshops, and classes exist to help you in this process.

___ SNATCHING DEFEAT FROM THE JAWS OF VICTORY: THE FEAR OF SUCCESS

"Almost" is your middle name. You get going on a successful track and things are beginning to pay off . . . BUT . . . you decide to change careers . . . you get sick . . . you get into a fight with co-workers . . . your work goes downhill . . . you get strangely bored with whatever you're doing . . . you get depressed . . . you're late for important meetings . . . _____ (fill in your favorite creative method of self-sabotage).

If you dig down deep, you may uncover some of the causes of this sort of self-sabotage: (1) "I'm not good enough (my family told me so) and I don't deserve good things. So I'll get rid of anything good that comes my way." (2) "Dad nor Mom ever succeeded. I'm afraid to become more successful than they were, which might hurt their feelings and alienate me from the family." (3) "If I don't really try, I'll save myself the possible pain of finding out that I don't have what it takes." Your motto: "I coulda been a contender!"

If you read *People* magazine, you know how common a problem this brand of self-sabotage is in Hollywood. Shane Black wasn't the first or last resident of Tinseltown to undercut his own success. Roseanne Barr-Arnold jeopardized her career by mangling "The Star-Spangled Banner" on prime-time TV. Producer Julia Phillips (*Close Encounters of the Third Kind, You'll Never Eat Lunch in this Town*

Again) self-destructed on cocaine. Delta Burke gained weight and fought with her producers.

THE IMPOSTER SYNDROME

When your self-esteem is low, you *know* you're not lovable and you don't deserve success. After all, your own parents didn't love you the way you needed them to. You tried to win their love in various ways (your "survival strategies"): you became an overachiever or a people-pleaser or an entertaining clown or a hostile rebel or a surrogate spouse or whatever they needed. But even if they liked your act, they still didn't love the underlying, real you. You felt as though you were conning them, which made you even more ashamed of yourself.

Your big hope is that if only you can make it in Hollywood everything will be all right. At last people will love you and appreciate you. But what if you make it? If people begin to treat you as if you're wonderful, talented, lovable, and valuable before you've changed your own opinion of yourself, you feel as if you have conned them. You live in terror of them finding you out.

The cure for the imposter syndrome—as for every other brand of self-sabotage—is learning to love yourself the way your family was never able to love you.

UNRESOLVED MONEY ISSUES

This is a close relative of the "I don't deserve good things" phenomenon. Once again, low self-esteem is the culprit. Before you come to Hollywood, you need to clean up your attitudes toward money, because this town will challenge every bit of financial sanity you have.

Psychotherapist Eric Berne used to talk about three kinds of people: losers, nonwinners, and winners. Applying this to money issues, losers are people who never seem to let themselves have any money in their lives. They keep themselves perennially poor and even if they were to win the lottery, they would find creative ways of getting rid of the cash as quickly as possible. Nonwinners are willing to get by but don't feel they really deserve to get ahead. Winners are ready to accept all the good that comes their way, and to share it with others. In Hollywood it is especially important to be ready to win, because if you start to do well, the industry will throw money at you in astonishingly large amounts. If you're not prepared, you may not be able to cope with it constructively. Some industry people get caught up in the frenzy of excess spending and high living, much to their regret later on.

If you find yourself struggling with serious money problems, you may want to contact Debtors Anonymous (see Resources) to resolve them before tackling a major push for success in Hollywood.

___ OVERCOMING A FAMILY LEGACY OF FAILURE: THE "FIELD OF DREAMS" SYNDROME

> He never made it as a ball player, so he tried to get his son to make it for him.
>
> —*Field of Dreams*

Bob, twenty-eight, was at a crossroad in his career and his life. His pop singing/songwriting career was stalled. He had a small measure of success, including a couple of mildly successful records. But his heart wasn't in it, and his last album was disappointing. Should he change careers?

Being a family therapist as well as a career counselor, I like to start my work with a new client by taking a family history—in this case a family career history. I asked Bob to tell me about each member of his family and what they did or had done in their career lives. I also asked what their career dreams had been and whether or not these dreams had been fulfilled.

Bob started with his father, Sam. The second son of poor Italian immigrants, young Sam became a pop singer in the Sinatra vein. Sam, like Bob, had some early success, but at twenty-eight (the same age as Bob was now), he was in a serious car accident. He was confined to a wheelchair and had to give up his singing career. He reluctantly turned to real estate investing, and became quite wealthy. He married, and fathered two children. The eldest, Steve, went into real estate sales and became successful. Bob, the second son, inherited his father's thwarted desire for a performing career.

When I heard this story I knew that Bob and I would need to work on the family career legacy that was blocking Bob's own life and career.

Phil Alden Robinson's film *Field of Dreams* explores the phenomenon of the thwarted career legacy. The hero, played by Kevin Costner, is haunted by his father's failed baseball career and subsequent life as an unfulfilled dock worker. The father had filled his son's heart and mind with stories of baseball dreams, trying to ease his own pain through his hopes for his son. As a young man, Costner's character had rebelled against his father's efforts to deal with his loss in this way, and didn't resolve his relationship with his father before the old man died. He deeply regrets his last conversation with his father, in which he had mocked his father's reverence for the legendary Shoeless Joe, one of the Chicago Black Sox who threw the World Series at the beginning of the century. Now a thirty-six-year-old farmer in Iowa, Costner begins to hear voices that direct him to create a space in his life (a corn field turned into a baseball diamond) within which he can resolve this relationship. The voices tell him, "If you build it, he will come," and direct him to "ease his pain." At first he is confused as to who "he" is. Perhaps Shoeless Joe? But as the film progresses we realize that it is his father's pain that Costner must ease before he can get on with his own life and career.

Both of these cases illustrate the deep, often unconscious power that the career history of a parent can have over the life and career pattern of a child. Family systems theorists believe that children who are born into a dysfunctional family take on roles to "ease the pain" of the family.

LIVING OUT A PARENT'S DISAPPOINTED DREAM

In Bob's case, as the second son of a second son, he was designated as his father's surrogate to live out Sam's tragically thwarted dream of a successful singing career. Perhaps neither Bob, his father, nor anyone else in the family was consciously aware that this role had been assigned to Bob. Possibly it was thought that Bob had just "inherited" his father's talent. But Bob, at the age when Sam had his accident, had hit a point in his life where he, too, had to confront the family pain that had long been "eased" by the dream of Bob's success.

I gently questioned Bob about his father and his father's career. As

Bob began to talk about Sam's disappointment, he started to sob. The intensity of his emotion shocked him. Bob didn't experience his father's pain as someone else's pain. He experienced it as though it had actually happened to him, to Bob. Even though he had not yet been born when his father's car and life crashed, he was able to feel what Sam must have felt. He had "eased" his father's pain by absorbing it and incorporating it as his own.

I asked Bob how he was similar to his father and how he differed from him. We discovered that Bob had a number of interests in addition to singing. In fact, he really didn't enjoy performing that much. Recently he had taken a course in video editing and thought he might like to cut music videos. He wanted to continue singing too, but only as a hobby.

We talked about how Bob could "ease the pain" in his family without pursuing a singing career he really didn't want. At my suggestion, Bob spoke with his mother and brother about his dad, and the family agreed to a special sixty-fifth birthday celebration for Sam that would include a videotape Bob would put together of his father's singing career, including old photographs, newspaper announcements, and recordings Sam had made in his youth. This became a very emotional project for everyone in the family and Sam was deeply moved at his children's efforts and acknowledgment of both his talent and his tragedy. Through this work, Bob was able to move on with his own life and to leave his family career tragedy behind him.

___ LACK OF FOCUS

I've worked with a number of people in my private practice who have struggled with this problem. Even though they have taken the time to explore their dreams, strengths, interests, and goals, they seem to find it impossible to focus. What we're dealing with here is another form of self-sabotage.

Here are a few of the many reasons people may have for not targeting a specific career goal:

"If I Don't Want It, It Won't Hurt If I Don't Get It." "If I actually target my specific goal, I'll have no excuse for not going for it. Since I'm not sure I'll be good enough to succeed, I'll protect myself from disappointment and rejection by not letting myself focus. If I don't want it, I can't be hurt if I don't get it. If I don't try, I can't fail."

Another variation on this theme: protecting yourself from possible rejection in the area that means most to you by pursuing goals that aren't the ones you really care about. This is like dating people you aren't attracted to so any rejections won't hurt as much. The problem, of course, is that success with someone or something you don't care about doesn't bring you the joy and satisfaction that come with attaining your heart's true desire.

"I Don't Approve of Who I Am and What I Want." "If I actually admit who I *really* am, I might not like or approve of that person—and my family and friends might not like him either. So it's better to try to be what they'd approve of, even if I'm not really happy."

The career patterns of people with this problem are often very erratic. Every time they focus on something they'd really like, the inner critic kicks in, shaming them for who they are and what they want to do. When they change their minds and pick a new, more "socially acceptable" target, they soon give that up in discouragement because it isn't satisfying. This can create a vicious circle of confusion.

James, a gay television director in his early thirties, came to me for help in focusing his career direction. He worked regularly, but with decreasing enthusiasm. He felt he was becoming a hack. We talked, we tested, but still couldn't find a way to pinpoint what James really wanted to do with his life. All we knew was that James wanted to find a way to express himself creatively on film. But every time we tried to talk about what it was that James wanted to express, we hit a brick wall. One night he had a dream in which he painted a picture of a beautiful young man on the sky. He was very disturbed by this dream, frightened to find out what it might be telling him.

Although James was open with himself and a few close friends about being gay, he realized that he had tried to separate his gay identity from his work. As he began to face the fact that he would dearly love to express his true nature on film, a whole new direction opened up to him. He began writing a spec screenplay about people and emotions he really cared about. He knew that getting it produced would be an uphill battle in homophobic Hollywood, but he felt freed up creatively for the first time in many years and was determined to do whatever it would take to bring his story to the screen.

"I Want It All!" Some people find it especially hard to face the finite limits of life and mortality. There are only so many years in a lifetime, so many hours in a day. As children we rejoice in infinite possibilities and we don't want to lose that optimism and "can do" spirit. But it's also important as we grow older to learn to make choices and to prioritize. This is part of growing up. Balancing boundary-free dreams against the practicalities of the human condition is a delicate matter. Without giving up anything that you love, try to boil your career choices down to (at most) two or three all-time favorites.

Some people are content with one career, but others need to have a few things going at once to be happy. This is especially true of extroverts, who often like a lot of variety in their lives.

This is certainly true of me. I like to counsel clients, and I also like to write books and to teach seminars. I'm establishing the Entertainment Industry Career Institute and, every once in a while, I like to do a little film or TV project development.

Here's a trick I discovered to help avoid grandiose thinking (imagining that I can juggle ten things at once): Think of your life as a stove top with five burners, two in the front and three in back, with a pot on each burner. If you move something from a back burner to a front burner, you'll have to move what was already in that spot back to the rear of the stove. If you move a new pot onto the stove, you'll have to remove one of the existing pots. You can do it all—but not all at once!

"If I Focus, I'll Remember." Sometimes people who experienced serious sexual, emotional, or physical abuse when they were children find it difficult to choose a career because they use defocusing as a way of protecting themselves from painful memories.

Monica, forty-five, had few memories before the age of ten. She kept her life very busy and jokingly referred to herself as a workaholic. But she had no particular sense of direction in her career, which disturbed her. In therapy, focusing on career choices was distressing for her. It gradually became apparent that Monica had been raped by her stepfather when she was nine. By staying busy and unfocused, Monica had been able to avoid remembering this dreadful event. Once she dealt with the ugly memory, the rest of her life gained clarity and focus.

___ THE LONE RANGER: THE ISOLATOR

Successful people know how to create support for their efforts. Unsuccessful people keep themselves isolated. Failing to build a support system for your career is a serious form of self-sabotage, especially in the entertainment industry where linking up with others and belonging to formal and informal networks of friends and colleagues is an essential part of finding work.

If you are an isolator, take the time to find out if this is a natural tendency toward introversion, which you can modify through learning to extrovert when you need to, or if your isolation is caused by fear of others and lack of trust based on early childhood trauma.

___ BLAMING OTHERS

You've tried to break into the industry (or, for industry veterans, the inner circle of heavy-hitting players) but it hasn't happened. You can't face the pain of looking at your own behavior or level of talent as a possible source of the failure, so you blame: (1) the Hollywood system; (2) your boss; (3) backstabbing colleagues; (4) unscrupulous producers, directors, casting people; (5) your agent; (6) your manager; (7) your ex-spouse; (8) your kids; (9) your mortgage; (10) your lousy childhood; (11) the unions; (12) _____ (you fill in the blank!); (13) anybody but yourself.

This stratagem may comfort your wounded ego but it won't solve the problem—in fact it makes it worse. In seminars I've taught at the Directors Guild of America and the Academy of Television Arts and Sciences I've run into a small minority of industry veterans who have turned this kind of blaming into a way of life.

___ A BITTER, NEGATIVE ATTITUDE

If the blaming-everybody-but-yourself syndrome continues for too long, it congeals into a permanently sour attitude that's a real turn-off to employers and co-workers. Successful people want to be around other winners—folks who like themselves and who have a positive, "can do" attitude. As screenwriting teacher Rick Pamplin sometimes warns prospective students, "No wimps, whiners, or losers" need apply.

WIMPS AND WHINERS

Hollywood hates people who aren't willing to pull their weight, people who won't buckle down and do the hard work it takes to get the job done. No one said the entertainment industry was an easy way to make a living.

HANGING OUT WITH NEGATIVE PEOPLE

If you spend a lot of time with folks who are self-sabotaging, you can find yourself drained of positive energy. If you choose to work with self-destructive partners, your projects will be doomed. If you put endless hours into trying to "save" people who have not yet found a way to give themselves permission to win, you may find yourself neglecting your own talents and enterprises.

MISCELLANEOUS PERSONALITY PROBLEMS

Under this heading include any self-sabotaging personality traits that might prevent people from hiring you or enjoying the experience of working with you: compulsive rebellion against authority, picking fights with people, constant lateness, an arrogant attitude, poor personal hygiene. . . . Whatever it is, clean it up before you try to make it in Hollywood. Unless you're unbelievably talented (and sometimes not even then), no one has time or energy for these unproductive hassles. Even Alec Baldwin and Kim Basinger got busted for bad attitude on *The Marrying Man*.

THE RIGHT ATTITUDE FOR A SUCCESSFUL HOLLYWOOD JOB SEARCH

If you find yourself becoming discouraged or negative as you pursue your entertainment industry career, try reading the following pep talk/meditation to raise your spirits and help you get back on track:

The most important thing to remember is that you already have a lifetime employer: yourself (and possibly your "higher power" or

God, if that's appropriate for you). You work for your best self: who you really are and who you are meant to be.

You are a permanent employee of _____ (Your Name), Inc. You are the Owner; Major Stockholder; Chief Executive Officer; President; Chief Financial Officer; Strategic Planner; Head of Marketing, Sales, and PR; Head of Production and Manufacturing—and the bookkeeper, secretary, and gopher (until you can afford to hire some helpers). Your gifts are the major assets of this corporation. It's your job to get out there in the world and give those gifts, sharing them with other people who would benefit from them.

This is a job from which you can never be fired. It will take you a lifetime to do it well. Your livelihood will come from giving these gifts—money is a natural by-product of meeting others' needs.

WATCH OUT FOR FLASHING RED LIGHTS!

Now that you're aware of some of the major forms of self-sabotage, keep your eyes open as you embark on this new push toward Hollywood success. Every month or so, go over this chapter again. Let a big, flashing red light go off in your head if you sense that you're starting to shoot yourself in the foot. If so, get help and nip the problem in the bud before it ruins your career.

20

☆

What If I'm "Different"?

★ ★ ★ ★ ★ ★ ★ ★ ★ ★ ★ ★ ★

When I worked for a prominent minority actor and would talk with agents about scripts for him to produce or star in, it was astonishing how frequently I was told that "we don't have anything with a black lead" or "the hero is Italian," not realizing that *any* script with a good strong main character could be played by my boss. These agents didn't think they were racist. It simply never occurred to them that a part written for a white male could just as easily be played (or produced) by a minority person—or a woman! (The Sigourney Weaver role in *Alien,* for example, was originally written for a man.) This is a "liberal" town. Hollywood people fancy themselves to be very enlightened. People aren't going to tell you they won't hire you because you're a woman, or black, or in a wheelchair. Definitely uncool. But that doesn't mean that discrimination doesn't exist in today's entertainment industry.

For example, when Rachel Talalay, who directed parts 3 and 4 of the grisly Freddy Krueger film series, was hired to do part 6 of the *Nightmare on Elm Street* franchise, she "would occasionally get internal memos telling me, 'Don't be too girly; don't be too sensitive.' " Certain assumptions were made about a "woman's sensibility" that had nothing to do with Talalay as an individual.

"People don't come up to you and say 'I'm not going to hire you because you're a woman,' " says director Martha Coolidge *(Valley Girl, Rambling Rose).* "You have to look for it to see it, because it's around the corner. It's the people who aren't interested in having a meeting with me or other women. It's the producers who are friends or business associates who don't think of you for something considered a man's piece of material. It's the look of hesitation that comes across their faces when you suggest maybe they should."

BUT ISN'T IT TOUGH FOR EVERYONE?

Yes, Hollywood is tough for everyone. And if you're a member of a minority group of some kind, not everything that happens to you will be the result of discrimination. Everyone's struggling and experiencing rejection. It's like Vietnam; if you say, "I'm really hurting here," the person in the trench next to you will say, "Hey, buddy, they're shooting at me too." And that's true. It isn't easy for anyone to get a job in Hollywood, but when the industry gets a cold, members of the nondominant groups get pneumonia. There's a double standard.

NO SECOND CHANCES: ONE STRIKE AND YOU'RE OUT

Both women directors and African-American directors have remarked on the problem of "second chances." A white male who makes a flop may be given second or third chances, but members of nondominant groups seem to get the "one strike and you're out" treatment.

"There are double standards used for judging the work of black filmmakers," says director Roy Campanella II. "This is especially true when it comes to second chances. In general, a struggling white filmmaker who errs will often receive a second chance; but a black counterpart who commits the same mistake will usually be written off."

Also, even when a film by a person from a nondominant group does well, it often doesn't result in more work, as would be the case for a member of the majority.

GENERALIZATION

There is also unfair generalization. If Michael Cimino makes *Heaven's Gate*, studio execs don't conclude that all films made by white guys will go over budget and flop so let's not hire David Lynch or Marty Scorsese or Francis Coppola. But if a black director or a woman director flops, too many Hollywood execs might generalize that individual failure into a "trend" and claim that audiences will no longer be interested in films directed by blacks or women. The riot after a Westwood screening of *New Jack City* led to unwarranted generalizations by some exhibitors and studios about the difficulties of opening a "black film." *New Jack* producer Doug McHenry noted that the shooting deaths in a Valley Stream, New York, theater during the opening of *The Godfather Part III* evoked no similar generalizations about films by Italian artists on Italian themes.

THE FLUKE SYNDROME

Another unfortunate phenomenon is the fluke syndrome. When subject matter that industry executives are psychologically comfortable with does well at the box office, there is usually a rush to greenlight clones. As elsewhere, in Hollywood imitation is the sincerest form of flattery. But when a film with, say, female protagonists or a deaf star does well at the box office, it may be described as a fluke and other proposals for similar films can often be turned down.

The people doing the nay-saying don't think they're prejudiced. They always have "rational" reasons, like "Women's movies don't make money" (what about *Ghost*, *Pretty Woman*, *Steel Magnolias*, *Terms of Endearment?*) or "Audiences don't want to see sign language" (what about *Children of a Lesser God?*). Yet, no matter how many action films fall by the wayside, Hollywood guys seem to keep making more of them. They aren't aware of their own unconscious biases against people and projects that are "different" from what they personally enjoy, find familiar, or are comfortable with.

TOKENISM

There seems to be an informal ceiling on the number of "different" people in any given working environment. Sometimes Hollywood will accept one or two into the club or the studio or the movie, but may balk at more.

A SAMPLE OF ONE

Many Hollywood people may have met only one or two people from your group in their whole lives (or they have met folks like you, but in a subservient role). Your culture, your perspective, your take on material may be truly foreign to them. Their friends and colleagues may be mostly like themselves.

The result: they may start extrapolating from a sample of one or two. All black filmmakers are like Spike Lee, aren't they? So if you're black, why aren't you interested in the same subject matter as Spike? And why isn't your film like Spike's? A film critic recently called nineteen-year-old Brooklyn filmmaker Matty Rich "the real Spike Lee." Was Marty Scorsese the real Coppola?

Another example: when Steven Soderbergh's *sex, lies and videotape* won the top prize at the Sundance Film Festival in 1989, Soderbergh became the flavor of the month. But when black filmmaker Wendell Harris won the same award the next year, he couldn't get his film *Chameleon Street* opened in L.A. for eighteen months. Harris was told by a major distributor: "This is great, but it's not like an Eddie Murphy film and it's not like Spike Lee."

Similar attitudes are at work when a filmmaker like Mario Van Peebles, whose *New Jack City* grossed more than $44 million, shops a steamy script about two young, middle-class black lovers and is asked by a studio executive "if we could put the characters on crack and move it to Compton." Another studio guy said, "Could you put in some hip-hop and make it into a musical?"

"These people just don't get it," says Van Peebles.

ARE YOU "DIFFERENT"?

I once attended a seminar taught by the pioneer family therapist Virginia Satir. She led us through a powerful exercise on discrimination: she asked everyone in the large audience to stand up. Then she asked us to sit down if we were members of any of the following groups: women, ethnic or religious minorities, people under twenty, people over forty, people who were gay or lesbian, people with physical or mental handicaps, overweight people . . .

As more and more people in the audience sat down, we all started to laugh as we realized the absurdity of the situation: only a tiny fraction of the audience was still standing! How ridiculous we are when we limit the possible contributions of the large majority of the population. And, in this era of global competition, how shortsighted!

THE IN GROUPS VS. THE OUT GROUPS

The social penalties for belonging to the various nondominant groups vary in intensity, but all create pain, stress, and low self-esteem. Some of the categories carry much greater burdens than others, but pain is a difficult thing to compare. A broken leg is far more serious than a wounded finger, but if it's your finger, it hurts. It's only human to feel our own pain before that of others. For example, the results of 300 years of systematic abuse and dehumanization of African-Americans by our culture may be arguably far deeper and more pernicious than, say, the results of "looksism" or ageism, but all are painful forms of discrimination.

Discrimination varies with time and place as well. Being Jewish in Poland during the thirties and forties was a crime punishable by death. Being Jewish in the Hollywood of the nineties is a very different matter, thank goodness, although certain stereotypes and stigmas still persist that limit the opportunity to explore important subject matter about the Jewish experience.

Today, even straight, white, English-speaking, Euro-American, able-bodied males between the ages of twenty and forty-five are beginning to experience "nondominant" status as their cultural power and numbers dwindle and their traditional perquisites are challenged by the various "out groups."

LET'S FACE IT: WE'RE ALL PREJUDICED

I believe that we're all prejudiced to one degree or another, even if we belong to a nondominant category. We all absorb the dominant culture's prejudices against other groups that are different from us. We also absorb the dominant culture's prejudices against our own nondominant group, and we may find ourselves hating other people like us or even, tragically, hating ourselves for being who we are.

What's especially pernicious about Hollywood's discrimination is that it doesn't only affect the availability of work—although that's certainly a serious matter if you're the one looking for a job—but it also carries a double whammy in that it influences people in every other industry and culture through the power of its on-screen images.

It's a vicious circle: if industry executives and talent are mostly young white males, then that group's taste and stories are reflected disproportionately on the screen. Other groups are invisible or portrayed in stereotypes. Choice is limited.

Audiences, given a narrow range of choice, are cheated. They are prevented from experiencing a wide range of stories from a multiplicity of fresh perspectives. They may even come to believe that the stories they see are a true and complete reflection of how the world is or ought to be—creating prejudice in their minds and lowering their own self-esteem if they don't fit into the chosen group.

HOW MUCH DISCRIMINATION IS THERE IN HOLLYWOOD?

Researcher Sally Steenland, who did a Ford Foundation-financed study on how minorities are portrayed in the media, found that "a core of overwhelmingly white producers and writers are 'creating characters in their own images,' producing artificial portrayals of blacks and other minorities on TV." Even if a writer doesn't limit or specify the ethnicity of a character, too many Hollywood producers, directors, and casting directors will make the assumption that the character is white and cast accordingly. And if the role is specifically described as a certain sex or race, they will seldom be creative about going beyond that written description, even though to do so might enrich the production. In other words, if a doctor character is described as a man of Irish extraction, they may not be open to the possibility that the doctor could be played by an Asian man or a Hispanic woman or someone with a disability.

In 1989 women were performing only 29 percent of all roles in feature films, earning 40 to 50 percent of what male actors were making. As for directors, women make up one-fifth of the 9,000-member Directors Guild, but only a few have steady work.

MERYL STREEP FACES THE AGE POLICE AND THE THREE MONKEYS

Meryl Streep has said that female actors face the "age police." Streep blames "the three monkeys" for the lack of work for actresses: "the producer who says, 'I don't see any good scripts for women being written,' and puts his hands over his eyes . . . the writer who says, 'I can't write those scripts because they won't sell,' and puts his hands over his mouth . . . and the studio that says, 'We can't afford to make those movies,' and covers its ears."

Star salaries are eloquent. Few actresses earn over $5 million a picture (Julia Roberts is a recent exception: she was reportedly paid $7 million to do her latest film), yet many actors make well over that figure, including Arnold Schwarzenegger, Mel Gibson, Bruce Willis, Jack Nicholson, Tom Cruise, Eddie Murphy, Dustin Hoffman, Warren Beatty, and others.

THE DOOR OPENS A CRACK WIDER

As I write this book, African-American filmmakers like Mr. Van Peebles are the Flavor of the Moment. In 1990 and 1991, more films with blacks behind the camera were released than during the entire previous decade. (However, the number of films directed by black directors is still minuscule and the money these directors have made is a fraction of that paid to Hollywood's top white directors.) From the brouhaha in the press over the new "Black Pack," one might assume that Hollywood's racism is a thing of the past.

Unfortunately, the journalists and critics doing the cheering don't really understand how Hollywood works. Like all such Hollywood enthusiasms, today's heat on African-American filmmakers could quickly evaporate if there are one or two box office disappointments. The principles of no second chances and generalization could slam the door shut once more.

But right now studios and agencies are indulging in one of their periodic feeding frenzies, hiring and signing black talent almost indiscriminately—or discriminately, depending on your point of view. (An agent friend recently asked me frantically, "Do you know any young black comedy writers? Everybody's screaming for them.")

The good news is that a window of opportunity has opened, and

I can only hope that a few of the most talented people will become permanent presences on the Hollywood scene, in turn helping other newcomers to get in on the game and make it in show business.

THE HOLLYWOOD GRAYLIST

Prejudice is prejudice, of course, but Hollywood has its own style in this as in everything else. Age discrimination, for example, is particularly vicious in show business. Hollywood Conventional Wisdom says that the industry is a young person's game and if you haven't made it big by forty, you never will.

But one actor I spoke with recalled that when he entered the business in his early twenties he was told that he was too young and that people were looking primarily for men thirty-five and over. By the time he'd reached his thirties, films were courting the young audience and stressed young brat-pack-age actors. Somehow he was never the right age!

Age discrimination doesn't affect only actors, however. The Caucus for Producers, Writers, and Directors, a group of powerful, award-winning industry insiders, became so concerned at the tales of woe heard from its members that it produced a documentary called "Power and Fear: The Hollywood Graylist" with the International Documentary Association.

As the film reveals, even top producers and writers with extensive track records encounter age discrimination from young film and TV executives who have been hired to court the young audience. These young decision makers often believe the myth that veteran producers, directors, and writers aren't capable of creating programming or films that younger audiences can relate to. Or, even worse as far as the older person's ego is concerned, the junior decision makers have never heard of them! One veteran producer I know resorted to making a videotape describing his award-winning achievements so that he could send it along to new network executives who might not be aware of his illustrious track record.

In my private practice, I counsel many people who are dealing with the effects of discrimination in their careers and their lives. It's always painful, but I've discovered that one group of people seems to have the most difficulty facing and dealing with discrimination:

white men over forty-five. Perhaps it's because they have so recently gone from being part of the in crowd to being in the out crowd. Women and minority people have dealt with discrimination their whole lives. Men who've been spared that experience during their youth are shocked to find that they, too, can be on the wrong end of discrimination.

Entertainment industry technicians, for example, can start to have career problems in their early fifties. Frequently these are men who have had lucrative careers filled with achievement. They've been busy. They've worked hard. But when younger producers or directors start to talk about wanting "a young, hungry" technician who can take the eighteen-hour days, they pass over the older worker.

A statement I came to hate as a development executive was "Let's get a hot young writer in here who can punch this thing up." The implication: older writers can no longer create heat. They're tired, out-of-date hacks with nothing new to say. They can't write "with-it" stuff that young people will enjoy. Tell that to the creators of the film *M*A*S*H,* who were grandfathers when they made one of the hippest films of all time!

Ninety-one-year-old screenwriter Charles Bennett, dubbed "the oldest screenwriter on assignment at a major studio" by *Daily Variety,* offered his thoughts on this problem at a workshop hosted by the Writers Guild of America. Bennett co-wrote some of Alfred Hitchcock's classic films: *The 39 Steps, Foreign Correspondent,* and *The Man Who Knew Too Much.* "Nowadays," Bennett said, "it seems that experience is considered a disadvantage. These older writers—men of fifty or fifty-five—are just not employed, although they're highly experienced and very good writers. But they're not employed because they're considered too old."

Bennett's suggestion: putting together older and younger writers. He has taken his own advice—with his forty-two-year-old writing partner and producer, Stuart Birnbaum, he finished the first draft of an updated version of his 1929 Hitchcock classic, *Blackmail.* The project is at 20th Century Fox.

Less positively, a number of Hollywood writers and producers find they must use younger colleagues and partners as "fronts" to pitch their work if they want to make a sale.

THE HOLLYWOOD GAYLIST

Hollywood takes a paradoxical attitude toward gay and lesbian workers. On the one hand, the industry can be very accepting of different life-styles. Many prominent people in show business are "known" to be gay, and few showbiz folks are shocked or upset by this. Most fancy themselves to be very open-minded about such matters.

On the other hand, job discrimination on the basis of sexual orientation is far from a thing of the past. This problem is particularly acute for actors, especially leading men and romantic leads. Somehow the industry can accept heterosexual actors playing a gay role but finds it more difficult to cast an openly gay actor in a straight role.

LOOKSISM

Hollywood is the home of the hip and the land of the gorgeous. Looks count. More than they should. Hollywood is a visual industry, and even for nonacting roles employers often want to hire people who "look the part" or make them look good. Unfortunately this often means they shun the overweight or the dowdy or the "different."

OK, NOW THAT I'M DEPRESSED, WHAT CAN I DO ABOUT IT ALL?

What can be done to break the cycle and let more people into the club? And what action should you as a job seeker take to overcome discrimination?

Let's assume that you've taken a long, hard look at the people at the top of your particular target niche in the entertainment industry—and you've discovered that you're different in some way from most of the people who could help or hire you. What should you do?

The worst thing you can do is pretend discrimination doesn't exist. Face up to it realistically so you can deal with it. Don't pretend the situation is any less tough or wrong than it is. Unless you're prepared for it, this kind of rejection can attack your self-esteem, no matter how thick your rhino skin is. But don't let this news depress, discourage, or dissuade you from pursuing your chosen career either. Barriers are made to be broken. You *can* break through—if you make the right moves. Nobody said it would be easy. Don't turn the anger inward, where it can fester. Get pissed. Then channel this energy into constructive action, on both an individual and collective level.

The people I know who deal most effectively with discrimination follow a simple plan: they admit it exists. They don't pretend it doesn't. They get appropriately angry about it, but don't blame every problem in their lives on it. They know that not every setback in their Hollywood career is the result of prejudice.

When they decide to take action against discrimination, they don't try to fight it alone, but make every effort to join with others and act collectively. And on a personal career level, in job interviews and on the job, they focus on being positive, doing outstanding work and developing a reputation for that work. They have a sense of humor and use it to their advantage, to defuse difficult situations and to preserve their own sanity. They find a comfortable balance between fitting into the Hollywood community and not losing their special uniqueness. They're fun to be around and easy to connect with, in spite of differences. But they won't take outrageous crap, and they have developed creative ways of letting people know if they're out of line.

ACT COLLECTIVELY

There are many worthwhile organizations in Hollywood that work (with greater or lesser effectiveness) to fight job discrimination. Join one or start one. Pitch in. Help them out, however you can. If you're nervous about going out front on the issue, lick stamps, work on a film they're making on antidiscrimination, answer phones.

Most of the guilds and unions have committees dedicated to combating prejudice. Women in Film has an Issues and Advocacy committee. Ethnic minorities have formed advocacy and support groups. (A bonus: you'll make some great contacts at these important organizations and you'll stay up to date on affirmative action programs at studios and production companies around town which may help you get a foot in the door.)

AND THEN—GET ON WITH YOUR CAREER

At a certain point you just have to ignore the statistics, block out the odds—and get on with your career. If you have the talent, you must find a way to get it out there. Spike Lee and Robert Townsend, for example, didn't spend all of their time in protest groups—they found the money and made some films. It's the only way to protect your sanity.

MAKE IT EASY FOR YOUR POTENTIAL EMPLOYER TO SEE BEYOND YOUR DIFFERENCES

In an ideal world, you shouldn't have to take on the job of helping your future boss see beyond your differences. But this being the real world, it's a fair assumption that sooner or later you'll have to do just that.

So prepare for the possibility that your potential employer may look at you and see that you're "different." If you've been different for a while, you've probably developed your own repertoire of clever ways of getting around this and disarming your prospect. If he or she seems to be truly uncomfortable with your "differentness," humor is probably the most effective tactic. It relaxes everyone, including you. It names the elephant in the room and you can get on with things. This is especially important if no one in your "category" has ever been hired to do this particular job. Never having seen a Korean film editor or a director in a wheelchair, for example, your boss may have trouble imagining such a possibility. Make it easy.

Try to find areas of commonality. Prejudice is an "us and them" kind of thing, and you want to get your potential employer to see you as one of the "uses," not the "thems." Connect, connect, connect— whatever it takes. If there are pictures of a five-year-old on the desk and you have a five-year-old, by all means start a conversation about kids. If you're both writers, a little "ain't it awful . . ." about network or studio executives always helps. You're both on the same side of that one—and, sadly, there's nothing like a shared enemy to unite people.

You won't, of course, change your boss's prejudices, even if you work together. Your employer still may not like most older writers or

Asian technicians or handicapped actors or gay editors or African-American sound mixers or older women casting agents with Eastern European accents. But he or she will make an exception for you, as in "I don't like [or feel comfortable around] most 'different' people, but you're an exception." Yes, this attitude sucks, but you've got the job and you'll have a greater chance of effecting change if you have a little clout.

WHAT IF IT'S REALLY BAD?

If you find yourself in a situation where serious, clearly illegal discrimination is happening and is damaging your career and your self-esteem, something has to be done. Only you can decide if you want to take legal action against your employer. Get advice on this from your guild, your lawyer, your support group, and your career counselor. It's a big step, but it may be the right step. After all, at some point someone just has to say, "I'm mad as hell and I'm not gonna take it anymore!" The question to mull over is: am I the right person to take this stand and is this the right case? A lawyer familiar with civil rights litigation can help you make that determination.

But make this a last resort. It's important to pick your fights carefully. Put your energy where it will do the most good. A lawsuit will take time away from your career, and it won't make you friends. Members of "the club" will tend to stick together when threatened and if you're suing Warner Bros. or Disney, other industry players may fear that if they hire you, they'll incur the wrath of their friends at the studios.

A less radical move is simply to begin looking for work elsewhere. Find a better job and take it.

ADVICE FROM DIRECTOR ROY CAMPANELLA II

Roy Campanella's directing credits include many television movies, episodes, commercials, and documentary films. He directed, produced, and co-wrote the story for the CBS movie "Body of Evidence." Among his more than forty hours of prime-time episodic directing credits are "Frank's Place," "Wiseguy," and "Life Goes On." He is an honors graduate of Harvard College, has an M.B.A. from Columbia

University, and is an associate editor of *Black Film Review*.

Campanella says, "Talent alone isn't enough. As the film director John Huston observed, 'I don't believe cream always rises. I've seen too many talented people not get that one lucky moment. I don't believe that everyone who is supposed to make it does.'

"The 'one lucky moment' Huston speaks of invariably has to do with relationships. This is the area where I feel we as African-Americans are most at a disadvantage."

Campanella stresses the importance of building relationships and maintaining a positive attitude. "For the African-American filmmaker, who at every level will be rejected many times more, in general, than his white counterpart, it is crucial to have a constructive perspective that allows you to function in both mainstream and independent production circles. Continual rejection and lack of opportunity can give birth to a destructive bitterness and paranoia. We must struggle to turn this negative condition into a positive one.

"Once you get an opportunity, it's up to you to use your talent and knowledge to prove yourself. Each individual's circumstances will be different but the positive working relationships you establish and the way you take advantage of each opportunity will help determine the path of your career. But relationships are very often the key to the survival and development of your career. Whoopi Goldberg's outstanding talent and working relationship with Steven Spielberg and Quincy Jones helped to ensure she didn't drift back into obscurity after *The Color Purple*. However, had she lacked box office appeal, we wouldn't be seeing many Whoopi Goldberg movies.

" 'Persistence of vision' is a phrase used to describe the technical phenomenon of viewing a motion picture. It is also an accurate description of what is required for us to achieve our goals."

21

☆

The Luck Factor

★ ★ ★ ★ ★ ★ ★ ★ ★ ★ ★ ★ ★ ★ ★

THE OPPORTUNITY YOU PREPARED FOR

Let me say it right up front: I don't really believe in "lucky breaks." Luck is the opportunity you have prepared for.

Entertainment industry people often tell gullible talk show hosts and journalists that their success is the result of "a lucky break" or "being in the right place at the right time." Perhaps they want to appear modest. Or perhaps they sense that audiences don't really want to see the wires and ropes behind the theater curtains, or to know about the hours of sweat and preparation involved in putting on a magical show. Many fans like to see their Hollywood heroes as larger than life, blessed by the gods—and to believe that stardom can happen to them too if only Lady Luck discovers them in Schwabs.

When you hear one of these "How I Made It" stories on Arsenio Hall that attributes Hollywood success to a lucky break or great timing, dig deeper. You'll discover that being prepared for opportunity is the secret to good luck.

A SHAGGY DOG "GOOD LUCK" STORY

Once upon a time my friend Sascha Schneider, who won an Emmy as one of the producers of "Hill Street Blues" and who went on to produce "Scarecrow and Mrs. King" and many other top TV shows, was walking down the Third Street Promenade in Santa Monica with his wife, Laurie, and little daughter Hannah.

He saw another couple coming toward them, with two children. Sascha, who escaped from the former Soviet Union when he was thirteen, turned to Laurie and said, "Russians."

"Oh, come on," said Laurie. "There's no way you could tell that just by looking at them."

"I'll prove it," said Sascha.

He walked up to the couple and began speaking Russian to them. Their eyes lit up.

They told their whole story to Sascha. They had just arrived from the city of Tashkent in Uzbek, and they desperately needed work. Alex was a computer programmer.

Sascha loves to be the agent of "good luck." Many people helped him and his family when they needed it. So he decided to help Alex.

"You have to meet my friend Larry Saltzman," Sascha said. (Larry, a pioneer in applying computer technology to the entertainment industry, was then designing a database for Viacom Productions.)

Larry was happy to help Alex. He trained him on some new programs (the software in Tashkent was a little behind the times) and gave him his first job in America.

Alex worked hard and did well. On the strength of his first American "credit," he got a job at Shop TV, the J.C. Penney television shopping service.

Some months later, when Alex had completed that assignment and was looking for another job through a headhunter, the executive recruiter called Larry for a reference, which Larry was happy to give. Almost as an afterthought, Larry told the headhunter about his own background and experience. Within two weeks Larry was approached by the executive recruiter for a job as a consultant at a major studio in their consumer products division, with a substantial salary increase. And he then hired Alex to do some programming for him on this new job.

Some people might call this a story full of lucky breaks, but I see it as a tale of opportunities offered and taken. All the people involved had their eyes open for new possibilities, and were ready to seize them when they presented themselves. If these particular opportunities hadn't come along, they would have found others. And if they hadn't actively pursued the opportunities that *were* offered, this unique sequence of "good luck" wouldn't have happened.

HOW TO GET LUCKY!

Every day offers you many "lucky" opportunities. Whether or not you seize them depends on how prepared you are to really win.

Life is like a shooting gallery at a carnival, where brightly colored tin ducks parade in a never-ending display in front of your eyes. The choice is yours. You can decide to play or to walk on by. You can grump about the two bits it costs to pay for a ticket. You can stare wistfully at the stuffed purple rhinoceros and the cuddly pink teddy bear but take no action. You can grouse that the game is rigged, so why try? You can grab a pop gun and shoot wildly, trying the scattershot approach. You can get discouraged after missing a few ducks and quit in disgust. You can mutter to yourself that you never have any luck.

Or you can decide to win.

UNPREPARED PEOPLE SABOTAGE "LUCKY" OPPORTUNITIES

The principles of luck work both ways.

I have met many people in my practice who have had "lucky" breaks and opportunities and let them pass by.

I know an actor who was approached by a top agent after giving a terrific theater performance. The agent gave him his card and said, "Call me." The actor lost the card.

I know an editor who formed a close working relationship in the cutting room with a top director but didn't have the confidence to stay in touch after the show was over.

I know a casting director who had an important meeting scheduled with a director on the Monday after a major holiday. She chose to spend that holiday skiing on a slope that was too advanced for her. By Monday she was in the hospital with a broken leg. Was this "bad luck" or self-sabotage?

And is it "good luck" when a persistent actor happens to crash the right audition? Is it luck when a year of shmoozing pays off with a chance encounter with the perfect boss? Is it luck when three years of screenwriting finally result in a sale?

YOU CAN IMPROVE THE ODDS

At the beginning of this book I talked about the extraordinary level of competition in the entertainment industry, the hundreds of thousands of people you are competing with for the few available Hollywood jobs.

Now that you've read the book, I believe you've begun to turn the odds around so that they are more in your favor.

Imagine that you're in a giant baseball stadium, containing all the people who are presently working or who want to work in Hollywood. The place is jammed to the gills. The bleachers are full. The ball field is packed. More people are trying to get through the gate. Others are climbing over the fence. You're squeezed in between a burly grip with a pot belly wearing pink suspenders and a petite production accountant with red hair who looks like Bette Midler.

Now remove all the people who don't understand the game and how it works.

Subtract the folks who don't have the basic talent and training.

Take away those who have no focus and are wandering around aimlessly, hoping that chance and "luck" will hit them on the head.

Forget the people who don't know how to make the right moves— who can't pitch, track information, shmooze, and stay in action.

Scratch the group that doesn't have rhino skin.

Eliminate the people who sabotage themselves and aren't ready to let themselves win.

Now look around the ball field.

There's still a good crowd of well-qualified players who are formidable competitors, but things are definitely looking better.

This should be an interesting game.

Talk That Talk!

★ ★ ★ ★ ★ ★ ★ ★ ★ ★ ★ ★ ★ ★ ★ ★

A GLOSSARY OF SHOWBIZ JARGON

When in Hollywood, why not talk like the natives? The following is an incomplete but I hope interesting list of terms thrown around over power lunches all over town. To keep up with the latest jargon, you may want to catch the new issues of the trades and *Premiere* magazine.

Above the line: The "line" in question is one that appears on budgets for movie or TV shows which separates the "important creative talent"—actors, writers, director, producers—from the supposedly less important, less creative talent that actually does the hands-on production of the project—production manager, cinematographer, editor, the crews. These lowly creatures are known as the below-the-line folks. Unfortunately a sort of class prejudice has evolved in the industry separating the "powers that be" from the "worker bees." There is a faintly blue-collar connotation to "below-the-line," and it can be quite difficult to cross over from a below-the-line job to a "creative" job.

A-list: Of highest rank, as in "Get me an A-list director!"

Back end: Refers not to a starlet's derriere but to the percentage points in a deal that assure talent of a participation in the mythical profits. Gross points are most desirable (straight off the top of the studio's take) whereas net points allow the producers and studio to charge outrageous overhead against the project so that "profits" somehow never happen. Ask Art Buchwald.

Beat sheet: A beat-by-beat outline of the story. (*See* **Story beats**.)

Below the line: *See* **Above the line**.

Breakdowns: Breakdown Services is a company that "breaks down" scripts, detailing roles that are available. These breakdowns are available to managers and agents—for a fee, of course.

Buzz: Similar to **Word of mouth**. The talk around town. As in "The buzz is good on the new Costner film [or the new Disney regime]."

Calling card film: A.k.a. showcase or resume film. A film that demonstrates your special talents.

Castable: Describes a project that has desirable roles for name talent.

Character arc: The difference between where a character is at the beginning of a script and where she has advanced to by the end of the story. Actors enjoy the opportunity to play characters with this kind of "range of change."

Coverage: Story analysis of a literary property. Includes synopsis plus opinions on the property. If you want a story analysis or development job, you may be asked to provide samples of coverage you have done.

Creative differences: A.k.a. "warring egos." Sometimes a euphemism for "fired." "Director X left the film because of 'creative differences' with the star." Uh-hunh . . .

Dailies (or Rushes): The results of a day's shooting that are screened as soon as possible so that the director, studio, and producers can see how they're doing. "I can't meet you till ten. We have dailies."

Development hell: The often-protracted period between the creation or optioning of a literary property and the "green light."

D-person: Development person. A person who works on the acquisition and development of literary properties for films and television. This group includes everyone from the lowly readers and story analysts up through the story editors, and creative affairs vice presidents. Sometimes **D-Girl** or **D-Boy**, terms that are considered insulting.

Elements: The talent that is attached to a project to make it an attractive "package." Usually actors, director, (re)writer, name producer.

First look: An arrangement with a production company or studio whereby they get to see a producer's projects before anyone else does, with the option to get involved or not at their discretion.

Fish out of water: A Hollywood story formula that has often proved successful. The hero or heroine is thrown into a milieu or situation in which he or she is out of his or her natural element. *Beverly Hills Cop* and *Crocodile Dundee* are good examples.

Flavor of the Month: The newest person with "heat." *Premiere* magazine carries a regular "Flavor of the Month" column to keep you up to date on who's hot.

Franchise; Franchise continuity: In features, a franchise is a "brand name" character or story with presold elements that make marketing easier. Sometimes it's a character like Rocky who can be counted on for at least four sequels, or the Alec Baldwin character in *The Hunt for Red October*, who will appear in subsequent adaptations of Tom Clancy novels (sans Alec Baldwin). Sometimes it's a hit movie like *Back to the Future* or *Nightmare on Elm Street* that spawns endless offspring. *Star Trek* seems to be an endless franchise. In a business where making and marketing each new movie is like starting a new business, major studios lust after lucrative franchises. **Franchise continuity** is the buzzword for "heaven."

(In television, "franchise" sometimes refers to the arena in which the action takes place. "What's the franchise?" a network executive will anxiously ask the would-be series writer or producer.)

Going indie prod: Becoming an independent producer after holding a studio or production company job. Can be a euphemism for "unemployed" or "fired."

Go picture: A picture that is really going to happen, one that has gotten a "green light."

Green light: A yes. The most powerful people in the industry are those whose yes can put a film into production, or "green light" it.

Halo effect: The golden glow that shines on your career if you work on a hit, even if your efforts had nothing to do with its success.

Heat: What you (and your agent, manager, and publicist if you're fortunate enough to have them) try to generate about yourself and your talents.

Hiatus: The time in the spring when TV series are down. Also the time between the completion of last season's shows and the beginning of this season's shows.

High concept: A story idea that lends itself to a snappy, one-line description (*see* **Logline**) Often a concept or premise with a catchy gimmick, as in "Danny De Vito and Arnold Schwarzenegger are . . . Twins!" Instant green light. Walt Disney Studios Chairman Jeffrey Katzenberg's famous January 1991 leaked memo claimed to give the real "lowdown on high concept." He said that high concept is "one of the most misunderstood and misused phrases in the Hollywood lexicon" and that it was introduced by Michael Eisner when he and Katzenberg were at Paramount to describe "a unique idea whose originality could be conveyed briefly. The emphasis was supposed to be on 'originality' but has come to be placed on 'briefly,' so that today 'high concept' is thought to mean an idea that can be summarized in a logline in *TV Guide*."

History: (As in, "They have history.") Since Hollywood is such a small town, many of its players have history with each other—often unpleasant history, creative disputes, arguments, vendettas, lawsuits. This complicates the process of putting elements together on a project. Did Goldie quarrel with Zemekis on a previous film? Is the A-list cinematographer you're thinking of hiring a former lover of the production designer? Isn't the star's lawyer a sworn enemy of the studio's production exec? They have history.

Honey wagon: A very important trailer on location—it contains the rest rooms.

Hot set: A set that's ready for shooting. Don't touch!

Housekeeping deal: A deal whereby a studio or company gives a producer, producer-writer, producer-director, or producer-actor free space in return for first look at the properties they develop. May or may not also include salary of secretary, phone expenses, salary of a development staff, money for the producer, etc.

Hyphenate: A double- or triple-talented person. As in writer-director or producer-director-star.

The industry; the business: The entertainment industry, of course, which as we all know is the only business that counts!

Legs: Something a project has if it is considered to do well in the long run. As in "The movie opened well, but does it have legs?" Translation: "The movie did well in the all-important first few days, but will it continue to do business?"

Letshavelunch: Not to be confused with "Let's have lunch." The former is a pleasantry, not to be taken as reality or a sincere desire to sit across from you at the Ivy. The latter is really an invitation. Learning to tell the difference between these two terms can help save your sanity!

Logline: A one-line description of the plot as it might appear in *TV Guide.*

Movie cross: A shorthand way of describing a story, as in *Field of Dreams* meets *Robocop.* (Hmmm, that might be interesting. Let's take a meeting on it!)

Movie jail: Where you land when you've had a few bombs. The opposite of "heat"—no one will hire you. But movie jail, like Monopoly jail, usually doesn't last forever. Sooner or later, if you're persistent, someone will hire you and if your project does well—you're hot again!

Negative pick up: This sounds like a bad night on Hollywood Boulevard, but it's really a more or less independently produced movie that is picked up by a major (a major studio) for distribution.

One sheet: The poster for a movie.

On the nose: Obvious or trite. Casting or writing that is too on the nose is considered unimaginative or uncreative.

Open: A movie that opens is one that attracts an audience in the all-important first few days.

Orphan project: A project whose champion at the studio or production company has left or lost favor.

Over the top: Excessive, exaggerated. Acting or writing that is over the top is embarrassingly unsubtle.

Packaging: Putting the elements (see definition above) together on a project to make it a more attractive property.

Pay or play: A deal whereby a studio or company is obligated to pay a talent whether or not that talent is actually used in the project ("played"). For example, the studio holds ("nails down") a director with a pay-or-play contract, but the film never gets made or the studio decides not to use her. According to this deal, she must be paid her full salary anyway. Nice work if you can get it, you might say! But actually, most showbiz people would much rather make the film than be paid off.

Phone it in: To make a merely perfunctory effort. "His performance was really disappointing. He phoned it in."

Phone monkey: A derogatory term for Hollywood people who spend the day shmoozing, deal making, and hustling on the phone. Reportedly this term was invented by Alec Baldwin to describe a Disney studio production executive who annoyed him on the troubled set of *The Marrying Man.*

Property: Literary material that forms the basis for a movie or TV project. Book, script, treatment, etc.

Short list; short-listed: As in "She's short-listed to direct *Slimy Critters from Mars* at Fox." When producers or studio people are putting together a picture, they create lists of possible creative talent. These lists are then shrunk to a short list of prime contenders.

Show runner: A TV term for a writer-producer with enough clout, talent, or experience to run an entire series. Who determines if a writer-producer is a show runner? The buyer, of course.

Sides: Pages of script that actors read during audition. As in "I only had five minutes to go over the sides before I was called in."

Spec script: A screenplay written on speculation, not commissioned by a studio or producer.

Story beats: The major plot points in a story.

Stunt casting: Attaching very strong actors to a project to make it a more desirable "package."

Suit: An executive (creative or business), sometimes a lawyer or an agent. A disparaging term for meddling folks who aren't hands-on creative or production people.

Taft-Hartleyed: As in "I was Taft-Hartleyed into SAG [the Screen Actors Guild]." If you're not a guild member but a producer wants to hire you on a union project, you can be Taft-Hartleyed into the union because no union can prevent a producer from hiring you. The casting director or producer will send a report to SAG giving their reasons for hiring you and not a union member. This is a fast way to get into the guild.

Take a meeting: Have or attend a meeting.

Tent poles: The tent poles of a production slate are the supposedly surefire blockbuster pictures that hold up the tent, making room for lesser pictures under their sheltering presence. Often wishful thinking, of course.

Topper: *Variety*-ese for "top executive," as in "Fox topper Barry Diller."

The town: Hollywood, of course. Is there any other town on the planet Earth? A synonym for the entertainment industry community at large. As in "She's perceived in the town as an up-and-comer."

Turnaround: A bump on the road through development hell. A script has been commissioned or optioned by a studio, which then decides against producing it. They put it back on the market. This is called putting it into turnaround. Turnaround scripts are very desirable to many other studios that hope that by cracking whatever story problems remain they can get a property that is nearly "shootable" and thus shorten the stay in development hell.

Web: *Variety*-ese for broadcast network.

Weblet: *Variety*-ese for the Fox network.

Word of mouth: What people are saying. Good word of mouth is the best marketing a film can have.

Wrap: As in "It's a wrap!" The end of the principal shooting of a picture. Usually followed by a wrap party, a great opportunity to get in a last, frenzied round of networking and bonding to help you land your next job. Even if you didn't work on the picture, try to wrangle an invitation. And even if you've worked long and hard on a miserable project, don't succumb to the temptation to overimbibe and make a fool of yourself—the town has a long memory.

Additional writer's jargon:

★ Back story

★ Deep characterization

★ Exposition

★ Foreshadowing

★ Progressive complications

★ Story spine; story backbone

★ Subtext (also used by directors and actors)

★ The inciting incident

★ Upping the stakes

Screenwriting classes will fill you in on these important terms.

HOLLYWOOD YIDDISH

Among the founders of the movie industry were a number of Eastern European Jewish immigrants who discovered this new field open to them, as corporate America was not. As a result, a rich fund of delightful Yiddish expressions are commonly used around town. "Shmoozing" and "chutzpah" you've already discovered. Here are some additional terms you may hear thrown around:

Bubkes (or Bopkes): Something trivial, worthless. As in "His word on this doesn't mean bopkes."

Cockamamy: Ridiculous. As in "Don't bring me your cockamamy schemes!"

Dreck: Garbage. The exact English equivalent: crap. Describes a worthless film, TV show or performance.

Macher: An important person, a big shot, an operator.

Mench (or mensh): A person of integrity. A compliment. As in "He's a real mench" (He's a real, upright guy).

Meshugge: Crazy. "Mishegoss" is craziness, as in "What's her mishegoss? ("What's her problem?").

Shlep; shlepper: To drag. Casually used for distance, as in "Burbank is a shlep from here." A shlepper can be a not-too-complimentary term for a laborer, as in "Let's get a few shleppers in here to carry the equipment."

Shnook; Shlemiel: Uncomplimentary names for ineffective people.

Shtik (or shtick): The first Hollywood term I ever learned, and I still love it. Leo Rosten's *The Joys of Yiddish* defines it as "a studied, contrived or characteristic piece of business employed by an actor," "a prank," "a piece of misconduct," and "a devious trick." You see the problem with these expressions! They can mean whatever the speaker wants them to mean. But it's usually used as in "What's Sam's shtik?" or "Don't pull a shtik like that on me." A *Premiere* magazine article (March 1990) on mogul Jon Peters explained that "Peters does his street-shmooze shtick: 'Aaayyy, sweetie!' he'll yell into the phone. 'How ya doin?' "

Yenta: Originally a gossipy woman but now used for anyone who gets involved in others' business and is a good matchmaker. An agent, for instance, might be described admiringly as a yenta who's great at getting everybody together on a project.

To enjoy more Hollywood "Yinglish," I recommend buying a copy of Leo Rosten's book *The Joys of Yiddish* (New York: McGraw Hill, 1974).

Resources

★ ★ ★ ★ ★ ★ ★ ★ ★ ★ ★ ★ ★ ★

(Note: Many of the publications mentioned below can be ordered through entertainment industry bookstores and catalogs. Double-check all addresses and phone numbers. Be aware that as this book is being published, Los Angeles is dividing the (213) area code in two, with many numbers moving to the (310) area code, so if a number doesn't work as (213), try (310). Information may change between the time a book is published and the time you read it. And, in spite of our best efforts, mistakes and typos can occur. Be especially careful before sending out letters or money. To help me update this book for future editions, I'd appreciate your sending any additions, changes, or comments to: Linda Buzzell, Entertainment Industry Career Institute, Box 108, 3435 Ocean Park Blvd., Suite 206, Santa Monica, CA 90405.)

CHAPTERS 1–2

The Bad and the Beautiful, starring Kirk Douglas. MGM, 1952. Director: Vincent Minelli. Douglas portrays a Hollywood type still much in evidence: the ruthless producer who is both loved and hated by those who work with him. But even those who hate him have to admit he spurs them on to do their best work.

The Big Picture, starring Kevin Bacon. Columbia Pictures, 1988. Director: Christopher Guest. A sardonic look at how a film school graduate is corrupted by the Hollywood system.

Fleming, Charles. "Failing Upward in Movieland." *M*, January 1992.

Goldman, William. *Adventures in the Screen Trade.* New York: Warner Books, 1983.

Harmetz, Aljean. "Glory and Humiliation in the Screen Trade," *Esquire,* July 1991.

Head Office, starring Judge Reinhold. Silver Screen/HBO/Guber-Peters, 1985. Director: Ken Finkelman. Word is that the character played by Rick Moranis was based on a well-known Yeller/Screamer film producer. "You're killing me here!" he screams at a colleague on the phone, "but I love this business." A wicked impersonation. And the office politics depicted in the film aren't that different from studio politics in Hollywood. Another character admits, "I love the action."

Hughes, Kathleen A. "Phony Power: Technology Leads to New Absurdities in a Hollywood Obsessed with the Telephone," *Wall Street Journal,* 9 November 1990.

Litwak, Mark. *Reel Power: The Struggle for Influence and Success in the New Hollywood.* New York: William Morrow, 1986.

Matthews, Jack. "The Ethics of Hollywood," *Los Angeles Times,* 22 April 1990.

McClintick, David. *Indecent Exposure: A True Story of Hollywood and Wall Street.* New York: Morrow, 1982. A behind-the-scenes look at Hollywood politics through the David Begelman/Columbia Pictures embezzlement scandal.

Phillips, Julia. *You'll Never Eat Lunch in This Town Again.* New York: Random House, 1991.

Salamon, Julie. *The Devil's Candy: "The Bonfire of the Vanities" Goes to Hollywood.* New York: Houghton Mifflin Co., 1991.

"Sexual Harassment: Hollywood's Dirty Little Secret." *Entertainment Weekly,* 6 December 1991.

S.O.B., starring Richard Mulligan, Julie Andrews. Lorimar, 1981. Director: Blake Edwards. Although marred by some offensively stereotyped characters, this film depicts the Hollywood game as it was played in the late 1970s—and was made by a true Hollywood insider. Robert Vaughn plays a wonderfully sleazy studio exec, and other characters include the insincere Hollywood agent, the cringing publicist, the mad director, and the neurotic star. Some hilarious moments.

CHAPTER 3

Association of Independent Video and Filmmakers. 625 Broadway, 9th Floor, New York, NY 10012. (212) 473-3400. Resource center and library for independent filmmakers.

Independent Feature Project. 132 West 21 Street, 6th Floor, New York, NY 10011. (212) 243-7777. Fax: 212-243-3882. Independent Feature Project/West, 5550 Wilshire Blvd., Suite 204, Los Angeles, CA 90036. (213) 937-4379. Independent Feature Project/Northern California, P.O. Box 460040, San Francisco, CA 94146. (415) 826-0574. Independent Feature Project/Midwest, P.O. Box 148026, Chicago, IL 60614. (312) 549-7989. Independent Feature Project/North, 1401 Third Avenue South, Minneapolis, MN 55404. (612) 870-0156.

Sundance Institute. c/o Drea Hoffman, 4000 Warner Blvd., Producers Bldg. 4, Rm. 11, Burbank, CA 91522. (818) 954-4776. Also R.R. #3, Box 624-B, Sundance, UT 84604.

CHAPTER 4

Hirsh, Sandra, and Jean Kummerow. *Life Types: Understand Yourself and Make the Most of Who You Are.* New York: Warner Books, 1989. This is my favorite book for helping people determine their temperament code.

Keirsey, David, and Marilyn Bates. *Please Understand Me: Character and Temperament Types.* Del Mar, Calif.: Prometheus Nemesis, 1984.

Kroeger, Otto, and Janet M. Thuesen. *Type Talk: How to Determine Your Personality Type and Change Your Life.* New York: Delacorte Press, 1988.

Sinetar, Marsha. *Do What You Love: The Money Will Follow.* New York: Paulist Press, 1987. This book has a great chapter on the difference between work as play and work as addiction.

CHAPTER 5

Books That Describe Entertainment Industry Jobs

Blanksteen, Jane, and Avi Odeni. *TV Careers Behind the Screen.* New York: John Wiley & Sons, 1987.

Brouwer, Alexandra, and Thomas Lee Wright. *Working in Hollywood: 64 Film Professionals Talk About Moviemaking.* New York: Crown Publishers, 1990.

Hines, William E. *Job Descriptions: Responsibilities and Duties for the Film and Video Craft Categories and Classifications.* Los Angeles, Calif.: Ed-Venture Films/Books, 1984.

London, Mel. *Getting into Film.* New York: Ballantine Books, 1986.

Rachlin, Harvey. *The TV and Movie Business: An Encyclopedia of Careers, Technologies, and Practices.* New York: Harmony Books, 1991.

Reed, Maxine K., and Robert M. Reed. *Career Opportunities in Television, Cable and Video,* 2nd ed. New York: Facts on File Publications, 1986.

Resources for Writers

Beil, Norman, ed. *The Writer's Legal and Business Guide: For Motion Pictures, TV and Books.* New York: Arco Publishing. 1989.

The Hollywood Scriptwriter newsletter. 1626 N. Wilcox, #385, Hollywood, CA 90028. (818) 991-3096. Kerry Cox, editor.

Independent Writers of Southern California. P.O. Box 34518, Los Angeles, CA 90034. (213) 470-9654.

Robert McKee. McKee, a well-known screenwriting teacher, can be reached at Two Arts, 12021 Wilshire Blvd., #823, Los Angeles, CA 90025. (213) 312-1002.

Rick Pamplin's Screenwriting Workshop: How to Sell Your Material to Hollywood. 8306 Wilshire Blvd., #294, Beverly Hills, CA 90211. (213) 465-0993. Pamplin is one of the most savvy teachers in town about what ideas and concepts will sell to Hollywood. He helps his students develop sellable movie premises. If he likes a student's idea, he may option it himself.

Performance Writing Workshop. Helps actors write a one-act play to showcase their particular talent. Led by playwright-director-actor Bruce McIntosh. (213) 285-9480.

Sautter, Carl. *How to Sell Your Screenplay: The Real Rules of Film and Television.* New York: New Chapter Press, 1988.

Seger, Linda. *Making a Good Script Great: A Guide to Writing and Rewriting by a Hollywood Script Consultant.* Hollywood, Calif.: Samuel French Trade, 1987. Seger is a well-regarded "script doctor."

Truby Writer's Studio. 1739 Midvale Avenue, Los Angeles, CA 90024. (213) 575-3050 or (800)33-TRUBY. Founded by story structure teacher John Truby, TWS offers classes, audiotapes, books, and software. Special programs on genres, TV writing. Also offers a "Writers' Black Belt Program," in which a consultant works with students to complete a script and then (according to the brochure) helps you get it to industry players.

Writer's Boot Camp. 1950 S. Pelham, #1, Los Angeles, CA 90025. (213) 470-8849. If you're having trouble getting that script written, Jeff Gordon's program is designed to sweat it out of you.

Additional Resources

American Federation of Musicians (AFM). 1777 N. Vine St., Suite 410, Hollywood, CA 90028, (213) 461-3441. FAX: (213) 432-8340.

Paul Gray's Film Directing Seminar. (213) 556-3516.

Katahn, T. L. *Reading for a Living: How to Be a Professional Story Analyst for Film and Television.* Pacific Palisades, Calif.: Blue Arrow Books, 1990.

Premiere magazine's "Cameos" section gives excellent portraits of people in many entertainment industry jobs and describes the career track they took to get where they are.

Judith Weston's Acting for Directors. (310) 396-1765.

See the bookstore catalogs (Chapter 8 Resources) for additional books and tapes on entertainment industry careers. Also watch the trades for seminars.

CHAPTER 6

Assistant Directors Training Program. Kate Tilley, Chairperson, Training Plan Board of Trustees, Directors Guild of America, 7920 Sunset Blvd., Los Angeles, CA 90046. (213) 289-2000.

Hubbell, Joan. "Celluloid Sheepskins." *American Film*, April 1991.

CHAPTER 7

Birnbaum, Jane. "Learning to Throw the Inside Pitch." *New York*, 25 March 1991.

Dworski, David. "The Pitching Workshop" (audio cassette), Dworski & Associates, 309 Santa Monica Blvd., Suite 420, Santa Monica, CA 90401. (301) 394-3900.

Kosberg, Robert, with Mim Eichler. *How to Sell Your Idea to Hollywood*. New York: HarperPerennial, 1991.

CHAPTER 8

"Inside Everything: The Modern Mania for Knowing More Than You Need to Know About the Way Everything in the World Works," *Spy*, June 1990.

Obst, Lynda. "To Live and Die by the Trades," *Premiere*, April 1991.

"Power in Hollywood: The Sequel," *Premiere*, May 1991.

Toffler, Alvin. *Powershift: Knowledge, Wealth, and Violence at the Edge of the 21st Century*. New York: Bantam Books, 1990.

Directories

Academy Players Directory. Academy of Motion Picture Arts and Sciences, 8949 Wilshire Blvd., Beverly Hills, CA 90211. (213) 278-8990. A visual telephone directory of actors, listing their agents. Categories include: young leading man/lady; leading man/lady; character actors and comedians; children. Expensive to buy. Can be consulted at the Academy Library.

Directors Guild of America Directory. Directors Guild of America, 7920 Sunset

Blvd., Hollywood, CA 90046. (213) 289-2000. Lists guild members with their credits. Free to members.

Hollywood Creative Directory: The Complete Who's What and Where in Motion Picture and TV Development and Production. Hollywood Creative Directory, 3000 Olympic Blvd., Suite 2413, Santa Monica, CA 90404. (213) 315-4815. FAX: (213) 315-4816. Includes 2,000 cross-referenced names. Expensive but worth the price. Published three times per year by Hollywood Creative Directory, which also publishes the *Hollywood Agents Directory*, a listing of both talent and literary agencies by agent's name, specialty, and agency; *The Complete Reference Guide to TV Movies and Minis, '84–'89;* and *Feature Writers '80–'89.*

Hollywood Personnel Directories (Feature Script Submission Directory; Overall Deals at the Studios: Producers, Directors, Writers, and Stars; TV Producers; TV Syndicators). DVE Productions, 3017 Santa Monica Blvd., Suite 304, #149, Santa Monica, CA 90404. (213) 281-7637. Call for sample.

Hollywood Reporter Blu-Book Directory. Available from the *Hollywood Reporter* (see below). Lists addresses and phone numbers for production companies, support services, postproduction, film and tape, distribution companies, law firms, international companies. Updated and published annually.

International Documentary Association Membership Directory and Survival Guide. International Documentary Association, 1551 South Robertson Blvd., Suite 201, Los Angeles, CA 90035. (213) 284-8422.

LA 411. Detailed resource of L.A. film and tape production (especially commercials). Includes free-lancers from directors of photography to production assistants; where to find equipment, props, wardrobe; location information; postproduction; and just about everything else. Updated and published annually. Available from LA 411 Publishing, P.O. Box 480495, Los Angeles, CA 90048. (213) 460-6304. Accepts listings from free-lancers.

Lone Eagle Directories. Lone Eagle Publishing, 9903 Santa Monica Blvd., Beverly Hills, CA 90212. (213) 471-8066. Call for brochure. Books include: *Film Directors: A Complete Guide,* by Michael Singer; *Film Producers, Studios, Agents and Casting Directors Guide,* by Susan Avallone and Jack Lechner; *Cinematographers, Production Designers, Costume Designers and Film Editors Guide,* by Susan Avallone; *Film Writers Guide,* by Susan Avallone; *Television Writers Guide,* by Lynne Naylor; *Special Effects and Stunts Guide,* by Tassilo Baur and Bruce Scivally; *Film Composers Guide,* by Steven C. Smith; *Television Directors Guide,* by Lynne Naylor; and *Film Actors Guide,* by Steve LuKanic.

Los Angeles Entertainment Industry Fax Directory. J. Belsher Co., 2606 El

Cerrito, San Luis Obispo, CA 93401. (805) 542-0800. For those of you who believe in faxing resumes, this may be worth checking out.

Pacific Coast Studio Directory. Lists addresses and phone numbers for agents, studios, TV stations, production companies, guilds and unions, special effects people, stunt people, suppliers of unusual products and services (aircraft, animals, etc.) Publishes quarterly. Available from Pacific Coast Studio Directory, 6313 Yucca St., Hollywood, CA 90028. (213) 467-2920.

Producer's Masterguide. Gives much the same info as *LA 411* but includes international listings as well. Intended for production managers. Worldwide info on permits, guilds, festivals, etc., but practical for location work as it includes rental houses listed by states in the United States and in other countries. Updated and published annually. Available from the Producer's Masterguide, 330 W. 42nd St., 16th Fl., New York, NY 10036-6994. (212) 465-8889.

Ross Reports. Lists contact people for TV shows currently in production. Published monthly. Available from Samuel French, 7623 Sunset Blvd., Hollywood, CA 90046. (213) 876-0570.

Variety Who's Who in Show Business (1989). Gives short biographies and lists credits for industry notables from all categories. Available from R.R. Bowker, 245 W 17th St., New York, NY 10011.

Who's Who in the Motion Picture Industry: Major Studios, Production Companies and Distributors, 6th ed. Rodman Gregg, Packard House Books, P.O. Box 2187, Beverly Hills, CA 90213.

Writers Guild of America Directory. Lists guild members with their credits. Includes separate listings for ethnic minorities, women, and writers over forty. Available from the Writers Guild of America, 8955 Beverly Blvd., Los Angeles, CA 90048. (213) 550-1000. Free to members.

Entertainment Industry Libraries

The **Academy of Television Arts and Sciences Library,** 5200 Lankershim Blvd., Suite 340, North Hollywood, CA 91601. (818) 752-1870. Files, books, archive materials. Open to the public.

The **American Film Institute Library** is located on the AFI campus at 2021 North Western Ave., Los Angeles, CA 90027. (213) 856-7655. I have been told that this library has been temporarily closed to the general public, serving only AFI students, but I hope that it will be able to offer its excellent services more widely again soon.

The **Lincoln Center Performing Arts Library**, 111 Amsterdam Avenue, New York, NY 10019, (212) 870-1630. An excellent library for all the arts. Includes archive.

The **Margaret Herrick Library** and the **Academy Film Archive** are located at the Academy of Motion Picture Arts and Sciences' Center for Motion Picture Study, 333 South La Cienega Blvd., Beverly Hills, CA 90211. (213) 247-3000. Call (213) 247-3020 if you have a research question. The center has clipping files on 60,000 films and 50,000 people; 18,000 books, pamphlets, and periodicals; 5,000 scripts; 5 million still photographs; and over 12,000 films.

The **UCLA Theatre Arts Library** is on the UCLA campus in Westwood, 405 Hilgard Ave., Los Angeles, CA 90024. (213) 825-4880.

The **University of Southern California's Cinema-TV Library** on USC's downtown campus boasts 60,000 clipping files on personalities and film/TV titles, plus 10,000 scripts. It also has a press book collection and stills, audio, and videotapes. (213) 740-8906.

Some of the libraries have limited hours, so be sure to check times.

Entertainment Industry Bookstores

Larry Edmunds Bookstore, 6658 Hollywood Blvd., Hollywood, CA 90028. (213) 463-3273. Also has a branch in the San Fernando Valley.

Samuel French's Theatre & Film Bookshop, 7623 Sunset Blvd., Hollywood, CA 90046. (213) 876-0570. FAX: (213) 876-6822. Also has a branch in the San Fernando Valley. I recommend that you order "The Samuel French's Theatre & Film Bookshop Catalog," which will be mailed to you for a modest charge (check current rate). The catalog includes industry directories plus books on every aspect of show business. Many of the publications mentioned in this book can be ordered through French's catalog. There's also a selection of scripts, T-shirts, mugs, and showbiz gift items.

Elliot M. Katt: Books on the Performing Arts, 8568 Melrose Ave., Los Angeles, CA 90069. (213) 652-5178. (800) 445-4561 for credit card orders outside of California. FAX: (213) 659-3521. Katt has an excellent catalog that you may want to order: "Technical & Reference Books On Cinema, Acting, Music & Writing."

Script City is a bookstore-by-mail. You may call them at (213) 871-0707 for a mail-order catalog that includes scripts of feature films, TV episodes and TV movies, computer software, how-to audiotapes, and Hollywood paraphernalia. 8033 Sunset Blvd., Suite 1500, Hollywood, CA 90046.

The Trades

Daily Variety
5700 Wilshire Blvd. #120
Los Angeles, CA 90036
(213) 857-6600

Hollywood Reporter
6715 Sunset Blvd.
Hollywood, CA 90028
(213) 464-7411

Entertainment Industry Databases

BASELINE, 8929 Wilshire Blvd., Suite 100, Beverly Hills, CA 90211. (213) 659-3830; (800) CHAPLIN. FAX: (213) 659-9890. New York office: 838 Broadway, New York, NY 10003. (212) 254-8235. FAX: (212) 529-3330.

Celebrity Service International, 8833 Sunset Blvd., Los Angeles, CA 90069. (213) 652-9910. In New York: 1780 Broadway, Suite 300, New York, NY 10019. (212) 245-1460. If you qualify, for approximately $200 a month you can make up to five telephone inquiries a day to a researcher who has been assigned to you. Industry insiders sometimes use Celebrity Service if they're putting projects together, casting talent, booking a talk show, or planning a party or fund-raiser. Celebrity Service publishes a "Contact Book," which contains over 5,000 listings of talent agents, PR people, personal managers, producers, etc.

Entertainment Data, 331 North Maple Drive, Beverly Hills, CA 90210. (213) 271-2105; (800) NAT-GROSS. FAX: (213) 271-2856.

Entertainment Industry Conventions

Showbiz Expo, 2122 Hillhurst Ave., Los Angeles, CA 90027-2068. (213) 668-1811. Held in the spring in Los Angeles and in the fall in New Jersey.

American Film Market (AFM). 12424 Wilshire Blvd., Suite 600, Los Angeles, CA 90025, (310) 447-1555. FAX: (310) 447-1666. Held in February or March in Los Angeles.

NATPE International Programming Conference, 10100 Santa Monica Blvd., Suite 300, Los Angeles, CA 90067. (301) 282-8801. FAX: (301) 282-0760.

Other Resources

Breakdown Services, 1120 S. Robertson Blvd., Los Angeles, CA 90035. (213) 276-9166. Provides script breakdowns to managers and agents.

Paul Kagan Associates, 126 Clock Tower Place, Carmel, CA 93923. (408) 624-1536. This is an independent research, publishing, and consulting firm, concentrating on the entertainment and communications media industries. The company publishes thirty-five U.S.-media-related and three foreign-media-related newsletters. The company also produces special reports covering cable TV, pay TV, motion pictures, broadcasting, and home video. They present seminars for executives and provide consulting services. Paul Kagan is a former securities analyst for E. F. Hutton in New York.

Writers' Computer Store, 11317 Santa Monica Blvd., Los Angeles, CA 90025. (213) 479-7774. The best source of information I know of about what computer programs are currently in favor in Hollywood for script word processing, film budgeting, scheduling, accounting, etc.

CHAPTER 9

Directors Guild of America Newsletter. "Elia Kazan: On What Makes a Director." January 1990.

Power Networking software is available from Dotzero, Jack Smith, President. Call (310) 376-7732 or FAX: (310) 379-5103.

Tierney, Randall. "16mm Resume." *Premiere*, May 1991.

CHAPTER 10

Hopkins, Tom. *How to Master the Art of Selling.* New York: Warner Books, 1982.

McCaffrey, Mike, with Jerry Derloshon. *Personal Marketing Strategies: How to Sell Yourself, Your Ideas and Your Services.* Englewood Cliffs, N.J.: Prentice-Hall, 1983.

Director's Guild of America Newsletter. "Elia Kazan: On What Makes a Director." January 1990.

CHAPTER 11

Cohen, Charles E. "Gerardo, One 'Rico Suave' Dude." *People*, 22 April 1991.

Des Barres, Pamela. "Dress Codes," *Movieline*, July 1991.

CHAPTER 12

Benson, Sheila. "The Standouts at Sundance—Kensit, Vasquez," *Los Angeles Times*, 24 January 1991.

Cerone, Daniel. "Waiter-Director . . . Nah, Nobody'll Believe It," *Los Angeles Times*, 14 April 1991.

Thomas, Kevin. " 'Big Dis' Puts Bigger Ones to Shame," *Los Angeles Times*, 21 December 1990.

Actors' Resumes

Henry, Mari Lyn, and Lynne Rogers. *How to Be a Working Actor: The Insider's Guide to Finding Jobs in Theater, Film and Television.* New York: M. Evans, 1989.

Lewis, M. K., and Rosemary R. Lewis. *Your Film Acting Career: How to Break into the Movies and TV and Survive in Hollywood.* Hollywood, Calif.: Samuel French Trade, 1989.

Filmmaker Programs

A number of resources are available to help you make your film or video project. In addition to excellent seminars offered through the American Film Institute, UCLA Extension, the academies, guilds, and other industry organizations, you may want to explore the following programs (as always, check addresses before applying; programs come and go).

American Film Institute Directing Workshop for Women. (213) 856-7722. For professional women with extensive experience in the media arts—writers, producers, assistant directors, actors. The program gives grants of $5,000 plus use of equipment for thirty-minute video projects, which must be done on a total budget of $10,000 (you fund-raise the additional $5,000). They fund a group of twelve every fourteen to sixteen months.

Discovery Program. c/o Chanticleer Films, 6525 Sunset Blvd., 6th Fl., Hollywood, CA 90028. (213) 462-4705. A crossover opportunity for industry professionals who want to break into directing. The program covers basic production costs of twenty- to thirty-minute films to be shot in approximately six days. The films have professional-level production values. Deadline usually in February or March. You need to submit a twenty-page script that you've either written or optioned and which you would like to direct. If you are accepted, the program will fund your project and produce it (shot on 35mm). They typically receive 700 applications, from which they select 6. You are judged on both your resume and the quality of the material you submit. Narrative films only. Write for information on how to get an application form.

Filmmakers Project, Women's Steering Committees of the Directors Guild of America and the Writers Guild of America. For guild members. (213) 289-2000. A new program, still being set up at press time, in which members of the two guilds can collaborate on seven–ten-minute 35mm showcase or "resume" films. Filmmakers selected by a blue-ribbon selection committee will be given $10,000 plus in-kind services. Films will be given an industry screening. Eight to ten films to be funded per year.

Independent Filmmaker Program. Administered by the American Film Institute. Funded by the National Endowment for the Arts. (213) 856-7787. Applications open 1 July, deadline changes every year but is usually in September. For independent filmmakers who have already directed. You must submit a work in progress plus past work. Their top grant is $20,000 for production or completion costs. They grant in four areas: experimental, animation, narrative, and documentary. Over 500 applicants, of which 12 receive grants.

Sundance Institute. c/o Drea Hoffman, 4000 Warner Blvd., Producers Bldg.

4, Rm. 11, Burbank, CA 91522. (818) 954-4776. Also R.R. #3, Box 624-B, Sundance, UT 84604. Encourages independent filmmaking. The Burbank office holds a screenwriting lab and a filmmakers lab (open to directors who don't write). Screenwriters submit scripts for consideration. Directors send tapes and resumes. Call to get on mailing list for application. They receive 600–700 applications, from which 10 are accepted. Since most screenwriters want to direct their own screenplays, eight out of the ten will tend to be screenwriters, only two will be nonwriter directors. The labs provide access to "resource" directors, writers, actors, etc., who advise filmmakers. Labs for playwrights, producers, composers, and choreographers are held at Sundance's Utah location. You may also want to attend the annual Sundance Film Festival, which showcases independent features and documentaries.

Women in Film Finishing Fund. 6464 Sunset Blvd., #900, Hollywood, CA 90028. (213) 463-6040. Some money is available to complete already-started film or video projects.

Grants

Foundation Grants to Individuals. Foundation Center, 888 7th. Ave., New York, NY 10019.

Jackson, Bruce. *Get the Money and Shoot: The DRI Guide to Funding Documentary Films,* Documentary Research, 1981. 96 Rumsey Rd., Buffalo, NY 14209.

The Program Fund News gives info on the Corporation for Public Broadcasting's grants plus application forms. Eloise Payne, Program Fund, CPB, 1111 16th St. N.W., Washington, D.C. 20036. (202) 293-6160.

Wagner, Susan, ed. *A Guide to Corporate Giving in the Arts,* ACA Publications, 570 7th Ave., NY, NY 10018. Also publishes *The Cultural Directory: Guide to Federal Funds.*

CHAPTER 13

Medich, Rob. "It's Not Only Temporary: Good-bye, Mail Room; Hello, Temping," *Premiere,* June 1990.

Major Entertainment Industry Employment Agencies

All Star Agency. 204 S. Beverly Dr., Suite 110, Beverly Hills, CA 90212. (213) 271-5217.

London Temps. 12424 Wilshire Blvd., Los Angeles, CA 90025. (213) 826-3828.

Our Gang. 554 S. San Vincente Blvd., Suite 101, Los Angeles, CA 90048. (213) 653-4381.

The Right Connections Personnel Service. 511 N. La Cienega Blvd., Suite 218, Los Angeles, CA 90048. (213) 657-3700. FAX: (213) 657-5524.

Also see the "Personnel Services" listing in *The Hollywood Reporter Blu-Book Directory.*

Hollywood Studio Job Hot Lines

Wherever you are right now, why not pick up the phone and call the studio hot lines to see what jobs are open?

Columbia Pictures Entertainment: (818) 972-8520; Columbia Pictures Studio, Culver City: (310) 280-4436; The Walt Disney Company: (818) 560-1811; Fox TV: (310) 467-JOBS; NBC: (818) 840-4397; Paramount: (213) 956-5216; 20th Century Fox Film Corporation: (310) 203-2804; Warner Brothers and Lorimar TV: (213) 337-4914; Universal/MCA: (818) 777-5627.

CHAPTER 14

Balzar, John. "Hollywood and Politics: A New Grit," *Los Angeles Times,* 10 October 1991.

Finke, Nikki, and Peggy Biscow. "Power Eating," *Los Angeles Times,* 30 June 1991.

Horowitz, Joy. "The Greening of Hollywood, 1990," *Premiere,* June 1990.

Roane, Susan. *How to Work a Room: Learn the Strategies of Savvy Socializing— For Business and Personal Success.* New York: Warner Books, 1988.

Sherman, Len. *The Good, the Bad and the Famous: Celebrities Playing Politics,* New York: Lyle Stuart, 1990.

Hollywood Organizations

Academy of Canadian Cinema and Television. Los Angeles Chapter, P.O. Box 4250, Sunland, CA 91040. A good networking group to join if you're Canadian, like I am. Many other countries have film and TV liaison organizations in Los Angeles. Germany has the Goethe Institute, Great Britain has a chapter of BAFTA (British Academy of Film and Television Arts). Check with an industry library to find the organization that caters to your country of origin or interest.

Academy of Motion Picture Arts and Sciences. 8949 Wilshire Blvd., Beverly Hills, CA 90211. (213) 278-8990. Oscar's family. If you qualify for membership, by all means join and get active. The most prestigious organization in Hollywood, and a great place to meet people.

Academy of Television Arts and Sciences. 5220 Lankershim Blvd., North Hollywood, CA 91601. (818) 754-2800. Gives out the annual Emmy

Awards and publishes *EMMY* magazine. If you qualify, by all means join and get active! They have special Academy Repertory Groups for writers, actors, directors, and producers, which help Academy members from many different areas of the industry to broaden their talents. An excellent place to meet and mingle with some of the most powerful people in television.

Al's Screen Room. Al's Bar, 712 Traction Ave. (between Second and Third Streets at Alameda Ave.) in downtown L.A. (213) 687-3558. Presents open screenings of "shorts, narratives, documentaries, animation, nonrepresentational film, pornography, et al," by independent film- and videomakers. Submissions invited.

American Cinematheque. 1717 N. Highland Ave., Suite 814, Los Angeles, CA 90028. (213) 461-9622. Supported by top industry people, the Cinematheque is building a "temple to film" next to the famous Mann's Chinese Theater.

American Film Institute. 2021 N. Western Avenue, Los Angeles, CA 90027. (213) 856-7600. Founded *American Film* magazine, currently published by Billboard. Each year the AFI honors a major entertainment industry figure in a televised ceremony. I highly recommend joining the American Film Institute, which presents classes and seminars for the public as well as offering a highly respected graduate level degree in film.

Association of Entertainment Industry Computer Professionals. 1341 Ocean Ave., Box 361, Santa Monica, CA 90401. For computer people who work at the studios and production companies and also for end users—people who use computers to write scripts, do budgets, graphics, musical scores, etc. Holds bimonthly meetings on a variety of topics.

Association of Freelance Professionals. 3607 West Magnolia Blvd., #6, Burbank, CA 91505. (818) 842-7797. FAX: (818) 842-8226. Its newsletter, *Freelancer*, has good nuts-and-bolts advice for film and video professionals on how to work as an independent contractor.

Association of Visual Communicators. 15125 Califa St., Suite E, Van Nuys, CA 91411. (818) 787-6800. Serves audiovisual industry professionals, industrial, corporate, and documentary filmmakers. Gives the annual CINDY awards.

Chicagoans in the Industry (CITI). For all you Windy City folks in Hollywood. Contact Jeff Gordon, who runs the Writer's Boot Camp, at 1950 S. Pelham, #1, Los Angeles, CA 90025. (213) 470-8849. This active group has meetings with speakers (Chicagoans who've made it in Tinseltown), screenings, fun outings like trips to the races.

Cinema Cafe. A coffee house with cinema room. Has regular evening programming spotlighting the work of actors and emerging or independent directors, writers, and cinematographers. 7160 Melrose Ave. (one block west of La Brea Ave.) in Hollywood. (213) 939-CAFE.

EZTV. 8547 Santa Monica Blvd., West Hollywood, CA 90069. (213) 657-1532. A "video gallery" that holds regular video screenings of features, documentaries, works-in-progress, etc.

Financial and Administrative Management in Entertainment (FAME). 500 S. Buena Vista, Burbank, CA 91521. (818) 650-1245 or (818) 560-7650. Financial and business people within the industry belong to this group.

Hollywood Radio and TV Society. 5315 Laurel Canyon Blvd., Suite 202, North Hollywood, CA 91607-2772. (818) 769-4313. FAX: (818) 509-1262. HRTS is an organization of West Coast executives in broadcasting, broadcast advertising, program and commercial production, and allied fields. It holds regular "Newsmaker Luncheons," which are great for networking, plus an annual holiday party at the Century Plaza Hotel. Among the companies that have season tables or reservations for the luncheons are the TV networks and stations, major studios, independent producers, advertisers, ad agencies, cable and pay TV, publicity agencies, talent and management agencies, services, and suppliers. A Who's Who in TV.

Independent Feature Project/West. 5550 Wilshire Blvd., Suite 204, Los Angeles, CA 90036. (213) 937-4379. Publishes *Montage* magazine. Ask them to send you information on membership and current seminars and activities. If you want to be involved in independent film, joining this organization is a must.

International Documentary Association. 1551 S. Robertson Blvd., Suite 201, Los Angeles, CA 90035. (213) 284-8422. Publishes a monthly newsletter/calendar and a membership directory. Ask them to send you free calendar and membership information. Holds "shmooze" events to help you meet other people interested in nonfiction film and video. Board of Trustees includes representatives of HBO, the Discovery Channel, Arts and Entertainment Network, Lifetime, and the Turner Network. If you want to work in this area, joining the IDA is a must!

International Television Association. 6311 N. O'Connor Rd., #LB-51, Irving, TX 75039. (214) 869-1112. Organization of nonbroadcast video producers working in-house or free-lance in corporate, educational, government, medical, military, and other settings where there is a need for professional video communications. Has more than 8,000 members around the world. Local chapters. Publishes *Corporate Television* magazine. Gives Golden and Silver Reel awards in categories such as employee communications, information, interactive video, public service announcement, PR, sales/marketing, training, and videoconferencing.

Residuals. 11042 Ventura Blvd., Studio City, CA 90068. (818) 761-8301. A bar in the San Fernando Valley at which your residual check (which guild members get when a film or TV show receives a repeat showing), no matter how small, may entitle you to a free drink. This could be a better deal than it sounds, because many residual checks are for pennies.

Telefilm Canada. I'm from Montreal, so this one's for me! Call Sam Wendell at (310) 859-0268. 9350 Wilshire Blvd., #400, Beverly Hills, CA 90212. Telefilm keeps lists and resumes of Canadian talent in L.A. on file. FAX: (310) 276-4741.

University of Southern California Cinema-TV Alumni Association. 7944 Capistrano Ave, West Hills, CA 91304. (818) 340-0175. Presents seminars.

Vidiots. A video store that features hard-to-find independent, foreign, and documentary films. holds regular programs with filmmakers. 302 Pico Blvd., Santa Monica, CA 90405. (310) 392-8508.

Hollywood Charities/Political Organizations

Why not combine networking with doing some good for the world? Membership in some of these organizations is by invitation only, but volunteers are often welcome.

American Oceans Campaign. 725 Arizona Ave., Suite 102, Santa Monica, CA 90401. (213) 576-6162. Founded by Ted Danson, this organization is a lobbying group dedicated to the restoration and preservation of America's oceans. Supporters include Jeff Bridges, Carol Burnett, Emilio Estevez, Danny De Vito, Sally Field, Leonard Nimoy, Ally Sheedy. AOC works closely with ECO (see below).

Caucus for Producers, Directors and Writers. P.O. Box 11236, Burbank, CA 91510-1236. (818) 792-0421. Formed during the 1973 writers' strike to defend the rights of writer-producers and hyphenates. Goal is to be the conscience of the creative community. They have addressed a number of literary and ethical issues, including the depiction of the use of alcohol and drugs on TV, environmental issues, promoting the use of seat belts, and ageism in the industry. Not open to the general public, this organization is made up of some of the top producers, directors, and writers in Hollywood. You may not be able to join, but perhaps you could explore the possibility of volunteering to assist on a project.

Earth Communications Office (ECO). 1925 Century Park East, Suite 2300, Los Angeles, CA 90067. (213) 277-1665. Started by entertainment lawyer Bonnie Reiss, ECO is a $50-per-person membership organization open to everyone in the entertainment industry. ECO takes action on a wide range of environmental issues.

Education 1st. 1990 S. Bundy Dr., Los Angeles, CA 90025. (213) 442-3582. Founded by industry insiders Lynda Guber and Carole Isenberg. Cynthia Robbins, Executive Director. This organization works to convince Hollywood writers, producers, and directors to include pro-education themes in their films and TV programs.

Environmental Media Association (EMA). 10536 Culver Blvd., Suite C, Culver City, CA 90232. (213) 559-9334. Founded by Norman Lear, his wife, Lyn, and other top industry people, including Fox's Barry Diller, Disney's Michael Eisner, CAA's Mike Ovitz, and Robert Redford. President is Andy Spahn. Encourages media people to express positive environmental messages in their films and TV programs. A rather exclusive organization, so you may not be able to join, but you may want to find out if you could volunteer your assistance on any of EMA's projects.

Hollywood Women's Political Committee. 10536 Culver Blvd., Culver City, CA 90232. (213) 559-9334. Members include the top liberals in show business, including Morgan Fairchild, Jane Fonda, producer Paula Weinstein (A Dry White Season), and songwriter Marilyn Bergman ("The Way We Were"). Recently hired Washington's Margery Tabankin to spearhead fight for pro-choice abortion rights.

The Show Coalition. 270 N. Canon Dr., Beverly Hills, CA 90210. (213) 859-1778. Hollywood producers, lawyers, and managers hold weekly early morning breakfast meetings at which they question political leaders. A real Hollywood power breakfast!

Women in Show Business. P.O. Box 2535, North Hollywood, CA 91610. (818) 994-4661. Entertainment industry charity for children.

Young Artists United. 7095 Hollywood Blvd., #499, Los Angeles, CA 90028. (213) 281-7515. Membership is open to people who work in the industry and have a commitment to community service. YAU raises money for programs for youth. They send speakers to schools to talk about subjects like illiteracy and safe sex. Also direct public service campaigns. They have education committee forums that raise important social issues. Founded in 1986 by actress Alexandra Paul. Most members are between twenty and thirty. Some are well-known actors like Robert Downey, Jr., Marlee Matlin, Esai Morales, Sarah Jessica Parker, and Ione Skye; others are behind-the-scenes people and agents, producers, studio execs.

For additional listings, see the "Associations" section of the *Hollywood Reporter Blu-Book Directory* and see chapter 20 Resources below. Also watch the trades.

CHAPTER 15

Cieply, Michael. "Inside the Agency," *Los Angeles Times*, 2 July 1989.

Hollywood Agents Directory. Hollywood Creative Directory, 3000 Olympic Blvd., Suite 2413, Santa Monica, CA 90404. (213) 315-4815. You can also order this through an entertainment industry bookstore.

CHAPTER 16

Klugman, Ellen. "That's Entertainment: Executive Recruiter Says Show Biz Board Rooms No Place for Fish," *The Penn Stater*, March/April 1991.

Personal Managers

National Conference of Personal Managers/West Coast. 10707 Camarillo St., Suite 308, North Hollywood, CA 91602. (818) 762-NCPM. FAX: (818) 980-8212. National Conference of Personal Managers/East Coast, 210 E. 51st. St., New York, NY 10022. (212) 421-2670. FAX: (212) 838-5105.

Entertainment Law Referral Services

Beverly Hills Bar Association. 300 S. Beverly Drive, Suite 201, Beverly Hills, CA 90212. (213) 553-4022, 553-6644.

Los Angeles County Bar Association. 617 S. Olive Street, 4th and 6th fls., Los Angeles, CA 90014. (213) 627-2727.

West Hollywood Bar Association. 1605 W. Olympic Blvd., Los Angeles, CA 90015. (213) 938-0418.

Public Relations

See the "Public Relations" section of the *Hollywood Reporter Blu-Book Directory*, which can be ordered from the *Hollywood Reporter*.

"Willa Clinton," *Black Face*, vol. 1, no. 2, 1991. This is an excellent Q&A with publicist Willa Clinton, who has worked on films like *Batman, Driving Miss Daisy*, and *Crossing Delancey*. She discusses exactly what a publicist does, the qualifications required, and the role of the free-lance publicist, the unit publicist. *Black Face* is the quarterly journal of the Black Filmmaker Foundation, Tribeca Film Center, 375 Greenwich Street, New York, NY 10013. (212) 941-3944.

Davis, Ivor, and Sally Ogle Davis. "Flacks Fatales," *Los Angeles*, August 1991. Not-too-flattering portrait of some of Hollywood's top publicists and how they work.

Entertainment Industry Executive Recruiters

Citron, Alan. "Hollywood Gives Headhunters a Recruiting Role," *Los Angeles Times*, 29 October 1990.

Delugach, Al. "Hollywood Headhunters," *Los Angeles Times*, 7 November 1988.

Bryant B. Crouse Associates. Bryant Crouse, Ph.D., 1732 Deloz Ave., Los Angeles, CA 90027. (213) 664-8382. Mr. Crouse is a trained psychologist and former Korn-Ferry executive. Retainer search. Works with all functions and sectors of the entertainment industry, creative and traditional functions, including business affairs, finance, legal, marketing, human resources. Entertainment areas include film, television, home video, cable, music.

Fell & Co. Robert Fell, 10550 Wilshire Blvd., #1105, Los Angeles, CA 90067. (213) 556-2372. Retainer search. Specializes in entertainment and communications areas, legal, finance, marketing. Does not do searches in creative areas. Fell is a pioneer in executive search for Hollywood; founded Fell & Co. in 1975.

W.F. Hay & Co. Bill Hay, 10100 Santa Monica Blvd., Suite 2075, Los Angeles, CA 90067. (213) 557-3624. Retainer search. Specializes in entertainment and broadcasting, senior level searches. Legal, financial, creative affairs executives. Mr. Hay was formerly a partner at Korn-Ferry.

Heidrick & Struggles. Judy Havas, 300 S. Grand, #2400, Los Angeles, CA 90071. (213) 625-8811. Retainer search. One of the largest executive recruiting firms. Thirty-five-year-old firm, offices in principal cities around the world. Specializes in all areas at significant salary levels. Does not do searches for production staff or for employees at salary levels that do not warrant a company paying executive search fees. Willing to receive resumes from high-level employees.

P.B. Izzi & Co. Patti Davis, Julie Templeton, 1142 Manhattan Ave., Suite 327, Manhattan Beach, CA 90266. (213) 546-6000. FAX: (213) 546-9162. West Coast-based entertainment industry executive recruiter. Works on retainer basis. Specializes in middle- and upper-management positions. Does not do searches in creative, engineering, computer programming areas.

Gary Kaplan & Associates. Gary Kaplan, 201 S. Lake Ave., Suite 600, Pasadena, CA 91101. (818) 796-8100. Retainer search. Works in all entertainment areas, finance, broadcasting, radio, television, theme parks, hardware and software suppliers (over $60,000). Does not do searches for creative positions.

Korn-Ferry International. William Simon, Worldwide Entertainment Group, 1800 Century Park East, Suite 900, Los Angeles, CA 90067. (213) 879-

1834. Korn-Ferry may be the largest executive recruiting firm in the world. It has forty-two offices, ten specialty practices. It does retainer search only. It has an expanding entertainment department, with a focus on globalization of the media. K-F specializes in all senior-level entertainment industry searches worldwide. Will accept resumes only from senior-level executives.

Lipson & Co. Howard R. Lipson, Ph.D., Harriet Lipson. Affiliates: Neil Fink, Helene Rand. 1900 Avenue of the Stars, Suite 2810, Los Angeles, CA 90067. (213) 277-4646. Five-year-old firm, multiple (ten to twenty-five) retained searches for several key clients. From CEOs to systems analysts. Broadcasting (TV, radio), cable, financial, MIS, real estate—domestic and international.

Brad Marks International. Brad Marks, Leslie Hollingsworth, 1888 Century Park East, Suite 1040, Los Angeles, CA 90067. (213) 286-0600. Retainer search. Mr. Marks, a well-known pioneer in entertainment industry executive search, began his own executive search firm in 1982 and merged with Korn-Ferry in 1986, where he headed the entertainment division.

Helene G. Rand Associates. Helene G. Rand, Ph.D., 12 Tara View Road, Tiburon, CA 94920. (415) 435-2699. Retainer search. Types of searches: corporate middle and senior management, including operations and business management, presidents, CEOs, directors; VP business affairs, marketing, finance, MIS, sales in the entertainment industry as well as high technology industries that interface with entertainment. Computer graphics, audio, video, and electronics technology. Does not do searches for engineers, computer programmers. Will receive resumes. Does searches for new and established firms.

Search West. Sheldon Metz, Entertainment Industry Specialist, 1875 Century Park East, Suite 1350, Los Angeles, CA 90067. (213) 284-8888. Large recruiting firm. "Number one recruiting company in California." Seven offices in California. Contingency search. Middle and upper management, from director-level up. Does not handle creative and technical positions.

Entertainment Practice. Spencer Stuart, Karen Folsom, Stephen Unger, 400 S. Hope, #2430, Los Angeles, CA 90071-2825. (213) 620-0814. Retainer search. Worldwide executive search firm, 140 consultants in sixteen countries. Entertainment a major specialty area.

As always, double-check all facts and addresses before submitting anything. Also, be aware that much of this information was given to me by the companies themselves, so take it with a grain of salt.

CHAPTER 18

Entertainment Industry Career Institute. Box 108, 3435 Ocean Park Blvd., Suite 206, Santa Monica, CA 90405. (213) 396-3920. Linda Buzzell, M.A., MFCC, Founder/Director. Classes, support groups, consultations.

Robinson, Bryan E., Ph.D. *Work Addiction: Hidden Legacies of Adult Children.* Deerfield Beach, Fla.: Health Communications, 1989.

Weinstein, Steve. "The Worrying Man of *Marrying Man.*" *Los Angeles Times,* April 5, 1991.

CHAPTER 19

Alcoholics Anonymous World Services. *Alcoholics Anonymous: The Big Book,* 3d ed. New York: Alcoholics Anonymous World Services, 1976.

Berne, Eric, M.D. *Games People Play.* New York: Random House, 1964.

Bradshaw, John. *Healing the Shame That Binds You.* Deerfield Park, Fla.: Health Communications, 1988. A book about overcoming low self-esteem and "toxic shame."

Bradshaw, John. *Homecoming: Reclaiming and Championing Your Inner Child.* New York: Bantam Books, 1990.

Burka, Jane B., Ph.D., and Lenora M. Yuen, Ph.D. *Procrastination: Why You Do It, What to Do About It.* Reading, Mass.: Addison-Wesley, 1983.

Burns, David D., M.D. *Feeling Good: The New Mood Therapy.* New York: Signet/New American, 1980. This book helps you overcome depression and negative thinking.

California Self-Help Center Directory. (800) 222-5465. By calling this directory, you will be able to find the telephone numbers for self-help groups like Alcoholics Anonymous, Adult Children of Alcoholics, Arts Anonymous, Co-Dependents Anonymous, Al-Anon, and Debtors Anonymous in California.

Carter-Scott, Cherie. *Negaholics: How to Overcome Negativity and Turn Your Life Around.* New York: Fawcett Crest/Ballantine, 1989.

Debtors Anonymous. General Service Board, P.O. Box 20322, New York, NY 10025-9992. (212) 642-8222.

Field of Dreams, starring Kevin Costner. Written and directed by Phil Alden Robinson, the Gordon Company/Universal Pictures, 1989.

Greenberg, James. "Portrait of the Artist as a Young Millionaire." *Los Angeles Times Magazine,* 19 August 1990.

Hyatt, Carole, and Linda Gottlieb. *When Smart People Fail: Rebuilding Yourself for Success.* New York: Penguin Books, 1987. A good book to read if you've been fired or had a painful job experience.

May, Rollo. *The Courage to Create.* New York: Bantam Books, 1975.

Miller, Alice. *The Drama of the Gifted Child: The Search for the True Self.* New York: Basic Books, 1981.

Mundis, Jerrold. *How to Get Out of Debt, Stay Out of Debt and Live Prosperously.* New York: Bantam Books, 1988.

Steiner, Claude M. *Scripts People Live.* New York: Grove Press, 1974.

The 12 Steps for Adult Children of Alcoholic and Other Dysfunctional Families. San Diego, Calif.: Recovery Publications, 1987.

Whitfield, Charles L., M.D. *Healing the Child Within: Discovery and Recovery for Adult Children of Dysfunctional Families.* Deerfield Beach, Fla.: Health Communications, 1987. If you're from an alcoholic or dysfunctional family, this book can help you avoid self-sabotaging your career because of unresolved issues from your childhood.

Woititz, Janet Geringer, Ed. D. *The Self-Sabotage Syndrome: Adult Children in the Workplace.* Deerfield Beach, Fla.: Health Communications, 1987. The strengths and weaknesses of adult children of alcoholics and dysfunctional families in the workplace. Workaholism, burnout, "family heroes."

CHAPTER 20

Bielby, William T., Ph.D., and Denise D. Bielby, Ph.D. *1989 Hollywood Writers' Report: Unequal Access, Unequal Pay.* Writers Guild of America/West, 8955 Beverly Blvd., West Hollywood, CA 90048.

Campanella, Roy, II. "Persistence of Vision: Surviving in the Film World," *Ebony Man*, June 1987. Portions of this article reprinted by permission of Mr. Campanella.

Dawes, Amy. "Screen Seems No Place for Women: Men Get More Roles, Earn Higher Pay in All Types of Film, TV Prod'n, SAG Says," *Daily Variety*, 2 August 1990.

Dutka, Elaine. "Meryl Streep Attacks Hollywood's Gender Gap at SAG Conference," *Los Angeles Times*, 3 August 1990.

Easton, Nine J. "Hey Babes! How Old is Too Old for Hollywood?" *Los Angeles Times*, 17 November 1991.

Farber, Stephen. "Female Trouble," *Movieline*, July 1991.

Horowitz, Joy. "Hollywood's Dirty Little Secret," *Premiere*, March 1989. An excellent overview of racism in Hollywood.

Leland, John, with Andrew Murr. "New Jack Cinema Enters Screening," *Newsweek*, 10 June 1991.

"Power and Fear: The Hollywood Graylist," a documentary produced by the Caucus for Producers, Writers and Directors with the International Documentary Association (see chapter 14 Resources).

Robb, David. "Bennett, 91, Urges Older Writer 'To Keep Going'," *Daily Variety*, 11 April 1991.

Rohter, Larry. "Are Women Directors an Endangered Species?" *New York Times*, 17 March 1991.

Sadnowick, Doug. "The Hollywood Closet," *L.A. Weekly*, 21–27 June 1991.

Steenland, Sally. *Unequal Picture: Black, Hispanic, Asian and Native American Characters on Television*. Ford Foundation/Wider Opportunities for Women, 1989.

Steenland, Sally. *What's Wrong with This Picture? The Status of Women on Screen and Behind the Camera in Entertainment TV*. Women in Film/Wider Opportunities for Women, November 1990.

"Study: Racial Reality 'Invisible' on TV," *Hollywood Reporter*, 24 August 1989.

Thompson, Anne. "Battling the Big Boys: The Decline of the Woman Star," *Los Angeles Weekly*, 4–10 May 1990.

Weinstein, Steve. "Maybe He Should Have Impersonated a White Studio Boss," *Los Angeles Times*, 14 July 1991.

"Women: 10 Years of Action," Women's Steering Committee Special Issue, *DGA News*, Directors Guild of America, December 1990–January 1991.

Zeitlin, Marilyn. "The Hollywood Graylist: Too Old To Be Hired, Too Young To Be Retired." *DGA News*, September–October 1991.

Organizations

Access Theatre. 2428 Chapala St., Santa Barbara, CA 93105. Voice # (805) 682-8184. Trains people with disabilities. Puts on performances. Also keeps casting files on working performers.

African-American Film and Television Association (AAFTA). 6565 Sunset Blvd., Suite 301, Hollywood, CA 90028. (213) 466-8221. An entertainment networking organization. They hold lunches and seminars on film production, distribution, etc.

American Indian Registry for the Performing Arts (AIRPA). 1717 N. Highland, Suite 614, Hollywood, CA 90028. (213) 962-6594. This nonprofit organization founded in 1983 acts as a support group, fights stereotypes, and promotes Native American actors. It encourages film and television companies to employ Indian people in creative and technical aspects. It publishes a monthly newsletter and an annual talent directory, the *Entertainment Industry Guide*, and holds workshops and seminars.

American Women in Radio and Television. Southern California Chapter, P.O. Box 3615, Hollywood, CA 90028. (213) 964-2740.

Association of Asian-Pacific-American Artists. 3518 Cahuenga Blvd. West,

Suite 302, Los Angeles, CA 90068. (213) 874-0786. The focus is advocacy. Monitors the industry to advocate a realistic portrayal of Asian Americans in movies. Puts on media awards recognizing individuals, production companies, and corporations that have promoted this realistic portrayal.

Behind the Lens (Association of Professional Camerawomen). P.O. Box 1039, Santa Monica, CA 90406.

Black American Cinema Society. 3617 Mont Clair St., Los Angeles, CA 90018. (213) 737-3292. This organization puts on an exhibit in April, gives out cash grants to student and independent black filmmakers (deadline and print specification information will be provided if you write or call), assists with job hunting.

Black Filmmaker Foundation. 80 Eighth Ave., Suite 1704, New York, NY 10011. (212) 941-3944. Founded in 1978, the BFF has assisted many emerging filmmakers and developed audiences for their work. In 1985, BFF acted as the fiscal agent for Spike Lee in securing the grant of funds to finance *She's Gotta Have It*. Today, Lee sits on the BFF Filmmaker Advisory Board, which was founded to address the unique obstacles and opportunities that these filmmakers will face in the 1990s. The board consists of many of the top African-American filmmakers working in Hollywood, including Debbie Allen, Robert Townsend, Keenen Wayans, Reginald Hudlin, and Suzanne DePasse. Each month BFF sponsors a screening, creative workshop, and artist showcase to encourage new talent. BFF plans to establish BFF/West in 1992.

Cinewomen. 9903 Santa Monica Blvd., Suite 461, Beverly Hills, CA 90212, (310) 855-8720. Nonprofit women's networking organization. Their goal is to provide professional and emotional support for women whether they are just starting out or are well into their careers. Recently produced a documentary on the homeless which Jodi Foster narrated. They are also working with other women's organizations to put together a summit meeting with heads of studios to promote a clear dialogue.

Deaf West Theatre Company. 5060 Fountain Ave., Hollywood, CA 90029. (213) 660-0877 for voice, TDD # (213) 660-8826.

H.A.P.P.I. (Handicapped Artists, Performers and Partners, Inc.). P.O. Box 24225, Los Angeles, CA 90024. (213) 394-6625. Holds workshops, keeps casting files on working performers.

Hispanic Academy of Media Arts and Sciences (HAMAS). P.O. Box 931418, Los Angeles, CA 90093-1413. (213) 964-1635.

Hollywood Supports is a new anti-homophobia and anti-AIDS-discrimination organization created by prominent members of the entertainment industry in the wake of actor Brad Davis's death from AIDS. Richard

Jennings, executive director of the L.A. chapter of the Gay and Lesbian Alliance Against Defamation (GLAAD), is the group's first executive director. No phone or address had been announced at press time, so you may want to call the offices of founders Barry Diller, chairman and chief operating officer, Fox Inc., (310) 277-2211, or Sid Sheinberg, president and chief operating officer of Universal Pictures' parent company MCA Inc., (818) 777-1000, for more information. Supporters include top Hollywood studio executives, agents and celebrities like Oliver Stone, Barbra Streisand, and Spike Lee.

Latino Writers Group. 6922 Hollywood Blvd., Suite 500, Hollywood, CA 90028-6125. (213) 269-1471. This organization was founded in response to the Bielby Report (see above). The LWG was cofounded with Nosotros and HAMAS. Their goal is to generate employment for Latino screenwriters. They offer training programs, job listings, speakers, and a script submission program.

Media Access Office. 8121 Van Nuys Blvd., Suite 214, Van Nuys, CA 91402; or P.O. Box 3778, Hollywood, CA 90078. (818) 781-1093. Nonprofit organization that acts as a liaison between the entertainment community and people with disabilities who want to be employed as performers and in creative positions. They put on workshops and keep casting files on working performers, acting as a referral service.

National Theatre Workshop for the Handicapped. 106 W. 56th St., New York, NY 10019. (212) 757-8549.

Nosotros ("Us"). (213) 465-4167. This organization provides classes and puts on actor/industry showcases in its own theater. Also sponsors the Golden Eagle Awards.

Walt Disney Minority Writers Internship Program. For information, write to Brenda Vangsness at the Walt Disney Studios, 500 S. Buena Vista St., Burbank, CA 91521.

Women in Film. 6464 Sunset Blvd., Suite 900, Los Angeles, CA 90028. (213) 463-6040. Holds annual Crystal Awards, film festival, "brown bag" lunches, networking events. Both women and men may join, but membership is not open to newcomers to the industry. Excellent opportunities for volunteering, networking. Also has an advocacy committee to improve the position of women in front of and behind the camera.

Also, check out the guild in your targeted niche to see if it has a special committee on minority concerns. Most guilds now do.

Acknowledgments

★ ★ ★ ★ ★ ★ ★ ★ ★ ★ ★ ★ ★ ★ ★ ★ ★

I am indebted most of all to my clients, students, colleagues, mentors, and friends in the entertainment industry, who have taught me about what it really takes to make it in Hollywood.

I also want to thank my agent, Lisa Bankoff, for her help and advice. She was wise enough to know that Craig Nelson at Harper-Collins would be the perfect editor for this book. She was right: his guidance has been invaluable.

I also owe a debt of gratitude to Lyn Benjamin for taking the proposal for this book to one of the most beloved agents in Hollywood, the late Ben Benjamin at ICM, who knew that Lisa Bankoff of the agency's New York office would be the right person to help me bring this book to life and who made the Godfather Call that counted. Lyn also contributed excellent suggestions.

And I want to express appreciation to everyone who has allowed me to tell their stories in this book, those whose names appear and those who remain anonymous or pseudonymous. And thanks to those whose contributions and stories space concerns didn't allow me to include.

Regarding preparation of this book, I want to thank Gary Frankford for his editorial and research assistance and Marla Poor and Margaret Black for research. Also author Nancy Baker for consulting with me on the preparation of the book proposal and Roy Campanella II for excellent editorial advice.

Many others have helped me. I will try to acknowledge as many as I can. Please forgive any omissions: Lucas Foster, a skilled and inspiring production executive who has been uncommonly generous in advising my students. Judith Grutter, M.S., N.C.C.C., for opening up the exciting world of career counseling to me and teaching me about psychological type and temperament. Also career counseling colleagues Maciek Kolodziejczak, Catherine Van Ness, Al Aubin, Arlene Levin, Phil Spinelli, Richard Knowdell, Dean Porter, and Elizabeth Schneider.

I thank the industry pros who have been panelists at my seminars over the last three years, including Patrick Read Johnson, David Lonner, Beth Swofford, David Goyer, Barbara Goodman, Cynthia Shelton, Sam Grogg, Jim Brubaker, Dale Launer, Bryant Crouse, Carol Faith, Mark Mueller, Michael Barlow, Larry Becsey, Alan Bergmann, Jeremiah Chechik, Jim Drake, Philippe Perebinossofs, Larry Turman, Phil Alden Robinson, Larry Mirisch, Carol Bennett, Jim Fargo, Ran Rapiel, Charlie Haid, Renee Valente, Deirdre Paulino, David R. Elliott, and Christine Foster.

I thank Ron Kramer, for showing me what a good manager can do for a show business career. The American Film Institute's Associate director, Emily Laskin, and the Public Service Programs staff. The Academy of Television Arts and Sciences' Activities Director, Linda Loe, and the Activities Committee. Directors Guild of America National Special Projects Officer Selise Eiseman. Composer David Bell of the Society of Composers and Lyricists. Carol Marcus Plone and Joelle Dobrow of the DGA Women's Committee and Sheryl Levine Guterman of the WGA Women's Committee. The many talented people I have had the privilege of working with, including Carl Weathers, David L. Wolper, Jacques Cousteau and his son the late Philippe Cousteau, Joel Silver, Jack Haley, Jr., Mel Stuart, Arnold Shapiro, Nick Noxon, Charles and Ray Eames, Peter Fowler, Carl Freed, and many others.

I thank attorney Michael Gendler for his wise advice and counsel. Agent Beth Bohn of the Cindy Turtle Agency. USC's Gabor Kalman, filmmaker and creator of the International Documentary Association's David L. Wolper Student Documentary Awards, and my other colleagues and friends at the International Documentary Association. Actor-writer George Furth, for helping me understand what it takes to be a successful actor in Hollywood. My friend producer-director Sascha Schneider, who has encouraged me since we first met in the research department at Wolper Productions in 1967, and my friend Laurie Zemelman Schneider, a talented therapist who co-led a pioneering "Hollywood Anonymous" group with me in 1986. Attorney David Dantes. Agent Debbee Klein of the Irv Schechter Agency. Ben Bennett, who supports a whole community of talented entertainment industry tenants and who taught me that for some of us, it is the love of the creative people in this industry that counts, not just the product we manufacture. Cliff Fenneman for the article on Elia Kazan. New Zealand film critic Mark Knowles, for antipodean encouragement and champagne at the Beverly Wilshire. Gabriele Zinke, Jesse and Dan Douma of the Writers' Computer Store. Karen Silverstein, for her efforts on my behalf. The Rev. Karen Buzzell-Frey and her husband, Walter Frey, for caring. Mary Jane Henderson and Randolph Howe for their support and encouragement throughout the writing process.

Index

★ ★ ★ ★ ★ ★ ★ ★ ★ ★ ★ ★ ★ ★